AMONG THE BOOKS BY

JAMES TRUSLOW ADAMS

THE AMERICAN

EMPIRE ON THE SEVEN SEAS

BUILDING THE BRITISH EMPIRE

THE LIVING JEFFERSON

AMERICA'S TRAGEDY

HENRY ADAMS

THE MARCH OF DEMOCRACY

THE EPIC OF AMERICA

THE ADAMS FAMILY

OUR BUSINESS CIVILIZATION

PROVINCIAL SOCIETY

NEW ENGLAND IN THE REPUBLIC

REVOLUTIONARY NEW ENGLAND

FOUNDING OF NEW ENGLAND

The American

The American

THE MAKING OF A NEW MAN

BY

James Truslow Adams

New York

CHARLES SCRIBNER'S SONS

1944

Printed in the United States of America

THIS BOOK IS
MANUFACTURED UNDER WARTIME
CONDITIONS IN CONFORMITY WITH
ALL GOVERNMENT REGULATIONS
CONTROLLING THE USE OF PAPER
AND OTHER MATERIALS

PREFACE

THIS BOOK is not intended to be another history of America. In the past, I have tried, in one work, to present that in the form of a factual narrative. In another, I tried to interpret the facts and to show how and why America developed as it did. In this third, and probably final essay, I devote myself solely to the American himself. For my own interest I wanted to discover, if possible, what geographical, historical and social forces had made the American different from the citizen of any other nation. For he *is* different. In the eighteenth century, Crèvecœur wrote of him as "that New Man." Recently, in a handbook designed to help British service men who find themselves associated with him, it is stated that they will find in America something they never met in Europe, the real "European." But if, due to the melting-pot, many an American is a better European than can be found among the stay-at-home people of any one European country, he is something much more than that. He is becoming, indeed, something wholly new.

He is not only "new"—he is becoming also an important factor to be considered in the future of the world, not merely from his numbers, the resources of his country, and his power in the future international balance, but in himself. What the American is like, what made him, and what he may do, are problems of sudden import to all the world, and not least to us Americans ourselves. I undertook the study because I wanted to, for myself, and in this volume I give my findings, for what they are worth. In delving into the American past, with which, from other standpoints, I had become fairly familiar, I have for the purpose of this study used only those items which bear on its central theme. Battles and other incidents, many of the Presidents and other leading figures, have remained for the most part unnoticed and unsung. I have wanted to discover, and record, only those factors which have combined to make the John Does and Richard Roes, of many different racial origins and backgrounds, into the American.

I owe, of course, as any author does, debts, often heavy and intimate, to others, but wish here to mention in especial Mr. Whitney Darrow, who has taken a great interest in the general plan and scope of the book from the start, and Mr. John Hall Wheelock, who has given invaluable and always friendly and courteous aid in his editing of the manuscript.

JAMES TRUSLOW ADAMS

Southport, Connecticut,
May 14, 1943.

CONTENTS

The American

PROLOGUE

I AM writing this book to please myself. It likely may not, and I have no idea whether it will please any one else. The point is I want to clarify something in my own mind. As an American I have written many books on American life and history. Before turning to writing, some twenty years ago, I was for many years in business of different sorts, starting as an office boy, and my work at different times took me into all but five states of the Union. Between these two phases of my life, I was in the army in the last war. I have done business with Americans from Canada to the Gulf, and from the Atlantic to the Pacific. I have been abroad many times, on government service and for research, so that I have been able to contrast the Americans with other peoples, and, as Kipling wrote of his own country, "What should they know of England, who only England know?"

Yet at the end of it all I come back to the question: "What *is* an American?" That may seem so obvious to many as not to be worth thinking about and certainly not worth writing a book about. We think we know him and may ask what is the use of analyzing him. But do we know him so well? Take myself to start with, just because I am nearest at hand. I think of myself as one hundred per cent American—not in the sense of making the eagle scream but just as "American." My first Adams ancestor came from England to Maryland in 1658, very soon passing over to Virginia, and we have been Americans ever since. For some generations they were farmers, or as they called it in the South, planters, though a "plantation" might be only fifty acres cut out of a wilderness. My father's mother, however, was Spanish, and my father himself was born in South America, where my grandfather was representing a New York business house at the time. My father did not speak English until sent back home to school when he was eight. Yet I never think of having any connection with South America or Spain but only with America.

My family has fought in every American war, from the French and Indian down to the present one. On the Spanish side my ancestors came to South America in 1585, long before the *Mayflower,* and in all lines of descent I am wholly New World. There is much in English history that I admire and much in English life that I find comfortable, but I could no more give up my American citizenship and go permanently to England and become British than I could change my body. I am American, whatever that may mean.

Let us think of a few Americans who had that quality we recognize as "American." For example, Washington was one of our greatest men and America owes him a debt it never can pay, but he was less in the American than the English tradition, the tradition of a Pym or a Hampden. We sense something new and different when we turn from a Washington and a Hamilton to a Franklin and a Jefferson. Abraham Lincoln was indubitably American. Other types come to mind, a Ford or a Rockefeller, not because of their success stories but for their odd combination of qualities. You would know Ford was an American if you met him in Tibet. Then there are Barnum and Mark Twain, or in fiction Natty Bumppo, Hosea Biglow, Daisy Miller, Huck Finn, David Harum, Mr. Dooley and scores of others.

Here we strike the first snag—unity in vast diversity. I am far from saying that birth, race or citizenship have nothing to do with it, but Americanism derives from things other than these. Of our continental population of 123,000,000 as given in the Census of 1930 (the total is now nearly 135,000,000), 14,000,000 were foreign-born, close to 40,000,000 foreign-born or children of one or both foreign-born parents, and 8,000,000 of our then actual or potential voters (one in every eight of the total) were foreign-born. We have always had the foreign-born. In the persons of ourselves, or our ancestors only a few generations back, we, every man Jack of us, came, as they used to describe outsiders in a small village I once lived in, "from away." This is true but it is evident that some of these and their descendants have developed into real Americans and that others have not, regardless of racial origin. What is the difference between the *real* and the merely *legal* American?

That is what I have been trying to find out. That is what this book is about. It is not just another history of the United States. We shall not be in the least concerned with a detailed narrative of events. Rather like a fisherman I am only "whipping the stream," casting my line here and there in the hope of a rise by the wary trout, which in this case is "the American." This book is not about what people—Americans or others—have done *in* or *to* America. It is about what America has done *to them*. It does do something. That is evident. "Ruggles of Red Gap" is a glorious example. What does America do and why? What has made this queer animal, this American, this NEW MAN as Crèvecœur in 1782 called him after close study?

The immigrants who from the beginning have come to America have been a picked lot. Together with a good deal of riffraff, they have been, in spite of innumerable cases of oppression and poverty in Europe, just those persons in their homelands who have had the energy and ambition to get away from that oppression and poverty and take their chances in a New World. As has been well said of Lincoln and his career, the main point is not that he was born in a log cabin but that he got himself out of it to become a leader of a great cause and people. America has been in large part the answer to the problem of what happens when unlimited human energy meets illimitable natural resources, especially under historical and political conditions which permit of unprecedented individual freedom of action. It is a sort of mathematical equation to which, in many of his aspects, the American is the answer. Q.E.D. The size and natural richness of our land is thus one of the factors with which we have to deal.

Minor points will be mentioned later in their places, such as the geographical conditions which, with the human elements in the case, helped to set off New England as a separate section; also the conditions of soil, climate and so on, which were to make the South slave and the North free, and bring on the Civil War. There was the range of the Allegheny Mountains, which played an important part; the great valley of the Mississippi, extending nearly 1,500 miles between the Alleghenies and the Rockies, which in its unexampled resources, remoteness and protection, had its influence in becoming the world's "Valley of Democracy" and the center of our isolationist sentiment. There were the vast forests of the East, and the prairies and plains of the West, which also played their parts in developing traits and types.

Many persons, the world over, say, some with hope and some with fear, that the future lies with us Americans and what we do. Perhaps it does and perhaps it doesn't, but at least it is worth while trying to find out what we are and why. To learn what a man is you have to know a lot about his background and life, so that, although this book is not a history, we shall have to go a long way back and follow the American through his experiences and consider the influences which have been operating to make him what he is. Then perhaps we can sum him up. It is worth trying.

CHAPTER I

THE FIRST AMERICANS

FIRST of all, let us take a swift glance at the land to which all these people "from away" have come. We shall not describe it in elaborate topographical detail but merely note some of the more outstanding features which appear to have been of prime importance in fashioning the American rather than in simply determining the history of some locality.

In the first place, it was remote from Europe. It was also huge. Even that strip across the continent now the United States contains 3,000,000 square miles. Not only was it huge, but it was full of incredible riches. It is true that the stores of metals, especially the copper, silver and gold, lay buried far to the west and were, happily, not to be exploited in our earlier period, as were the precious metals of Mexico and Peru by the Spaniards. But they were there, as were also the vast forests; coal deposits; the farm lands which Jefferson figured would last us for a thousand years; oil; and other forms of wealth to be garnered. I need not catalogue the whole list. The main point for us in our hunt for the American is that on or under the soil of our continent there was offered one of the most extraordinary chances, perhaps *the* most extraordinary chance, to attain freedom and wealth mankind has ever had.

Moreover, our whole future domain was almost empty of human life. There were, indeed, the Indians, barbarians mostly in the hunting stage. They gave the settlers plenty of trouble, as well as on occasion important help, and the story of our dealings with them forms one of the dark blots of our history. But there were only about half a million of them all-told scattered over the whole of the future United States. The riches of America were not like those of India or China, already in possession of old races and civilizations numbering hundreds of millions of people. Leaving out for the moment the problem of ethics—the question as to whether half a million barbarians and savages should have been allowed to retain as hunters a land now supporting 135,000,000 civilized people—we have only to consider the fact that there was no teeming population to conquer or supplant. One of the richest portions of the whole world lay more or less open to rapid exploitation.

On May 6, 1607, three little English vessels, the largest, the *Sarah Constant*, of 100 tons and the smallest of 20 tons, passed between the capes guarding the entrance of Chesapeake Bay after a voyage of over four months from the old country. America has had many famous ships of peace and war in her annals but these should be the most famous of all, for their passengers who were destined for permanent settlement were the *first Americans*. As they made a temporary landing on Cape Henry, the spirit of the continent might have said to them in the modern country vernacular, "Meet America!" It was indeed new, and a stranger, but the spirit might also have said to all the world, "Meet the American." America was to do wondrous things to these voyagers who thankfully scanned the shores in the next few days, breathing the blossom-scented air of a Virginia spring after the weary and dangerous weeks at sea. The continent was to do it likewise to the millions who in the centuries to come were to follow these first immigrants on their westward ocean-faring. All of them together in the future as Americans were to do extraordinary things also to the countries of the Old World from which they came, but none on either side of the Atlantic dreamed then of what the centuries had in store or that one of the greatest epics in history had its beginning in that month of May.

Before getting these first Americans settled on shore we may stop to note one all-important point about them. That is that they were English, as were to be practically all the immigrants who were to leave a deep impress on America during that seventeenth century. I am not forgetting the Dutch in New York, the Swedes on the Delaware, and individuals or small groups scattered here and there among the English until the German, Scotch-Irish and other immigrations in the next century. It is true that some of the earlier non-English stocks left traces in architecture, language, art and customs. The important fact for the American, however, was not the echoing of these things, interesting or romantic as they are, but the fact that in the early formative period our national language, law and political institutions and traditions, became practically all English because the bulk of the population, which was of molding influence before 1700, was and remained English. This was to prove of enormous importance.

What were they, and what were the traits which they had when the American branch shot off from the main trunk? It is not easy or safe to try to generalize about the characteristics of any people at a given moment, especially at a moment some centuries ago, but before we even make some tentative suggestions, we may note one or two points. The Englishman, or, in broader terms, the Britisher, of today, is in many ways quite different from his forebears of 1600, even allowing for much individual variation at both periods. Also, the American of today is in many ways different from his forebears among the first settlers. In a good many respects, some superficial and some not, but often leading to mutual misunderstanding, the English have developed along certain lines into what they are now, whereas the Americans, subjected to new influences of environment and circumstance, have developed along others into what *they* are.

They are different from each other, though more alike, in my belief, than any other two peoples in the world in spite of our later very large admixture of foreign bloods. If we size up the "real" Americans (including all those of alien races who have become Americans, in so far as they have become "real" ones), I think there is no question but that in fundamentals they are more like, though now in many minor ways *unlike,* the British than they are like any other people, such as the French, Italian, Germans, Russians, and others, to say nothing of such races as those of the Orient. By fundamentals I mean our general way of looking at life; our individualism; our beliefs as to what things are decent and worthy; our attitude towards law and individual rights; our political aptitude for self-government; and many other items of similar basic importance.

In all this, a continuing common language and literature have played no small part, but much also must be attributed to the fact that our own country in its formative period was chiefly molded by English settlers who had the same centuries of development of mind and character behind them which the English of the old country had had. It must be recalled also that, although the splitting-off process of American from English, or British, began for each generation when it left the Old World for permanent residence in the New, immigration to parts of the United States continued for many generations from Britain and Ireland, so that there was a steady infusion of new settlers from thence. Moreover, America in its colonial period was a part of the British Empire, frequently quarrelling with it but still connected by close ties and strong influences. We were a part of that Empire for a longer period than we have been independent of it. So firmly had we been set in the English mold, in spite of the steady changes going on which were making Americans out of former British, that even long after independence English thought, ways, fashions, society, politics and literature continued to exert strong pulling forces on us.

It was more than a mere accident of history, therefore, that the first settlements here were made by the English, and that by 1664, after the capture of New Netherland from the Dutch, the whole Atlantic seaboard from French Canada to Spanish Florida was part of the British Empire, open to English settlement and influence.

What were the English at the time of their first permanent planting here? One point about them was that they were not

Europeans. When we look at maps we are led to think of Britain as part of Europe because the map which gives us Great Britain and Ireland is usually called Europe, and we think of the British Isles as belonging to it. Roughly, from the invasion by Cæsar to that by William the Conqueror, say from 55 B.C. to 1066 A.D., Britain was scourged by invasions and settlements from the continent, but there has been no invasion since the Normans, nearly 900 years ago, though Philip of Spain tried it with his Armada, as others have threatened to do since. Thus on their "island fortress," a distinct race developed, with distinct traits.

Trying to consider what traits the English had, say, in 1600, and disentangling them from the present ones, we may speak of their casualness and amateurishness. It has often cost them, and sometimes others, dear, but they would rather be casual most of their lives and pay for it at crises than to spend all of their lives in planning carefully, and perhaps taxing themselves heavily, for possible future contingencies. They believe in "muddling through," and "losing every battle but the last one." The Englishman simply refuses to worry about what has not yet happened, and he always has done so. It is nothing new.

But when something happens, the Englishman—well, we cannot say perhaps that he *thinks* it out, but he has a sort of sixth sense, located not in his brain but diffused through his whole anatomy and all his organs, which somehow leads him, with his bulldog tenacity and courage, to do what suits his character and, in a clumping sort of way, to get him what he wants. And he has known pretty well what he has wanted and how to get it. What he had wanted from Magna Carta and down to and through our colonial period—to say nothing of the subsequent periods—was above all else to be able to have and go his own way. If there has been continuity of a sort in English history through the centuries, it has been because of a certain constancy in the English character and not because they have sat down and "planned it that way." The Englishman has hated planning and being planned for, by any paternal government, as we shall see when we come to the first settlements of Jamestown and Plymouth in the matter of the attempt at a sort of communism. The goose-stepping and regimentation of the Germans has always, as a system, been as abhorrent to the English as has been the logic-chopping of the French.

They have always had a practical way of looking at things, and getting them done. When their toes are stepped on by bad laws or the encroachments of a government on their personal liberty they do what is needful for the immediate occasion but do not wander off into a misty haze of political theorizing. When for example, in our own early days as a part of the empire while we were still English ourselves, they finally decided they had to cut off the head of King Charles, they did it with a minimum of blood-letting and, unlike the French in their Revolution, without changing the calendar and as far as possible the whole blueprint of ordinary life. In fact what they have liked has been ordinary life, and when they have been driven off the track of it by some emergency they want to get back to it as fast as they can.

Yet somehow, from Magna Carta down to perhaps their legalistic fumbling of the ball of statesmanship and common sense in the crucial decade preceding the American Revolution, their sixth sense instead of logic enabled them to make free institutions and self-government function better than any other people ever has. They had fought, down to the founding of America, not for some generalization like the French *liberté* but just for this or that particular liberty they had enjoyed in the past or which they thought they ought to have. When they got it, "that was that," and the thing was done.

And almost always there was the spirit of compromise, when a critical moment was reached. More than any other race they seemed to understand how—no, not quite that perhaps, but subconsciously to be able—to make self-government work without any one to govern them. I have quoted elsewhere the saying: "One Englishman, a fool; two Englishmen, a football match; three Englishmen, the British Empire." Allowing for wide exaggeration, the statement holds much truth. An individual Englishman may be almost any sort of fellow, but you get a group together and the spirit of sport and team-play emerges, and it may be noted that sport was never more popular than in the "Merrie England" of our own early settlement days. Get a good-sized group, the population at home or a few starting a colony, and the spirit of self-government comes to the top at once—freedom within the law—as we shall have ample occasion to observe with regard to our own settlements and frontiers.

They have always been a tough-fibered breed, disdainful of comfort and softness. They had been hammered on the anvil of Fate by many invasions in the earlier centuries, and they had come out of it hardened. Unemotional on the surface, because they had learned not to let themselves go, they were not so underneath, and had an intense love of tradition and of their country. Perhaps more than at any time before or since they *were* at the time America was being settled "letting themselves go" in expression. One has only to read Shakespeare's lines on England to understand the fervor of the patriotism of the period:

> This royal throne of kings, this sceptered isle . . .
> This precious stone set in the silver sea . . .
> This blessed plot, this earth, this realm, this England.

While we were yet part of the Empire, England was sneeringly called a "nation of shop-keepers" (not by Napoleon, to whom the term is usually ascribed, but a generation earlier by our own Samuel Adams), and it is true that they have always been great traders. The growth of the Empire, including the settlement of America, was due as much to that fact as to the other that, though attached to "home" with one of the deepest of their primal instincts, they have also loved wandering and adventure. The combination is happily expressed in the term "Merchant Adventurers" applied to some of the great business companies which did so much to build the imperial structure at the time of our own beginning, and if we Americans often love business ventures more for the sake of "the game" than the gain, we come by the trait naturally, though it has been much emphasized by the conditions of our American environment.

Yet these adventurous "shop-keepers" have been far from materialistic in other ways also. There has always been a very deep religious strain in them and in the early seventeenth century religion was one of the most important preoccupations of the national life. As we shall see, America was in part founded as a result of sectarian differences in England, but aside from the question of whatever sect they might belong to, the English who came here brought with them as part of their heredity an outlook on the world in which religion would be almost certain to be a leading influence.

We may add that these world-exploring shop-keepers somehow managed to create a body of literature which has included some of the finest poetry and imaginative literature in the world, and this flowering of the spirit was at its height just when the English settlement of America began. The English neither at that time, nor before nor since, can be said to have attained to the first rank in either music, painting or sculpture. They have been an imaginative but not an aesthetic race.

We may mention one more point and that is the fluidity which English life acquired from the nature of its institutions. In one aspect English social life—and that is true also of the period of American colonization—seems to be rigidly stratified. From King to pauper, each apparently had his place and knew it, from high society to servants' hall. But there has been another and much more important aspect, due to the law of primogeniture. Jefferson, who was to secure its abolition in Virginia because he considered it undemocratic, as it was under American conditions of his day, did not recognize the part it had played in democratizing England as compared with the Continent, in the Old World. Its effects were important for us.

Speaking broadly, according to the law in the period we are discussing and now, among the nobility not only the title but the bulk of the entailed estate goes to the eldest son. The younger sons become "commoners" and have to fend for themselves. There are distinguished, famous and powerful families in English history but no such thing as "noble blood" as understood on the Continent, where the titled noble and all his titled children form a caste apart from the rest of the population. The English younger sons and daughters scatter among all classes of the people and over all parts of the Empire. There is a profound difference between nations which have merely strongly emphasized *social* classes and those which have rigid *castes.* Even if only slowly certain kinds of work ceased to be looked down upon socially in England, yet the freedom, and necessity, to do and be what one wanted in the shifting social life of that country has been of immense importance in developing the love of personal liberty and the releasing of the energies of all individuals, as contrasted with the case in caste countries. In this respect, England was a sort of half way house between the rigidity of the remnants of the feudal system on the Continent and the complete unshackling which was to be one of the effects of the American wilderness and frontiers. Life in any new country tends to become fluid socially and economically, as the British Dominions bear witness, but the way was smoothed for them and for us by the partial fluidity already attained by the English system.

It is a point of great significance for us that the first settlements by the English in America occurred at a time when England herself was in ferment. The great age of Elizabeth, with the immense fillip it had given to the enterprise and self-confidence of individuals, had just come to a close. It had been the age of Drake and the "sea dogs," the "singeing of the beard of the King of Spain," the defeat of the Armada, and the rush of English commerce to far quarters of the world. Elizabeth, great Queen that she was, had been facing a world against her, and had known it. The resources of her government were small, as were the taxes she could raise. She did not spend money to build the most powerful naval fleet or the greatest army on earth. Her subjects would not have stood for it. What she did was to give them all the freest rein she could to use their own resources to the utmost, and to save and build England themselves—farmers, fishermen, adventurers, merchants, all the various types who made the England of her day.

The result was that Englishmen, from top to bottom, had the chances of their lives, and took them. Elizabeth's subjects won their prizes or, often, died violent and heroic deaths, but they placed the little island on a pinnacle of glory, built a nation, and defended it against apparently overwhelming odds. They did it as individual men, hankering for adventure, wealth and power, not as government employees or officials, and they knew themselves *men.*

It was almost at that moment that the first lasting English settlement was made in America, from which the American was born. The *Sarah Constant* had sailed at the end of 1606. The East India Company had been chartered six years before; Elizabeth had died in 1603; Shakespeare was still living and a few months before the "first Americans" sailed he had produced his *Macbeth* and *King Lear* in London. Perhaps some of the passengers had seen the first performances of them. In 1533 Henry VIII had made the break with Rome, and anti-Catholic and anti-Spanish bitterness were still at their height. Elizabeth had tried to find a "middle way" for the new English Church. The Puritan movement had developed, and sects were multiplying. The year after the three vessels had reached Virginia, the first group of those who later became our "Pilgrim Fathers" left England for Holland. In 1611, five years before the death of Shakespeare, there was published the King James version of the Bible which, with the Shakespearean plays, has maintained its profound influence on English speech and thought, a link between all the English-speaking nations of the world. Never had Englishmen been more keen to have their own way and go their own ways, despite any and all. As Europe had had a magnificent outburst of energy and individualism after the Renaissance, so England was enjoying hers. On the death of Elizabeth, James of Scotland had ascended the throne, and with the attempted usurpations of the Stuart dynasty were to come the great struggle for liberty and the Civil War. In all English history a more fateful and propitious moment could hardly be found for settling America and beginning to hatch Americans.

Crossing the ocean again to Jamestown, we may note one more factor which was to be of great and continuing influence on Americanism from the very beginning down to the isolationists of the present day. That factor was the three-thousand-mile stretch of stormy sea which separated the home country, and its power to enforce its authority, from the colonists who came to live up and down our own coast. The dangers of the Atlantic crossing, the slowness of communication for many generations, and the remoteness of the English government, all helped to give the American a cockiness and self-assurance which have had much to do with his character, outlook on life, and international reputation.

CHAPTER II

A NEW WORLD

ON BOARD the *Sarah Constant* was a box the contents of which must have aroused great curiosity. It contained instructions from the Council of the Virginia Company in England and also the King's orders as to how the government of the first English colony in America was to be organized. The plan was simple in the extreme. The government was confided to seven designated appointees who were to form a local Council on the spot and run things, with power to add to their number (though they never added more than one). The charter, however, had provided that the colonists and their descendants were forever to "have and enjoy all liberties, franchises, and immunities within any of our other dominions, to all intents and purposes as if they had been abiding and born within this our Realm of England or any other of our said dominions."

The period was one of economic expansion and exploitation, and the mercantile chartered company, as exemplified by the Muscovy, Levant, India, Guinea, and Virginia Companies, among others, in England, was used in the rush for international trade by other nations also. Yet the governments of those nations, including that of liberty-loving Holland, gave their colonists no such guaranty of personal freedoms as did that of England even under the Stuarts. Back of the terms of this Virginia charter of 1606, back of the instincts of the colonists, was the long struggle of Englishmen through centuries past to do as they chose.

A vast proportion of immigrants to America have paid dearly in suffering for the chance of a fresh start in a New World, and those of this first group were no exception. There had been the mental strain and anxiety. These men had left all that was familiar in settled England (and we have noted how the English loved their home surroundings) to undertake what might well have seemed the hopeless venture of trying to establish a civilized community on the edge of a barbarous and almost unknown continent where four previous attempts had failed. Two earlier groups had been able to return to England, a third had been massacred and a fourth had disappeared forever. Great courage or deep despair must have been the motives of many of this fifth group who were trying once again. The four-month voyage, with its terrific storms, its shortage of food and fresh water, its mutiny on shipboard, must have emphasized for these adventurers the remoteness and loneliness of their situation.

Scarcely had they reached shore when they were attacked by Indians, and between the ocean, with its dangers behind them, and the savage natives on shore in front of them, their chances must have seemed precarious indeed. Moreover, fear of the still mighty power of England's deadly foe, Spain, pursued them also. The Spanish Ambassador in London had kept a close watch on what he deemed English intrusion on his King's claims to the two Americas, and it was believed that Spain might wipe out the new settlement. When a fortnight's exploration was undertaken to find a suitable place for the colony, ten men were left at Cape Henry to give warning of any Spanish approach.

Nor did the settlers know anything of pioneering. This was no mere voyage of exploration or buccaneering by sailors who felt as much at home on the waves as on the downs of their native Devon or other English maritime counties. It was not a trading expedition to cities, far and foreign perhaps but nevertheless not inhabited by savages nor destitute of food and shelter. This new colonizing task was one not to be undertaken with a light heart or by weaklings. The men who were risking and suffering so much to make new homes and carve out new lives for themselves would not be the sort to brook much interference when they got started. If, as Pitt later said, the King in old England could not enter the house of the poorest man without his consent, the omens were clear that, three thousand miles away from the King's palace and the King's troops, house doors might become shut still tighter against royal, and all, authority.

There were more experiences in store which were to play their part in the building of America and the breeding of Americans. On the exploring expedition a place was finally decided on for the settlement. Partly for the sake of safety from the natives and partly from ignorance of pioneering, the spot chosen was a small peninsula, almost an island, projecting into the James River. There a fort, some dugouts and a few rude huts were built before the two larger ships departed for England leaving less than a hundred and ten Englishmen to face the continent and found a nation.

The river water was bad and brackish, and no well was dug the first season. Indian attacks occurred, leaving a toll of killed and wounded. Shortage of food and disease wrought havoc, and more than sixty of the hundred or so colonists died. In January, 1608, succor arrived from England. Captain Newport, who had been "admiral" of the first little fleet, returned to find only forty or less survivors but he brought with him about a hundred and twenty more. Five days after the arrival of these newcomers, however, fire swept the settlement, destroying all but three of the makeshift dwellings. The palisades, the fort and the storehouse for food went up in flames. Buildings were only partially rebuilt during the winter and more colonists died from exposure. Later in the year, on two different ships, some hundred and ten more immigrants arrived, including two women, but in 1609 the growing colony was almost wiped out by the famine which is still known in American history as "the starving time." The few survivors, having stood all they could, decided to try to return home. Fortunately a new Governor sent out by England, Lord De La Warr, arrived in the river with fresh supplies, at the critical moment, and the colony regained courage and life. Even by 1616, however, there were only about three hundred and fifty inhabitants, many of them discouraged, as they well might be. Thereafter fresh adventurers to the New World increased the numbers fairly rapidly, although they were to be at least decimated in the "Great Massacre" by the Indians in 1622. Meanwhile settlers had expanded far beyond the confines of the ill-chosen Jamestown, a site so unfortunate that it is today an overgrown waste, and even the land would have disappeared had not the Society for the Preservation of Virginia Antiquities built a seawall to protect it. By 1625 it has been estimated that there were a thousand white people in Virginia, but to leave that residue *four thousand had perished*. People who had gone through all these trials, and with the English background of self-reliance and wanting to do as they pleased and to be let alone, would evidently be still more individualistic than if they had remained in their accustomed places, socially and geographically, in the old country.

We may now consider what sort of people they were. In the first place we must distinguish sharply in early American history between those in England who formed companies, received charters, and had great plans, personal or national, as to what could be done in America, and those who actually came and remained in America. This is true of all the colonies. We might as well compare some of the great American landowners in the eighteenth century or business magnates in the nineteenth, who induced immigrants to come here as tenants or laborers and factory workers, with those same immigrants as to compare the great merchants and noblemen in earlier days, who tried to plant colonies from England, with the colonists who actually came and settled. The great noblemen, courtiers, and prominent merchants who had the influence and money to secure the "charters" and "grants" and "patents" by which they hoped to make fortunes in America did not themselves come here. Nor did the kings who granted their favors to the great in England consider much the people on the spot. It may be said that, with almost no exceptions, in the forming time of

America and the American not a single titled nobleman, merchant of means, or noted scholar came here as a permanent colonist. A small percentage of cultivated persons of the upper middle class, often connected with good families, did come, but the great mass who worked and suffered and bore the burden of the day were of the lower middle and poor classes, to say nothing of the "criminal" in days when stealing even sixpence or a loaf of bread might mean transportation overseas.

A recent and able historian of Virginia speaks of certain men of distinction who came with the first lot of colonists, such as Captain Edward Wingfield, Captain Gabriel Archer, who had been a student at Gray's Inn, Captain John Smith, the clergyman Robert Hunt, and so on, but, after all, these were quite unimportant persons in England. The fact that these men, and some of the Massachusetts settlers later, are considered of real importance is the best evidence as to the sort who really founded America. I have already spoken of the younger sons of the nobility, and there was one of these in Virginia, George Percy, the youngest of the eight sons of the Earl of Northumberland. He left, however, a dubious record, after holding several official posts. All of these men mentioned above disappeared from the American scene in a very few years, either from death, return to England or the seeking of adventure elsewhere.

We are not here concerned with the social picturesqueness of the earliest days of Virginia but with the sort of people who built up that colony. Of these it may be said that even allowing for the much over-rated influx of "Cavaliers"—an over-rating which was to have serious repercussions in the nineteenth century—Virginia for the first few generations was peopled, led and defended by those who at home would have been rated as middle-class and lower. The almost complete lack of the aristocracy and of those who in England would have been considered as distinguished, undoubtedly had a great influence on the development of the American. The Virginian yeoman farmer who, in all sobriety, called Lord Baltimore a liar to his face and threatened to knock him down, even though the offender *was* put in the pillory for it, would probably not have ventured on such a rash break with all he had been accustomed to had he been in England instead of Virginia, three thousand miles away from where every one "knew his place." The yeoman had found *his* own place in a veritable new world.

There were other things that America was beginning to do to these Englishmen who had been through the starving time, the fire, the deaths of thousands by disease, and the Indian massacres—things as unexpected by them as by the courtiers, capitalists and monarch at home. As almost always in history, the motives of those engaging in the enterprise had been mixed, and as also frequently happens, the plans laid went astray and the results were far wide of those anticipated.

When the Virginia Company was chartered, England was in the throes of a growing economic crisis which was dangerously threatening the great position she had attained in the world. To maintain that position, for a small island, demanded control of the seas and an expanding trade. These called for ships and for cutting the claws of other maritime powers. Spain had been defeated but her rise to power had come from the riches she had drawn from the mines and peoples of Mexico and South America, and she claimed North America. She would have to be blocked there if England were to survive. There might be more mines of fabulous wealth in the northern continent, or a passage through it to the riches of the East. No one knew but all believed it might be so. If these fell into Spanish hands England and the Protestant religion would be in dire peril. To establish a colony in Virginia was to place a dagger at the heart of Spain, and if, in spite of previous failures, Raleigh's boast that he would yet see North America "an English nation" could be made true, that would build one strong bulwark against the growth of a new and perhaps even more dangerous Spanish peril than England had yet met. That was one reason why the Virginia venture took on the aspect of a great national undertaking, one that appealed to the new and glowing patriotism which Elizabeth had aroused, and made Virginia, named for the "Virgin Queen," a popular topic even on the London stage.

There were other reasons. There was the pressing need for ships and ever more ships. From various causes, the old nearby trades had been shrinking, those with France and the Low Countries for example. New markets and sources of materials far overseas had to be tapped. Ships were needed for these, and in the absence of a great Royal Navy it would be these merchant ships which would have to be called on to defend England, as they had been in the defeat of the Great Armada. But the home resources for shipbuilding in England had also been shrinking, and she had become largely dependent on the Baltic countries. These, however, were not only foreign; to reach them required the consent of Denmark, which controlled the entrance to the Baltic, and war among the "northern countries" might at any moment strangle the British in both trade and defense. All the materials required seemed to be found in America—the "masts, cordage, pitch, tar, rossen." This was one of the chief reasons for making another essay to claim and settle a part of the New World. Aside from these and other reasons of state, there were the numerous selfish ones of the many individuals embarked on the undertaking. As for the Virginia colonists—rather than the government or the backers of the Company in England—they were clearly making a great adventure to better their personal fortunes, which at the time were steadily getting worse at home.

Such were some of the motives and the well-thought-out plan for the American venture. A little England was to be established, supporting the old with needed materials but also having its farms, towns and diversified industries. All sorts of ship stores were to be produced. Foreigners, such as Dutchmen and Poles, conversant with such matters, were sent over to begin the making of them. It was hoped too that fishing, the manufacture of glass and iron, of dyes, the raising of hemp for cordage and of flax for linen, even perhaps the discovery of silver and gold, would all play their parts in the life of the new colony, which was to be varied but supplementing and not competing with the economic life of the old country.

The great men in England and the ordinary men who came overseas had not reckoned with America.

The hopes of the first were all to be dashed, and those of the others to be realized only in altered form and after suffering of which the adventurers had never dreamed. America stepped in and took charge. Virginia was found to offer no precious metals or jewels; no dyes or hemp or flax. No glass or iron works developed as permanent industries. Even in a land of great trees, including forests of pine for resin, the vision of ship stores disappeared. In Russia, Poland and Scandinavia, labor was abundant and cheap. The voyage was short to England. In America labor was expensive and almost unobtainable. The voyage was perilous, long and costly. The three thousand miles of watery wilderness was our first tariff barrier, and on shore America had spoken to the common man.

"This long almost empty land," we might imagine her as saying, "is for you, the poor and the oppressed, the weary and the heavy-laden. It is not for those who would live softly and easily or from the toil of others. America is not a pampering land. You must have fortitude, high courage, and willingness to work. You and your families may have to suffer and take great risks, even to your lives. You may have to forego much that has made life seem normal and safe and pleasant in the homelands from which you and others may come, but in exchange you will find a new life, a life of freedom to be yourselves, to make the most of yourselves that you can, to win perhaps great prizes, and above all to take your place as free men and women in the building of a better life for all than has yet been dreamed of in the war-torn, and shacklebearing nations of the past. I welcome you with open arms to my wide expanse, three million square miles of woods and mountains, of fields and prairies and plains, of riches unthinkable. Take me and use me for yourselves and all humanity. Yours is the opportunity of all the ages. Use it well and a new Heaven and a new earth may dawn for man. Misuse it and man's last hope may break. For you—and you—and you—the chance has come."

The ears of the carpenters, the brickmakers, the leather workers, the farmers and others may have caught no such words on the breezes which swept over the mosquito-infested malarial marshes along the James from the western mountains, but the spirit of America and the molding forces of the new land began to work on them.

At first the prospect held little cheer. Moreover, the blueprint planning for the colony by the theorists at home had included the idea of communism, which has never worked in a civilized community but which crops up every now and then to allure certain types of mind which ignore the realities of human nature. The colonists were to work not for themselves as individuals but for a "common store" into which the results of their labor were to be placed and from which they would draw for their necessities. The experiment went on disastrously for some years. Without the incentive of personal gain for personal thought and work, ambition disappeared and the morale of the community fell to almost zero. Anything more different from the wisdom of Queen Elizabeth in enlisting the energy of every man in the state by allowing the able and adventurous to reap the full rewards of their energy and daring could not be conceived.

When under the rule of Sir Thomas Dale as governor a new course was taken, and each man was allotted three acres of his own and, as John Rolfe wrote, they could sit under their own "fig tree in safety, gathering and reaping the fruits of their labors with much joy and comfort," the effect was instantaneous. Captain John Smith commented that "When our people were fed out of the common store, and laboured jointly together, glad was he [sic] could slip from his labour, or slumber over his taske, he cared not how, nay the most honest among them would hardly take so much true paines in a weeke, as now for themselves they will doe in a day: neither cared they for the increase, presuming that howsoever the harvest prospered the generall store must maintaine them, so that wee reaped not so much Corne from the labours of thirtie as now three or four do provide for themselves."

A man could at last work for himself and his own. The free winds of America were blowing.

We have spoken of the "starving time." The distress had probably been due in part to the lack of knowledge of what would grow, and in part to the fact that a large part of the colonists, who were not farmers, knew nothing of agriculture. There was one crop, however, for which Virginia was particularly adapted and which has made her famous. That was tobacco. Its use was just becoming general in England, thanks to Sir Walter Raleigh and his pipe. All other hopes, even for food enough for the colony, had failed but tobacco could be shipped home. It would bring money to the colony and create credits in London to be used in buying the English goods which were needed. When John Rolfe, the first founder of an American industry and of American foreign trade, discovered the proper method of curing tobacco for shipment, the future of Virginia was assured.

Almost every one started to raise tobacco. It was one of the critical moments in the history of America and the creation of the American. Those who object to the use of tobacco may reflect that if it had not been for the "filthy weed" the Virginia colony would have failed. If *it* had failed there would probably have been no Plymouth and Massachusetts, and a derelict North America might have fallen to Spain. Rolfe's discovery or invention of how to cure tobacco so as to make it a product in the world's markets was, like Whitney's invention of the cotton gin nearly two centuries later, to have profound effects on American history and character. Tobacco was to create a unique type of society; to bring in slavery; to cause the great schism of the Civil War; to bring us our greatest racial problem; and to do many other things. The discovery of a commercially valuable product which could be raised by the discouraged colonists, combined with the impetus given to individual ambition by the return to the system of private property and personal reward for personal effort, gave life and courage to the community.

Another important factor in our story is the coast line of Virginia and Maryland, which is peculiarly integrated with the ocean, more so than any other section of the entire United States. Passing from the dangers of the Atlantic between the sheltering capes of Henry and Charles, one sails into the magnificent Chesapeake Bay, a protected inland sea. Into this, with its many inlets, flow numerous rivers which were navigable for even the ocean-going vessels of the period we are considering. It was far easier to use these waterways than to expend labor on building roads through the wilderness. So, forgetting the dangers from Spaniards and even Indians, the settlers in steadily increasing numbers left the fever-ridden little Jamestown, and spread themselves, wherever they chose, on small farms (which as we have noted were called "plantations") along the shores. Ships from London could call directly at the docks of each separate plantation, and the owner could ship his tobacco overseas straight from his curing houses with no cost of land transport.

As the canals and dykes of Holland have greatly influenced Dutch life and even character, so the peculiar physiography of Virginia and Maryland influenced from the start the type of civilization developed in those colonies. The ease of water transport, for one thing, made road building seem largely unnecessary labor and expense. This idea became more or less ingrained, and although conditions changed greatly in the next three centuries, Virginia was notably backward in road building until the motor age of the last few decades. Another effect of the early location of plantations on the shores of the Bay or banks of the rivers, was that no towns worthy the name grew up. It was easier for the planter to roll his hogsheads of tobacco from his own wharf onto the ship which would carry them to London, and to order his clothes and furniture and other things from the merchant there who credited him with the sale of his crop, than to do business both ways through a local merchant in a local town, even had either such existed.

It may be noted as a point of minor interest and coincidence, rather than of major influence, that during the Elizabethan period at the end of which Virginia was settled, the metropolis, London, was still dependent within itself on water rather than road transport. The river Thames flowing through it was the "Main Street" of the city and was largely used instead of the narrow and winding unpaved roads of the town. Along it, much like the palaces in Venice, were the great homes of the nobles, each with its landing stage and "watergate." Processions and state funerals floated up and down the stream, along with the small boats and their boatmen, which like the taxis and their drivers of the present day served the needs of ordinary citizens. Those who settled the Virginian shores and who had known London were accustomed to a great extent to going to and from their destinations by river and not by road, and would find nothing unusual about it.

The absence of towns and local business had its own effects, in turn, of many sorts. The social, intellectual and economic influences of town life were almost wholly lacking. A prosperous class of local manufacturers, merchants, clerks, artisans, tavern keepers and others did not develop. Life on scattered plantations, moderately prosperous but often remote from neighbors, bred certain traits. For example, the absence of towns and "places to stay," combined with loneliness (an ever-recurrent note, with many variations, in American life), developed the entertaining of strangers or friends in one's own house, and laid the foundation for what is justly called "Southern hospitality." Moreover the fact that cities did not grow up with a working-class population had two effects which greatly influenced the colony. It tended to reduce the number of workers who could readily be engaged for casual employment, and to accelerate the movement towards the land and independence.

In a word, America had set in motion two of its great molding forces:—the desire for owning land and the scarcity of labor even at high wages. A passion grew on the part of all, even the humblest, to own their own acres, however few they might be. Settlers refused to work for any one else when they could get land and work for themselves, which in the seventeenth century was not difficult. Lack of labor helped to keep down the size of plantations and to raise wages. There were, of course, artisans and laborers of various sorts in the colony but their wages were said to be "intolerable" and were perhaps four or five times those for similar work in England. Such wages easily led to the acquisition of a bit of land, and thus the great American magnet began to draw the poor from the Old World—wages undreamed of there, and free land with personal independence. Moreover, tobacco was a simple crop to raise, a fact that was to aid in the rush to the land then and in the growth of African slavery later.

But there were no slaves in the beginning, and indeed few until the next century. It was a period when there was no moral scruple against making slaves of savage or barbarous peoples; and it is a point often not sufficiently noticed that the American savage proved to be of no use as a slave. Indian slavery was tried in various colonies, including the Puritan ones of New England, but wholly without success. Had the North American native, like the South American, proved to be adaptable, as even some of the wildest of African tribes were to prove themselves later, the whole history of the United States might have been different. With an ample labor supply from the start the economic, social and political development of the colonies and subsequent states would have been on different lines, with no Negro problem and perhaps no Civil War.

In the air of North America even the native savage was no good when he lost his freedom.

So, as it was, there were no slaves, and a great shortage of labor, obtainable at only very high cost. On the other hand, there were large numbers in England who either longed for a chance in the New World or might perhaps be unwillingly sent thither. Changes in trade conditions at home, already alluded to, had not only thrown vast numbers out of work but had wrought havoc with the incomes of those who before had been fairly well-to-do. The contrast between the opportunities in America and the heavily reduced scale of living in England made thousands long to cross the sea.

The cost of passage, however, was heavy and the system grew up of ship captains carrying emigrants to America and reimbursing themselves by selling the services of the passenger for a term of years—usually five—on arrival. In the seventeenth century probably 100,000 came to Virginia alone in that way. They were of all classes and social grades. A considerable part of them were educated and ambitious but without means. These willingly sold their time (it is quite incorrect to say "themselves") for a few years in order to become independent and prosperous in a new country instead of remaining where there seemed to be no chance to get ahead. Some, especially younger ones, were kidnapped by unscrupulous captains. Some paupers were got rid of in this fashion so as not to be a burden on the taxpayers in their home localities. A small proportion were "criminals," as the term was then used, and transported by the government.

As a whole, however, these "servants" were good material for building up the new country. The time of service was, after all, only about the term of an apprenticeship then or a college training today, and when finished the world was crowded with opportunities such as most of those who came would never have had in England. Once in America, depending on their capacities and training, their positions while still servants, as they were called (though the connotation of the term was not that of the modern domestic servant), might be anything from that of tutor in the home of a well-to-do family, where he would be accepted as one of themselves, to that of a worker in a tobacco field.

The system was to be long continued and not only are some of the most distinguished families of today descended from such indented, or indentured, servants (both terms were used), but not a few themselves rose to national importance even up to the period of the Revolution and after. Thus Charles Thomson, secretary of the Continental Congress, two signers of the Declaration of Independence, as well as Maryland's great lawyer, Daniel Dulany, and the redoubtable Matthew Lyon, all came to America in that way—to mention only a few.

Once finished with paying for their passage by their time and work, the servants were free to hearken to the spirit of America in any way they chose. About fifty per cent of them appear to have become small landed proprietors. Even when land was not given to them, it took only a year or two of wage-earning when service was completed, to save enough to buy a few acres, and no more stigma attached to the fact that these new citizens had paid their way as they did for the chance to have a stake in America than would attach today to boys or girls who work their way through college. The success and social position of these 100,000 or so men and women who, with their descendants, formed by far the largest part of the population of Virginia by 1700, depended almost wholly on what they were and what they could do for themselves—the authentic voice again of the American spirit.

In the lower House of the Legislature for example, in 1629, sixteen per cent of the members were men who had appeared in the muster roll of five years earlier as "servants." Although in the latter part of the century, after 1660, the conditions for a poor man's getting ahead were less favorable, there is every evidence to support the statement of Governor Berkeley that hundreds of examples testified to the fact that no man in Virginia was denied the opportunity to rise and to acquire both property and honor.

Although the great numbers of immigrants of the type described above built up the population, they could not solve the labor problem. That difficulty has, for three centuries, harassed those intent both on making private fortunes and developing the country, but it has also given the worker a standard of living that would have seemed incredible to seventeenth-century Virginia, or even twentieth-century Europe or Asia. Whether it would have been better not to have built fortunes and used up the country so rapidly is a problem we may touch on later, but what interests us here is that until practically 1700 Virginia was not made up of magnates and great landed estates with troops of slaves as many romantic Southerners would have us believe, but, at least nine-tenths, of yeoman farmers tilling their own fields or at most with the help of a white indented servant or two, each of whom would be free to go his own way and become a farmer himself in a few years if he wished.

The lives they lived and the property they owned would have been carved out by their own efforts. There were some incapables, some poor and shiftless, a growing number of wage-earners, and, towards 1700, some Negro slaves and a few wealthy planters, but for the most part the early Virginians were as independent a lot of yeoman farmers as could be found on the rocky soil of all New England. There were many and important differences but not in this respect.

There had evidently been some unruly spirits among the first colonists, as indicated by the mutiny on the voyage over, of the details and causes of which we know little, as Samuel Purchas, who edited the letters and accounts from Virginia in his collection of voyages, deleted the evidence he had. Fortunately, what happened in America is of more importance. As later, on the *Mayflower*, the prospective settlers were evidently a mixed lot, but it is of interest to note how the two English instincts for "rugged individualism" and for liberty under law operated in each case when small mixed groups found themselves far removed from any government armed with authoritative power.

We have spoken of the hardships of the first summer, and of the fact that Newport had left the smallest of his three ships, the pinnace *Discovery* of twenty tons, behind when he returned to England. Evidently there was a minority group in

Jamestown who favored abandoning the enterprise, while the majority wanted to stick it out. A Captain George Kendall was accused of plotting to seize the pinnace and to scuttle for home, leaving the colony with no boat. Accused of treachery he got a fair trial and was shot. Legal justice, not lawlessness, on the American frontier had begun. At the same time Wingfield, the President of the Council, was deposed and another Councillor chosen as President in his place. Wingfield was a Catholic and for that reason, in those days, not overtrusted but he was an important man. His father had been close to Cardinal Pole and to Queen Mary, and he was the only one of the colonists whose name appeared in the charter of the Company. Nevertheless he was ousted. He had also made charges against John Robinson and Captain John Smith, both much lower in the social scale and royal favor than himself. Their very names are redolent of the ordinary man. The President was sued for slander, and in the starving colony there was held the first trial by jury in America, Robinson winning £100 damages and Smith £200, from the influential President.

We need not discuss the alterations in the various charters of 1606, 1609 and 1612, but in 1619 there was a governmental change of far-reaching effect for our story. A new form of government had been determined on in "the great Charter," and when Governor Yeardley arrived he announced it to the settlers. Government was henceforth to consist of a Governor and Council chosen by the Company in England, and (of enormous importance) of a Lower House made up of burgesses elected two from each subdivision of the colony, of which there were at the moment four.

Although this charter was wholly revoked in 1624 and Virginia became a Royal Colony, the popular element in the government was not disturbed, and the plan became the general one for all future Royal Colonies, viz.: a Governor and Council appointed directly or indirectly by the Crown, and a popularly elected Assembly, a rough copy in miniature of the then English Parliament. The importance of thus introducing in

America the element of self-government cannot be overrated. The Assemblies in each colony became the local equivalent of the English House of Commons and played a similar rôle. They were made up of the people, and held the purse-strings over the Royal or otherwise privileged part of the governmental machine. From the beginning, until the Revolution, a continuing thread in our history was the constant succession of squabbles between the popular Assemblies on the one hand and the Governors and Councils on the other. It was a struggle for control of government by the people, of the people, for the people, emphasized by many factors different from those involved in the similar struggle in England itself.

The men on the spot, in Virginia and later elsewhere, were convinced that they knew better what was good for them than could rulers or bureaucrats three thousand miles away. In this they were largely right and occasionally wrong. The affairs of local government were for the most part simple, and like matters which might arise in parish or town meetings. In imperial affairs each colony was inclined to take in general the provincial view of its own apparent local good without considering imperial problems as a whole. However, that is aside from the main point, which is that the colonial Assemblies, like the smaller political meetings named, were incomparable schools for teaching citizens to govern themselves and to control their own affairs.

How popular in make-up the Assembly, or House of Burgesses as it was also called, was from early days in Virginia has already been suggested by the number of "servants" who soon appeared in it after their terms of service were over. The spirit of revolt appeared at the very first session when two members who had been elected from "Martin's Brandon" were rejected by the other members on the ground that although Martin's patent to his lands was legal he had in it received certain privileges not accorded to other patentees. The ordinary American, on the first occasion allowed him, thus raised his voice against any form of special privilege. It was an English note, if you will, but it was to resound even louder on frontier after frontier in the remote American wilderness.

To some extent privileges of many sorts were accorded to classes and individuals in the old country, but on American frontiers there were no castles, no huge estates or aggregations of capital, no tenant farmers, no hereditary aristocrats who could claim privileges from the mere fact of birth. With labor and domestic service almost unobtainable, the old English question from the time of Wat Tyler's Rebellion:

> When Adam delved, and Eve span,
> Who was then the gentleman?

received for answer "everybody and nobody."

On frontiers where practically every one was making his own clearing, building his own house, working his own farm, and doing his own shooting, whether of game or Indians, with only the willing help of neighbors (if there were any), the demand for privilege would have short shrift. As we shall see, privilege came in as frontiers changed to old settlements and established communities, but almost all of America started as frontier, and the revolt against privilege became as ineradicably ingrained in the real American as did his insistence on doing as he would with what he made for himself.

A foreigner has been quoted as saying that Americans make too much of the frontier as an excuse for or explanation of everything, but it must be recalled that although the extreme frontier may have lasted only a few years in any one locality, we have had a succession of thousands of frontiers in our westward advance over three thousand miles across the continent, and have had a background of frontier life from 1607 until the frontier was officially declared ended in the Census of 1890. The frontier for America was not a brief period, like a national childhood, to be outgrown and forgotten but was an ever-continuing influence from the settlement at Jamestown up to the time of my own boyhood, when Indian fighting was still going on.

The form of the colonial governments was also of importance. The fact that the royal, and often titled, governor represented to ordinary Americans an almost foreign and frequently annoying hindrance to their own will not only made Americans fear the power of any executive, while they clung to the rights of a popularly elected legislature, but also made them resent privilege. The governor's noble title, when he had one, and at least his office, set him above ordinary folk socially. Also he was the fount of land grants and wealth which represented privileges beyond what the ordinary man could get by his own efforts without influence in the "governor's set." Although there were not a few good and conscientious governors, they were all too frequently merely bankrupt courtiers and royal favorites, who inspired no respect. The relation to them of colonists who felt that what they themselves were and had was the result solely of their own work and hardships was very different from even that of tenants, on an estate in England, to some nobleman or gentleman who, or whose family, had at least done something in the past for them and for the nation. Pride in serving a family whose name had come down through centuries, and a certain mutual dependence which had come from feudalism, often in England obscured the more naked facts of privilege.

In America the Royal Governors had no claim on the respect or gratitude of the ordinary man, who regarded them often as dishonest grafters, themselves of no real standing, the dispensers of graft to their personal friends, and enemies of the people. The governors had not even learned the technique of the modern city politician who gives picnics, hands out food or coal and shoes when times are hard, and has gradually developed a form of feudalism of his own. On every American frontier, at each advance, titles and other privileges came to be abhorred and feared by those who had left the settled order of the mother country or older settlements to work out their careers in a wild country.

When the Virginia Legislature met under the new form of

government it proceeded to set its seal of approval and acceptance to the Charter, an action which may have caused King James to smile. They then went on to make, as they put it, "such Lawes as might issue out of each man's private concept." The growth of the American was not altogether a matter for kings to smile at. We may skim over a dozen years or so during which the Virginians were engaged in altercations with King James and his much disliked Governor, Sir John Harvey, and come down to 1635.

Tobacco, for various reasons, had been playing the tricks of most staple crops and had been varying much in price, declining, on the whole, more or less continuously. The King had counted on the revenues from the crop as a considerable item, for the needs of the national exchequer and his own personal ones, and had from time to time attempted to fix its price and to prohibit the settlers from shipping it anywhere except to England. There had been protests and evasions. In fact there is much evidence to show that in spite of orders from home the colonists managed, by methods known to themselves, to enjoy more or less a world market for what was until 1660 almost their sole export.

The colonists moreover had had many quarrels with the Governor over local affairs, and the whole situation came to a head in 1635. The King had demanded a monopoly on all American tobacco at a price to be determined by himself or his councillors, and the Virginia Assembly passed an act refusing to agree, which Governor Harvey declined to forward. This was followed by the drawing up of a petition for redress of grievances, which he also declined to send on to the government at home. The Council in Virginia was working with the Assembly, and after an unseemly personal encounter, in which the Governor struck one of the Councillors, His Excellency was arrested by forty musketeers conveniently placed, and told that the "people's fury is up against you," and that he would have to leave for England to answer to their charges. He refused and ordered the Assembly dissolved, but both Houses of the Legislature continued to sit. When informed that the people were ready to move against him, he sailed, and the Council elected a governor *pro tem.* until a new one should be sent from England.

The episode was nothing less than a revolution. The stage was small but the facts remain that the Americans had refused to obey the King's orders, that the Legislature had met in defiance of the commands of his representative, who had been deposed and shipped out of the country, and that "the people" had taken matters into their own hands. "The people" were nearly one hundred per cent small yeoman farmers, and there was no difference in attitude between the Assembly and the Council. If we take an historical magnifying glass, and move it across the map from the colony in Virginia to England, and consider the affair in terms of Parliament and the King, instead of a colonial legislature and the King's representative, we shall understand it better, though the analogy may not be pressed too far.

The American could do this sort of thing bloodlessly and with more or less immunity. The Englishman at home could not. Why? In part because the stage was small, and the setting simple. In a similar case in England, as was to happen in another decade or so, parties would form and armies would march. There the social structure was complex and the interests of classes and parties divergent. In Virginia the parties were "the people," all much alike in their interests and positions, and instead of the King himself there was only a royal representative with no troops to unfurl the royal standard above *them* and with no traditional sanctity or powerful aristocracy to rally around *him*. And then there was that ever-present factor, the three thousand miles of the Atlantic. An uprising in an English county might be quickly suppressed, but to send some thousands of troops overseas to fight, in an unknown country, some twenty thousand or so of Englishmen defending themselves in their own homes, behind those doors which a King could not enter, was another matter.

Colonists then, and for long after, might be loyal to England and the Crown. They might also have a realistic sense of the value to themselves of the imperial connection. Nevertheless when they wanted to run their own affairs, when they wanted to be themselves in their own way, they evidently, as we may say, had it "all over" their fellow citizens at home. Old institutions, old inhibitions, old fears of force against them should they venture too far, old "kow-towing" to a graded social hierarchy, had somehow largely disappeared beneath the waves of the stormy Atlantic which was to be considered by them and generations of their descendants as a kind of protection in doing as they pleased with no possibility of serious interference.

The fledgling Americans of Virginia after only a quarter of a century were beginning to grow the eagle's feathers.

We must again skim over some years without noting details of the relations of the young American eagle with the British lion. The lion was in trouble. The period of the Civil War in England, the Cromwellian regime, and the Restoration, lay ahead. It was a period which affected the various American colonies quite differently. In Virginia its duration was mostly coincident with the regime of Governor Sir William Berkeley (1642–1677).

Berkeley was a fanatical Royalist but at first he had favored the colonial popular cause and had even allowed the Assembly to become the final Court of Appeal in Virginia, with the right to review with himself as governor judgments of the Legislature as a whole. Nevertheless he was evidently something of a narrow-minded fool, persecuting relentlessly Quakers and Puritans, and thanking God that there was not a free school in the colony—a statement which was far from true.

Except for one incident, of which we shall speak presently, his influence on the growth of the American, or perhaps we should say of the southern group of Americans, was rather psychological than political. With his fanatical loyalty to the House of Stuart, he was furious when the head of Charles I rolled from the block in Whitehall, and when he got the news he induced the Virginia Assembly to pass a violent denunciation of the act. During the Cromwellian period there was no governor. Berkeley retired to his plantation but he did help to defend Virginia against the ships which Cromwell despatched, and only a nominal surrender of the colony was made. When Charles II returned to the throne, determined never to "go on his travels again," he renewed Berkeley's commission as governor, and conferred on Virginia, for its loyalty, the title of the "Old Dominion," which it has ever since retained.

Berkeley also induced many of those who had followed the cause of the Stuarts to remove to the colony when Cromwell came to power, and these were the "Cavaliers" who were to loom large in Virginia tradition, though comparatively few in number.

Berkeley, on his return to office after the Restoration, tried to copy the reactionary policy of his royal master in England, and unfortunately the American spirit seems to have evaporated for a time from both Houses of the Virginia Legislature. Finally, however, the people again took matters into their own hands. The Governor had refused to help those who were suffering from severe attacks by the Indians in the outlying sections. A force was raised by a certain young Nathaniel Bacon, who had been in the colony only two years, and to whom the Governor refused a commission. Bacon defeated the Indians and destroyed their stronghold, only to be arrested by the Governor. When he attempted a second expedition against the savages, he was declared an outlaw but marched on Jamestown, with the people back of him, and forced Berkeley to flee. Unfortunately, Bacon died after a very short illness, and the rebellion broke down, but the Governor took such bloody vengeance on Bacon's followers that he was recalled, and King Charles is said to have remarked that "the old fool has killed more people in that naked country than I have done for the murder of my father." Virginia had paid high for its title and its loyalty to the Stuarts, and Berkeley himself died in England soon after without having been granted the interview he had craved at the hands of his royal master.

A vast change was now impending, due to the introduction of African slavery on a large scale; the creation of great estates; the loss of equality; the lessening of opportunity for the yeoman farmers who had been the backbone of the "Old Dominion"; and the growth of a colonial aristocracy based on land and wealth, entail and primogeniture. Meanwhile other colonies had been founded, along the southern coast, which we must disregard for the moment as we are merely taking soundings here and there to find the "American," and we shall now turn to the Puritan strain of the North.

CHAPTER III

THE BEGINNING OF NEW ENGLAND

AFTER a few years in Virginia, the picturesque John Smith returned home, to be sent out to America again by those interested in our northeast coast with orders to explore it and to report on its resources. His map and his numerous writings established the name of "New England" for the general section, and such, from 1616, it has always remained. The name has distinct connotations for us all, and the region has had an influence both on "the American" and his history out of all proportion to its size and population. We sense instinctively that "New England" means something very definite as contrasted with the group of "Middle Colonies," the "South" or the "West," but, although New England has its own individuality, it has always been complex. Yet if there is much diversity among the peoples of its present six states, as there was also in the more numerous and differently delimited early colonies, there is still a unity.

Both the unity and diversity have to be traced back to the environment and the people. I do not take my stand with such historians as claim to have found single keys to unlock the mystery of the human story, whether their key be climate, geography, economics, religion, the great man, or vaguely, the "great social forces." All these and others play their parts, but, to change the metaphor, the skein is so tangled that we are fortunate if here and there we can pick out for a short way some one guiding thread. For example, when Roger Williams, after being exiled from Massachusetts, travelled in mid-winter through snowy forests to Rhode Island to found a new colony, it was partly because of his religious beliefs, partly because the Bay people were afraid of his theory of land ownership (which threatened their property), and partly for the simple reason that, having to escape to some place, he knew an Indian there. Yet environmental, economic and other general influences do count in the long run. If the native friend to whom he fled had happened to live somewhere else, the whole Rhode Island experiment in government and religious toleration might have been played on a wholly different stage in another locality. Individuals and the accidents of individual life do count, but so also—and heavily in the long run—do the more general influences, geographic, economic, and others.

Topographically New England is very diversified. On the east and south there is the long coast line, which invited those dwelling near it to become seafaring. North and west are upthrusts of the Appalachian chain of mountains, which tended to shut the section off from the rest of the continent. Between the sea which served as a highway and the mountains which served as a barrier, the land was minute and rough for the most part, calling for much labor on small farms to make it suitable for agriculture. The varying soils were often poor, and the meadows scattered here and there were highly prized and had not a little to do with the compact form of settlement in towns, as had also the human factor of church government which we shall note later. When a group in a town asked leave to go elsewhere because they were "straitened for land," it was not for lack of empty acres but for want of usable ones, or from religious and political reasons.

Stressing the geographical rather than the human elements, A. B. Hulbert in his suggestive volume on *Soil* says that:

The New England "town" as a factor in American history is explained by nothing so much as by the New England meadow. These rugged states must be seen in the light of these innumerable spots of vivid green, spots only large enough for a limited number of families in which each one could have an anchorage, so to speak, in fertile meadow lands, but with a larger inheritance of upland, swamp, and forest. The small dimensions of these meadows and the variegated character of adjoining lands, made the raising of a great staple crop impossible; every farm raised every kind of produce which could be grown on the soils represented. . . . No one soil, even in the Connecticut Valley, extended in any direction more than a few rods or miles at the most.

Another very important influence exerted by the diminutive New England meadows . . . was the necessity of accurate surveys. Since the meadow was the lifeblood of each New England settlement, every foot of its soil became inordinately precious. . . . Surveys were carried out to inches and tenths with careful precision. . . . Being compelled to draw careful lines, to use circumspection with reference to limited meadow lands, to count inches, to guard jealously fences and corner posts, to avoid infraction of others' rights and to protect his own, was doubtless one basic reason for the Yankee's so-called penuriousness, his instinct for saving, his cautiousness, canniness, and "nearness."

Soils have played an extremely important part in the development of the American, a part too much neglected by most historians. The life of the frontier in time came to create a type of frontiersman who loved solitude and felt crowded if a neighbor settled within twenty miles of him, as contrasted with the more usual type who felt the loneliness and wanted neighbors or visitors. Too much, however, has been made of a mere love of wandering. Apart from the economic and social pressures exerted by the old settlements on those who could not make their way under the conditions existing in them, what led to a large part of our migrations and the settling of the wilderness was the search for *soils*, not only good soils but soils which would permit of a method of farming, dairying or whatnot to which the emigrant had been accustomed at home. As in the later industrial period a workman would naturally migrate to a region where he could find work to which he had been used (for example, as a miner to a mining region, a steel worker to a steel section, and so on), so in the early agricultural period the lure was a soil which the settler knew how to use. When we find Germans going to one section, Swiss to another, Scotch-Irish to another, we also find that the type of soil was usually the determining factor. Of course there have been others, such as cost, the tricks of advertising, or the presence of other members of the same race as the prospective settlers but the start was usually for soil of a certain sort. Moreover, as the paths to be travelled had been indicated first by the buffalo and other animals before the Indian, and then by the Indian before the white man, so the course of soil migration had been marked out by nature, ages before the coming of the first settlers from overseas. Vegetation, particularly trees, indicated the kind and quality of the soils in which they grew. Trees may be said to have been the first migrants in search of the soils that suited them, and the human pioneer looked for the trees—the many kinds of oaks, willows, chestnuts and others—and studied their variety, their size and age, to tell him where to find the soils which would suit *him*.

We must also not forget the vegetable needs of the domestic animals, which loomed large in importance. The cows, steers, horses, even the vast numbers of the humble razor-back hogs in the South, had to be given the land they needed, and the forage they required, and as America, until well after the Revolution, was ninety per cent agricultural, the need for land was not merely for *more* acres but for the *right kind*. Although it is only a rough estimate, we may say that perhaps only about one-fifth of the land in New England was of any use to settlers, and the acreage of the diminutive and sparsely scattered meadows was so valuable as to be worth as much and more than house lots, and about twice the price of upland.

Although we have stressed the meadow as an item usually neglected in the development of the New Englander, there were other molding factors due to geographical conditions. There was, for example, no such complicated and easy articulation of land and water as we have noted in Virginia and the Chesapeake Bay country. The river system was inadequate, with the fall line of rivers very near the coast, with the exception of the Connecticut. Even that river did not pierce the mountain barrier to the west, and from the direction of its course north and south emphasized the particularism of the New England region. There is another point which we may note. In studying the control which America has exerted over the American the suggestion of some leading anthropologists that he is gradually assuming some of the physical and psychological traits of the Indian cannot be wholly discarded. He is, for example, apparently growing taller, more wiry and more nervously high-strung. At any rate, Americans have followed the course of Indian migrations from the earliest age of the Mound Builders, in expanding *across* the rivers running north and south, rather than *up and down* them.

The river highways are less important than the isothermal lines which they cross. This was true of the Connecticut, along which climatic conditions alter fairly rapidly for agriculture as one ascends it. The first really important settlements on it were not made upward from its mouth but straight west overland from Massachuetts Bay. In addition the Connecticut crossed the claims or bounds of several colonies or later states. The Hudson would probably have had the same isolating effect except for its tributary Mohawk which gave those who used the Hudson access to the west. There was no such access for the group of colonies and states which have formed New England in different periods, and the geographical isolation of the section has had much to do with its intellectual and political provincialism, and the building up in it of a peculiar local culture.

In considering the influence of geographical conditions on this region we must not forget the climate which far more than offsets a brief and almost tropical summer with a long hard winter. Perhaps the most characteristic and loved idyll of New England, as well as one of the best depictions of our old Americanism, is Whittier's "Snow-Bound."

As we travel north from Virginia to Vermont we find a lesson in architecture which speaks to the thoughtful observer more convincingly than a whole essay on sectionalism. At the start, in the South, we find houses with large halls and rooms, with a kitchen separated from the main house, with old slave quarters and outbuildings at a distance. As we go northward, the halls and rooms shrink in size, the kitchen moves into the house and becomes perhaps its most important room; the hired "help" sleeps in the attic, if there is any help; the barn with the cattle and horses is no longer at a distance but is part of the house. The whole establishment, family and rooms and buildings, shrink together, as a man shrinks into his ulster in facing an icy wind, and the reason is the same.

Environment has great effect on ways of living. Ways of living in turn have their effects on attitudes towards life. Large-scale plantations, whether as they developed later in the South or as they existed until recently in the West Indies, tend to engender in the owner a belief in his own opulence, even if he is continually in debt to his agents or bankers. The large single annual crop, with its seemingly impressive value in credit, the extensive acres, the big house, the easy hospitality, the scores or hundreds of slaves or laborers, the climate—friendly rather than hostile—all make for an expansive outlook on life. There was practically none of this ever in New England. As we shall see in dealing with the next century, we have to draw a distinction in the South between the rich planter class and the small farmers, but there still remains a distinction as a whole between the Southerners and the New Englanders. It is based on climate, soil, terrain—geography in a large sense.

We have spoken of the heritage of love of individual liberty which the settlers brought with them from England, and of how this was emphasized by the sufferings and hardships they went through. Those in the Puritan colonies also had their sufferings and misfortunes—sickness, Indian raids and the rest—but what made the Yankee was more than these things, more even than the sort of person he was when he came. It was the environment—the soil, climate, lack of staple crops. It was also the ever-constant difficulty of making both ends meet, the need of always seeking some new way of saving money and labor, of getting shelter, heat in winter, warm clothes, of securing products from a harsh home-land or a foreign trade which did not fit in with the needs of the Empire but were necessary to provide exchange with it. The attitude towards money and small profits was to persist. Last summer a friend of mine met a man carrying a dead porcupine—a rodent very destructive to wooden buildings—on a New Hampshire road. The following conversation ensued:

"Are you going to eat it?"

"Nope."

"What did you kill it for?"

"Get twenty cents for each one."

"That isn't much."

"Mebbe it *ain't* much, but it's *that* much."

That is what New Englanders had been learning for three hundred years. They who fought their way, whether fishing on the stormy Atlantic, venturing overseas in their small ships (often to trade in forbidden quarters), or making a bare living tilling stony fields, would be, if anything, still less inclined than those of their fellow English colonials in the South to allow themselves to be interfered with by the government in England.

If the first Americans were those we have already written of in Virginia, in New England there was to be another group whose influence on the American has been perhaps even more deep and lasting. For better, and sometimes for worse, it is impossible to overrate it, and even the traditional picture of "Uncle Sam" is that of a typical New England farmer. Strong, with a "New England conscience" which often takes queer turns (notably economic), self-reliant and often conceited, provincial, morally meddling, shrewd, sure of his rightness, and with the other qualities we associate with him, he is the typical and traditional American.

The New Englander, although he has become the symbol of America, has never been taken to its heart. There is, oddly, no all-American hero from New England, in the sense of one known to all and loved by all, as well as merely known and respected. The section has given only four Presidents to the nation in over 150 years, and not one was reëlected by the people. Yet the section in its group life looms very large indeed. Americans have no intense affection for any particular Pilgrim, such as Bradford, yet "the Pilgrim Fathers" have a sort of collective niche in our popular Hall of Fame which is not merely sectional, and it is said that a hundred thousand tourists a year visit the traditional Plymouth Rock. It is as if, in our national hero-lore, New England had settled in it as the New Englanders did on the land—in groups and towns rather than as individuals. Yet the American cannot be understood without emphasis on the New Englander.

Obviously, unlike the South, New England could never have been a land of large plantations with slave labor and staple crops. It was forced to remain one of small farms which to be self-supporting called for diversification and skilled work, work requiring not merely brawn, but adaptability. The stone walls around the little fields still testify to the backbreaking labor demanded before ground could be cultivated and protected, but all the other factors also contributed to make the New Englander and the New England type of American. The variety of the tasks, practically all of them performed by the family itself, in a small self-sufficing household, demanded that each member should be something of a jack-of-all-trades and find as many ways to lighten labor as might be. Every possible way had to be sought for making or saving. A New England winter taught harsh lessons to the idle, lazy or thriftless. The Yankee character, inured to hard work, economical even to meanness, shrewd, stubborn, independent, individual, developing "notions" and inventions, was largely derived from the conditions in which it developed.

We have spoken of the environment and must now turn to those who came to it and what it did to them. Like those who founded Virginia, the settlers in New England were English, and we may take this opportunity of explaining again that if we stress these two English swarmings from the hive of old England in the seventeenth century it is not to ignore those of other races or nationalities who came to America. It is said that early in the century eighteen languages were spoken in

New York and there were many foreign names to be met with here and there, but the fact remains that it was the English who set the mold of our institutions, politics, law, language, ways of life and modes of thinking.

Efforts have been made by sectional historians to show that the earlier immigrants to the South or to New England were quite different—to the social or ethical advantage of either section as the historian's ancestry demanded. Careful and dispassionate examination would seem to show that socially there was little or no difference. From the beginning, America was made up of what they call in England the middle and laboring classes, and it has always remained so. This is, in fact, one of the important points about it.

The American is the result of the impact of America on the kind of people who came here, but we ignore too much, perhaps, the fact that those who were to become Americans, either real or merely legal, were not a cross section of *all* the life of the Old World but represented almost wholly only certain groups or types. To begin negatively, none of those of the highest grade in Europe, intellectually, socially, politically or economically, with rare exceptions, have come to America to throw in their lot permanently with us in the amazing American experiment.

It is true that almost from the beginning, and especially as life passed from the frontier to the settled stage, certain social gradations were formed. Some people have put on airs, prided themselves on their family, and worn different clothes, but these grades were largely based on money and personal success, because there was nothing much else to base them on. There have been no titles, hereditary distinctions, or government honors which gave prestige in the eyes of the public. These volatile social grades were quite different from the more rigid *classes* of England, just as that class system was less rigid, in turn, than a genuine system of perpetual *caste* on most of the European continent. It was the middle class and those below them who came here, as we have said, but those below quickly became middle class themselves as vast numbers of them acquired land, homes and other property. We are almost *all* middle class, in the English sense, and it is one of our greatest national achievements that we *are*. We have nothing *above it* and our failure, in so far as we have failed, has been in not lifting everybody *up to it*.

The effect of this on the American has been enormous. Matthew Arnold had no love for America, and in many ways was a fairly complete snob, yet he wrote of his own countrymen that "Our love of inequality is really the vulgarity in us, and the brutality, admiring and worshipping the splendid materiality," and that "On the one side in fact inequality harms by pampering; on the other by vulgarizing and depressing." America has been notably free from what Brownell called "these upper and nether millstones of materialism and brutality," and accordingly we developed differently from the English. Love of wealth and of personal distinction were certainly not left behind in Europe, but the idea of "class" was shed from the decks of every arriving vessel with the rest of the bilge water from the scuppers. We were to develop serious racial and economic problems but we never had that of class, in the European sense, in spite of efforts, North and South, to insist on social distinctions such as the mild forms of "Gent" versus "Goodman." This, and the fact that we, of all great nations, have never adopted or grown into democracy but simply as a whole have never known anything else, set the Americans apart and helped to breed their unique qualities.

America has never been Utopia and I am not here ignoring many of the blots and cross currents and minor influences but am referring to the great mass of genuine Americans during at least the first three centuries of their forming time.

It is not a trifling gesture that American railways have made to the public in refusing to mark cars of different costs for transportation, Classes 1, 2, 3, and even 4. If the public would not like this, as contrasted with European publics, it is because something has happened in America that had not happened over there. I once asked a young visiting Frenchman what struck him most about us, and after a moment he replied, "I think it is the way that every one looks you right in the eye and takes it for granted that all are on the same level." That is a quality of the American, a quality that enabled old Barnum to chat with the ultra-Victorian Queen Victoria without a qualm of self-consciousness or a thought of difference in rank or of his own possible vulgarity.

Of vulgarity there has been plenty in our country, as there is in others, but our being practically all of the same, and the middle, class has enabled our democracy to produce a distinction of its own which, at its best, is greater because it is more deeply human and genuine than any produced by an aristocratic society and tradition. I understand that Professor Copeland of Harvard once caused a rustle of resentment in his literature class by saying, "Gentlemen, we are *all* middle class." In spite of the flurry among some of the young scions of family and wealth, "Copey," as he was affectionately called, was right, and it will be only when his statement may no longer accord with fact that America will face real social danger.

If the term middle class is resented by some it is largely because Americans feel that they are as good as any one else, and the term has come to us from old societies in which the middle class is socially below a higher class, the aristocrats, and because there are some personally inflated Americans who would like to place themselves in a class above their fellows. Obviously some individuals are abler, more distinguished, and more cultured than others, but it would seem that in America any effort to claim distinction on account of mere membership in a self-appointed class would indicate that those doing so did not (in themselves) possess the distinction which they seek to claim. A democracy cannot have the same sort of social distinctions which belong, or we might say in these days, used to belong, to an aristocracy, and any attempt in America to create them on a class basis can result only in destroying that fine and high distinction which can be made in a democracy, without getting anything but a shoddy plutocracy based on cash, genealogies—real or manufactured—and newspaper society items, in its place. It is worth noting, even at this early period, as a forecast of the later America, that the expatriated Henry James, who spent a life in fascinated study of European society, found himself over and over in his stories and novels, almost as it were perforce, contrasting the genuine distinction of his democratic compatriots with the artificial distinction of many of his European aristocrats, even in the inmost circle of the Faubourg St. Germain.

But there is another point about those who came from the Old World to people the New.

From the beginnings in Virginia and New England to the present, American immigrants have in general possessed certain qualities to such an extent that it may almost be said that those who have come to us formed a potential America before they ever landed on our shores. This country has had enormous influence in creating the American but it has had chiefly selected material on which to work. America has been the "great adventure," for all, and only those who for the most part have been adventurous and ambitious above the average have undertaken it. Those who have come have done so because they hoped to escape from persecution, religious or political, and from barriers intellectual, social, and economic against their chance to rise, in their home lands. They have come, in a word, in order to be able to be themselves as men and women, and to make the most of themselves untrammelled by artificial hindrances built up in the past.

The star they followed westward was the star of freedom, freedom to be and do all that, as human beings and not as cogs in an outworn machine, they might prove themselves capable of. There have in the course of our history been millions on millions of them, not all of them desirable, not all of them understanding the meaning of the American Dream. Yet on the whole, although the material which the spirit of America has had to work with has been the common, not the uncommon, man, it has been the sort of common man who has glimpsed in the "New World" a really *new world* in which he could throw off the trammels of the Old and rise to his full stature as a man.

The dream has been different for many who have dreamed it, just as the New Jerusalem is for some a material city paved with gold in a land flowing with milk and honey, and for others a spiritual bliss ineffable, but it has been a dream of something far above the ineffectual baffling lives which they had been leading. Whether they were the religious refugees landing on Plymouth Rock, to whom we must now turn, or the flow of millions through Ellis Island, the dream has meant something new and wonderful and has called for courage, sacrifice, a break with the known and familiar, and willingness to stake all they had had in the old life for the sake of winning to a better one. That is the kind of common man, the uncommon sort of humanity, with which the American spirit has had to deal, whatever it may make of him in the end.

Another distinction, besides that already touched upon, which some historians have attempted to make between the settlers of the South and of New England has been that of religion. There is both truth and untruth in this, and we again encounter the problem of unity in diversity. On the whole, at the time of the first English settlement of America, England had become Protestant, though with a remaining Catholic minority suffering from many disabilities. The Protestants themselves had begun to split into sects, but in general they may be divided into those who stood foursquare with the established Church and its ecclesiastical doctrines and practices, and those known as Puritans, who considered themselves as still within the fold but who wished to purge or purify the Church of certain things to which they objected. Some went so far as to separate themselves entirely.

The age was one in which religion was still a leading issue, whether it was a question of Catholic Spain or France against a Protestant England, one between parties within England, or the more personal problem of the salvation of one's own soul. Religion, from various angles, had a deep interest for the ordinary man in the street—much as science has had in our own age—and all classes of Englishmen, from the most highly placed and cultured aristocrats down to the poorest laborers, were affected by the Puritan movement. As is shown by the early laws enacted there was a strong Puritan tinge to the Virginia colony. Indeed, Puritanism was, as we say, "in the air." The difference between the first South and early New England was not that the one was Puritan and the other not, but lay in the facts that the "straitest sect" of the Puritans went to Massachusetts, that its leaders were different, and that partly by accident they remained for long almost independent of local royal authority. There were also the geographical and climatic factors of which we have already spoken.

There were plenty of Puritans in Virginia. There were important and populous Puritan colonies in the West Indies and the Caribbean, but only New England developed in its peculiar way. The "if's" of history are often fascinating though futile, and it would be interesting to know what would have happened to, say, the New England conscience, if Bradford, Winthrop, John Cotton, Mather, and their fellows had found themselves established in the enervating climate of New Providence in the Caribbean or in Virginia, where signs pointed to the eventual building up of large estates with slave labor. Would so many of their descendants, for example, have turned out to be fiery Abolitionists a couple of centuries later?

Although we have called attention to the diversity in New England we have likewise done so as to its unity. As an entire region, if we blur details and think in a smudgy sort of way, it has always had certain generalized characteristics, but this does not answer the question as to why Massachusetts and the colony of New Haven should have been so intolerant, whereas Rhode Island and Connecticut should have been the national well-springs of tolerance, or why the leaders of the latter two colonies should have led the way to democracy and popular government while those in Massachusetts abhorred it. Perhaps the word "leaders" is our guide. In any case, we may now turn to those leaders and the peoples who wittingly or unwittingly followed them, and the part which not only New England but the distinctly marked sections of it played in developing the American.

For a long time, Massachusetts, as the saying goes, "stole the whole show," but that was to a great extent due to the fact that in the past century when American history was first being written in popular, and then supposedly scholarly, form it was being done so chiefly by Bostonians and Massachusetts clergymen. Massachusetts and the Puritans were exalted above all the rest of the territory and people of the United States at a very considerable cost to fair-play, accuracy and a national outlook. For many of these authors, "the American" for whom we are searching had to be not merely a New Englander but one steeped in the traditions of the early leaders of the Bay colony. That day has long passed, but that it existed and had its influence is in itself pertinent to our story.

It is more than likely, though no such inferential statement can be proved, that if the settlers whose fortunes we have briefly noted in Virginia had not won through to success, there would have been no settlement in New England, perhaps no English-speaking and English-liberty-loving America. In fact the first group settlement in the bounds of the present Massachusetts was never intended to be there, but within the boundaries of Virginia.

We have already mentioned the little group of religious refugees who left England for Holland almost at the same time that the first colonists left home for the Virginia venture. After a dozen years or so, first in Amsterdam and then in Leyden, these simple and pious folk decided that though they had separated from the Church of England they did not care to merge their English identity with a foreign nation, even such a one as that of the tolerant Dutch. Casting about for a place to which to emigrate, they thought of Guiana where, according to rumor, they might easily grow rich, but they feared both tropical diseases and the Spaniards. They also thought Virginia might be dangerous for them, because although that colony was strongly Puritan it was nevertheless Church of England. The final decision was to settle within the confines of the Virginia Patent but somewhat remote from the part already occupied.

What followed, how they got financial backing from merchants in London, sailed on the *Mayflower*, were forced ashore at Plymouth in the bitter cold of a New England December, and won through that first terrible winter is known to every school child. Plymouth was never an important colony in numbers or wealth. Absorbed by Massachusetts in 1691 it did not survive as an individual state of our Union, with all that this means for the growth of local pride and tradition, yet it looms large in the heritage of the American. As "group heroes" the "Pilgrim Fathers" probably lead all others.

For one thing they were very ordinary men socially, who nevertheless made a great place in history by risking all they had and were for the sake of a dream and an ideal. We have seen the beginning of the American in Virginia but with the Pilgrims a new element enters, that of a religious ideal, dominating and not merely mingling with the other impulses and ambitions. Otherwise there were similarities in the early years of both settlements. Following the preliminary exploration of the coast after the first landfall and the choice of the permanent site, there ensued the hardships which Americans have encountered so often in their long struggle to conquer and people a continent. The numbers of the original colonists, both north and south, were approximately the same (just over a hundred), and about the same proportion—one-half in each case—died during the first season, Plymouth suffering a great loss in the death of Governor Carver. In both cases a very small group of inexperienced pioneers were at first left to fend for themselves on the edge of the ocean in an unknown wilderness. Bradford wrote later of the first landing of the Pilgrims: "they had no freinds to wellcome them, nor Inns to entertaine, or refresh their weather-beaten bodys, no houses or much less townes to repair too, to seeke for succoure. . . . And for ye season it was winter, and they that knew ye winters of ye countrie, know them to be sharp & violent, & subjecte to cruell & feirce storms, dangerous to trauill to known places, much more to serch an vnknown coast. Besids what could they see, but a hidious & desolate wilderness, full of wild beasts, & wild men, and what multituds ther might be of them they knew not. . . . If they looked behind them, ther was ye mighty ocean which they had passed, and was now as a main barr, & goulfe, to separate them from all ye ciuill parts of ye world."

He then tells of the mutterings by the captain and others that if a place were not found for settlement immediately the Pilgrims would be put ashore with scant rations, to look after themselves without aid. "What could now sustaine them," he adds, "but ye Spirite of God & his grace? may not, & ought not the children of these fathers rightly say, our faithers were *English men which came over this great Ocean,* and were ready to perish in this wilderness, but they cried unto ye Lord, and he heard their voyce, and looked on their adversitie." It is interesting to note how Bradford in his simply told story of the Pilgrim movement strikes so many American notes from the beginning of the settlement at Plymouth. Here we find mentioned the great empty and unknown continent; its savage inhabitants and danger; the loneliness and the need of the new Americans, depending only on themselves; the idealism of the dream which they carried with them and the star which they followed; the barrier of the ocean; the belief in themselves as Englishmen; and the strength of the English tradition.

We have earlier observed what happened to the common-store notion when tried by Americans in Virginia. The communistic, or common-store, idea was part of the stock-in-trade of the blueprint theorists of the day then, as it is of many of the young humanitarian but ungrounded *intelligentsia,* so-called, of our own. A plan similar to the Virginia one was instituted by the business group which backed Plymouth but lasted, as in the South, only until empty stomachs settled the question against empty heads. After a couple of years or so, Governor Bradford of Plymouth noted, as John Smith had at Jamestown, that it was necessary to abandon the scheme and allot lands to individuals, whereby, as Bradford wrote, "more corn was planted than otherwise would have been by any means the Governor or any other could use."

The reason was no further to seek than it had been in Virginia. The Englishman is a thoroughgoing individualist, and the Englishmen who came to conquer a continent were no more Communists than their American descendants in general have been. As elsewhere in Plymouth, the "young unmarried men objected to having the fruits of their toil go to support other men's wives and children. Married men disliked having their wives sew, cook, and wash for others. Hard-working men thought it unfair that they should support the more idle or incapable. The older men, or those of the better class, declined to work for the younger or meaner." All this is very human, and, what many now too often forget, very American. Bradford was a simple but very sensible man, brought up as a boy to be a yeoman farmer following the plough but he had made himself well-read, and we may add his statement as to how Communism worked to that already quoted from Smith.

> The experience that was had in this commone course and condition [he wrote] tried sundrie years, and that amongst godly and sober men, may well evince the vanitie of that conceite of Platos & other ancients, applauded by some of later times;—that ye taking away of propertie, and bringing in comunitie into a comone wealth would make them happy and flourishing; as if they were wiser than God. For this comunitie (so far as it was) was found to breed much confusion & discontent, and retard much employment that would have been to their benefit and comfort.

The American is perhaps the most lavishly generous person in the world. Possibly it is partly due to some truth in the old saying contrasting the Americans and the French, to the effect that the French love to possess but not to acquire, whereas the American loves to acquire but cares little for possession. Jamestown and Plymouth were the earliest two successful settlements in America, and they both illustrate American traits at the very beginning. The settlers of each had shown their determination to make their own way, but they also showed that, although they did not intend to be forced by law or institutions to hand over to others the results of their own energy and work, they would nevertheless do so of their own volition when left to themselves. In 1622 Jamestown was far from being in a happy or secure position, but when its inhabitants heard that other new Americans had settled at Plymouth and were in desperate need they dispatched a vessel with food and seed corn to help the strangers who also were following the dream and engaging in the great adventure. Bradford, perhaps properly, thanked the Lord for it, but it was the Virginians who scrimped themselves to send the unsolicited aid.

Plymouth was never really democratic. Bradford, elected governor for thirty successive annual terms, had more autocratic power than any of the colonial Royal Governors but he used it on the whole mildly and with sense and honesty. In spite of the poverty and difficulties of the colony, the business men in London were paid off after some years, and although Bradford took a leading part in repaying the debt, the effect of the American frontier on ideas of "property vs. human rights" (as the problem has currently come to be called), can be discovered when, in the early days of the struggle, he wrote to the merchants that, "At great charges in this adventure, I confess you have beene, and many losses may sustain, but the loss of his [Carver's] and many other honest and industrious men's lives, cannot be vallewed at any prise." Without the money which the merchants had risked, the Pilgrims would not have reached the New World to die or prosper, and although on this early frontier that fact was recognized and the probity of the colonists was proved, we see nevertheless a new idea taking shape in the wilderness, as different from that regarding property in Europe as the savage-infested forests were from the peaceful villages and countrysides of Holland or England.

If Plymouth was neither democratic nor wholly tolerant, it was to form a great contrast to the intolerance of its later neighbor Massachusetts Bay, and was also to provide a landmark in the American democratic tradition. The latter fact was partly due to the character of the settlers and partly to the influences of the American environment and situation.

Both the Virginia and Plymouth colonists were mixed lots, but there was one important difference. The Virginians went to a designated part of America provided with a royal charter and a form of government which at least guaranteed that social order would be maintained by duly appointed authorities. When the Pilgrims, on account of unforeseen circumstances, landed outside the limits of the Virginia Company, they realized that they would be both without title to the land and outside the pale of any organized political society. Given the Englishman's instinct for order and government, it is probable that in any case the men of the *Mayflower* would have drawn up some sort of agreement as to how order should be maintained on shore after they had left the ship, where the captain had been in control. This became clearly the more necessary, however, since more than two-thirds of the passengers were not religious refugees, but included some, at least, of the sort who might start trouble when the authority of the captain, supreme on the high seas, should be removed. In fact some of the settlers had ominously boasted that once on land they "would use their own libertie."

It was a day when both political and religious "covenants" were familiar even to the common man, and the so-called *Mayflower Compact* was a simple extension of a church covenant. It was intended to cover only a temporary crisis, and was not meant to be a revolution in governmental theory. However, as Plymouth never received a royal charter, the Compact in fact remained the basic "constitution" of the colony for over seventy years. As the main body of this "constitution" consisted of only seven lines it is probably the shortest ever drawn up, and provided for practically a pure democracy. All but eight of the male passengers of legal age (and those eight may have still been ill), signed an agreement to make "just and equal laws"; to elect officers for a "Civil Body Politick," and to yield obedience to them. In other words, the settlers established voluntarily a lawful and peaceable self-government with majority rule. Although later the pure democracy was somewhat diminished in favor of the Church, Plymouth never became the sort of theocracy that was attempted in Massachusetts, and the form of covenant used was the precursor of the many other plantation and town covenants in New England.

It may well be said that there was nothing new in the Mayflower Compact. It did not promulgate a new theory of government but, as in so many other instances in Anglo-American constitutional history, it was merely a way chosen to meet a specific difficulty with a specific remedy. Likewise, as in so many other cases, its influence extended far beyond that dreamed of by the simple, practical and politically minded men who chose what for them was the natural way out of an unexpected complication. Tradition has much to do with molding the character and outlook of any people, and especially of a traditionally minded folk like the English. Although not intended to be such, the Compact, entered into that November day in 1620 by men who realized that they were soon to be left alone to found a settlement in an ungoverned waste, became in time the cornerstone of the American democratic theory, even if it was not widely quoted until the need of rationalizing our political ideas made itself felt in the years preceding the Revolution.

The main point for our present study is that it was due to America and the frontier. In Europe there would have been no need, as there would have been no possibility, for a group of ordinary men to have established a self-governing community. When the Pilgrims had left England for Holland, they had gained certain liberties but they had felt no urge to establish self-government. They obeyed quietly the laws of the country to which they had fled. It was only when they found themselves alone in the American wilderness, that the need arose to establish a government of their own. With no authority above them, with no charter or titles, they formed the first free state in the New World. The exigencies of their situation demanded that something be done, and it was done in accord with both their character as English and with the conditions of America. Heredity and environment combined in a result that was to have profound influence on the world.

The site chosen, under pressure of haste at the beginning of that New England winter when the captain refused to risk further voyaging, after a final effort to reach the mouth of the Hudson, was not well suited to either agriculture or trade. The colony thus remained poor, until eventually absorbed by Massachusetts, but it was of vast importance in forming the American. Legend is often of more influence than authentic fact, and although the Pilgrim legend in the popular imagination is in many respects far from accurate it contains much that is compact of the American Dream. All of it appeals to the old-fashioned American: the story of the simple, common men who left their homes for freedom to worship, who first founded New England, who established free government and a democracy, and who after their first harvest instituted our Thanksgiving Day. It is needless to point out that their ideas of religious liberty were narrow; that their democracy became limited; that if we owe Thanksgiving to them they forbade the celebration of Christmas and frowned on innocent sports. There is still, however, enough of truth in the legend to validate its influence and to explain why for a large part of America the American tradition begins at Plymouth Rock rather than at Jamestown. It must be recalled that New England influence spread across the northern half of the United States from Portland, Maine, to Portland, Oregon, and was of immense importance, in the nineteenth century particularly, when it dominated literature, publishing, and most of the new currents of thought.

The Virginians were the first Americans but the second group of settlers who, headed for Virginia, accidentally founded New England, added essential strains to our Americanism, qualities as in the earlier case partly derived from England but greatly modified by the conditions of the American environment. Moreover, just as Plymouth would probably not have been established had it not been for the earlier success of Jamestown, so the success of Plymouth, in spite of difficulties, paved the way for the planting of other colonies in New England. The transplanting of the English had become assured, and assured in regions so different as to develop two contrasting types of social and economic civilization. America, in so far as certain common factors of influence were concerned—such as the ocean, distance from England, the frontier, lack of labor, equalizing of wealth and status—was unifying the Americans as contrasted with the stay-at-home English, but regional conditions were also at work to bring about diversity.

There were also other variations, although the local conditioning American factors in Virginia were not to cause marked social and political cleavages for nearly a century. At first, the main conditions of soil, with the staple crop of tobacco, the waterways, and other factors already touched on, all tended towards making a more or less uniform type of life in the "tidewater section" of the South. In New England the diversity is notable even in little more than a decade from the start, but there, although some of the controls by physical conditions have been noted, the rapid diversity was due more to men and ideas. We may now turn to the rest of New England, which grew up after the Pilgrims led the way, and note particularly the strains in the American which were developed in Massachusetts, Rhode Island and Connecticut, as part of the composite New England influence.

CHAPTER IV

EARLY MASSACHUSETTS

THE influence New England was to exert was the result of a curious interlacing of the geographical environment and the outstanding individuals. The Pilgrims having led the way and shown that Englishmen could establish themselves on the inhospitable New England coast, other settlers followed in a few years, singly here and there, or in a small group such as the fishing company on Cape Ann.

Meanwhile, events were moving rapidly in the mother country, and the future there seemed ever more ominous—economically, religiously and politically. Many Puritans among the nobility and middle class, with their followers among the poor, were watching the signs of the time with anxious foreboding. Puritanism happened to be strongest where economic distress was most disheartening, that is, in the eastern section of England. There for a considerable period consultations were held and plans laid for possible emigration, either to the Caribbean islands or to the American mainland. In 1628 an influential group secured a patent for a strip of land about sixty miles wide, and running nominally from the Atlantic to the Pacific, which included the fishing settlement mentioned above. John Endicott with about sixty persons was sent out to take possession, followed by four hundred more the next year.

That same year the plans of the leaders matured and a charter, which probably the King and government regarded as similar to those of the customary trading companies of the period, was issued to the Massachusetts Bay Company, with the usual provisions for "freemen," a "General Court" to meet quarterly and elect annually a governor, deputy governor and board of assistants. In other words the more or less standard set-up was something like that of a modern business corporation, in which the stockholders elect a president and board of directors. In British colonial history these companies have played an important part and have had more power than would be accorded to mere business corporations but, on the other hand, their charters were never intended to be the constitutions of independent states. The colonies which the companies might plant were always considered subject to the home government which had chartered them, though owing to the ever-present factor of distance their "Courts" were frequently given the right to make such laws, rules or ordinances for use on the spot as might not be repugnant to the laws of England.

It seems clear, however, that the leaders of the Massachusetts movement had definitely thought out a very clever plan. After having had inserted in their charter a phrase which might be construed to have made the adventurers "a Corporation upon the Place" they signed among themselves an agreement that they would emigrate only "Provided always that before the last of September next, the whole Government, together with the patent for the said plantation, be first, by an order of court [the Company's Court] legally transferred and established to remain with us and others which shall inhabit upon the said Plantation." The whole matter was surrounded with much secrecy and it would appear to be obvious that the astute Stuart monarch would never have consented if he had realized what the Puritan leaders intended. This was nothing less than to transform a charter given them for business purposes into a political constitution with themselves in control of a new state almost if not wholly independent of royal and parliamentary authority. However, the trick was turned, and its advantages were used to the full in the next half-century.

Here we come on one of the interlacings of the human and geographic factors which make this period of American history so fascinating and complicated. The founding of Massachusetts was not, like that of Plymouth, based on an accident which took the settlers outside any organized part of the

Empire, but on a plan which was intended by legal chicanery to let them stay in the Empire but be as much as possible outside its control. It must have been clear to those who made the plan and who consulted counsel about it, that it would be questioned later—Stuarts or no Stuarts—and that a policy of "avoidance and delay" would have to be employed when situations became threatening. That is precisely what was to happen.

They took their chances, and they were evidently men who were willing to do so. Had they been democratic and tolerant, America might trace back with more accuracy its democracy and tolerance to them, but in fact these strains in the American, though they come in large part from New England, and in smaller part from the ordinary folk of Massachusetts, did not stem from the Puritan leaders. We shall speak more of them in a moment, but may note first the geographic factors in the case.

Because of what they did in the matter of the physical transfer of the charter, and because of what they were in their ideas of religion, government and desire for personal power, the history of Massachusetts divides itself into two streams. One was that of a constant struggle to prevent any control over its acts by England, and the other was that of liberalism in the colony itself against the arbitrary rule in politics and religion by a few. However, the opportunity to attempt what they did would never have occurred had Massachusetts not been three thousand miles overseas from the King and his forces. The importance which they attached to the physical transfer across the ocean of the charter is as clear an example as we could have of the significance of the factor of distance from the seat of authority which had so much to do with building up the American sense of freedom and isolation.

If distance from England was to be one of the constantly recurring factors of American influence on Americans, we may pause for a moment to emphasize, as we shall have to again, some aspects of the frontier, which have also had so much to do with forming traits in the American. We properly admire the courage which it takes to leave all that is familiar and go out to settle on the edge of a new country, but there is another side to the matter as well. The frontier is often a means of escape for those who find the complexities, social, economic or other, of a settled society too much for them. They have courage and perhaps ambition but instead of facing the difficulties of their old environment, which appear to them to have become insuperable, they prefer to cut through all the strings and start fresh where things are harder in some ways but easier in others. The question arises, to put it too bluntly perhaps, whether it is easier for boy or man to stay at home and think and fight a situation through or to "run away to sea"; or whether the Pyms, Hampdens, Cromwells and others who made English history by fighting the Stuarts in England itself were greater than those who dodged the problems there by emigrating to America.

The question is pertinent, at least to our story, for that story of the development of the American has constantly to include the frontier, and one point is certain. The man who prefers to stay at home is one type, and the man who prefers to go to waste lands or the fringes of civilization is another. Courage is called for in each case, but it is a different sort of courage. One man may prefer to be a political or religious martyr at home and take the consequences for the sake of a cause. Another prefers to face the hardships and dangers, the wild animals and savages, in order to avoid other dangers or complications, experienced already and better known. For three centuries the American has constantly been subject to the influence of successive frontiers, and has largely been formed by those seeking to *simplify their problems.*

The really great leaders of the Puritan and popular party in England did not emigrate with the two thousand or more settlers who came to Massachusetts Bay and founded Boston and its neighboring towns. Some men of ability came, such as John Winthrop, John Cotton, and others, but they believed in neither political nor religious freedom. Moreover they were of the strictest sect. They had their own ideas as to what a Puritan state should be. In England they had been rather unimportant individuals in a populous commonwealth. In New England they found themselves, to an extent even beyond what they had dreamed, *rulers,* and as their stage had shrunk and they themselves had swelled, they demanded, as is human, more and more power and became ever more reluctant to part with anything they could gain.

These Massachusetts leaders wanted very definitely certain things. They wanted both freedom to build a church according solely to their own ideas, and power to force all others to conform. They wanted to secure religious, political and social control of the colony they had helped to establish. It was soon well supplied with cattle and other resources and grew so rapidly that it was almost at once the largest and strongest English outpost in the New World. To rule it was heady wine for those who had left precarious positions of minor importance in England. Their "Theocracy" was to be a state ruled according to the Word of God, which meant, in practice, a few lay leaders working with the limited number of clergy to govern the rest of the thousands of Englishmen who had followed them for many diverse reasons, though religion had of course loomed large.

It is needless to discuss the moot question of just how the Congregational form of church started. The Pilgrims, who had been full Separatists, had it, and although the Puritans at first claimed not to be separating from the Church of England, as Cotton asserted as late as 1647, but only from certain impurities in it, in practice the Congregational Church soon came to be the general New England form. The odd part is that, although the obvious tendency of that Church is all towards democracy, the Puritan leaders, lay and clerical, hated democracy. Of this they have left us in no doubt. "Democracy," asserted Winthrop, "is amongst civil nations, accounted the meanest and worst of all forms of government," and a "manifest breach of the 5th Commandment." The Reverend John Cotton wrote to England that he did not conceive that God did ever ordain democracy "as a fit government for eyther church or commonwealth. If the people be governors, who shall be governed?" In other words, perhaps, what would become of the satisfying dominant position of the Rev. John Cotton?

The founders of Massachusetts were not students of political history or philosophy. The Old Testament, and largely the Mosaic period, formed for the most part the limits of their vision, in marked contrast to the leaders of America a century and a half later who framed our Constitution, and who took all history for their province. The Puritan state was a development from the Puritan church, and if the leaders hated democracy in political life, they came to do so no less within the Church itself. After the years of the reactionary Massachusetts Synod of 1646–48, the Church tended strongly to Presbyterianism rather than to democratic Congregationalism. The effect of this on the democratic beliefs of many of the ordinary colonists, as well as on the oligarchical policies of the clerical and lay leaders, was to cause a schism in the Theocracy which was to grow in importance until the struggle came to a head in the war of printed words between Cotton Mather and John Wise.

Nevertheless, if democracy was to emerge even in Massachusetts, it was to do so mainly as a result of the Congregational Church, the frontier and the local geographical conditions. When we seek New England influence across the continent to the western ocean, we look for the Congregational Church, the town form of government (which we have said was the result of the church and the meadow); the town meeting; the common school and the village green. But the leaders of Massachusetts gave us neither democracy nor religious toleration.

We cannot relate at length the detailed history of the most powerful Puritan colony. As for democracy, the frontier began its work almost at once. John Winthrop in a personal memorandum regarding his reasons for emigrating had indicated one of these in the question: "With what comfort can I [continue to live] with 7 or 8 servts in that place and condition where for many years I have spent 3; or 400l yearly and maintained a greater chardge?" Yet even in the first summer, although the colony had thought itself to be amply provisioned, 180 "servants" had to be given their liberty because food was too scarce. Evidently America was even less adapted to Winthrop's maintaining a household of seven or eight servants than England had been.

In England the problem for many had been that of avoidable expense. In America it often became that of starvation, and there is a big difference.

Our American saying "Root, hog, or die," has a sound historical foundation, and not a little to do with the genesis of the American. Apart from the democratizing process involved, the labor problem, lack of servants, and other points we have touched on, we may mention one more. The "root, hog, or die" of the American vernacular, our frontier version of "work or starve," may seem to have little to do with the more dignified Latin *caveat emptor*. In fact it has much, and also with one of the traits which, more particularly, from Charles Dickens down, foreigners have been inclined to attribute to an innate dishonesty in the American. Because almost every American "hog" had to root or die, "rooting," in one sense or another, became considered not only a duty, emphasized by the strands of the Puritan tradition, but "the hog," or the American man, was supposed to know *how to do his rooting*. In other words, it became deeply ingrained in our outlook on life that not only must a man work but that he must know *how*, and that if he did not do either—work or know—it was his own fault. This, in the simplicity of our early frontiers, was to a large extent true, except for sheer physical or mental incapacity.

The same was true of other colonies, but the Puritans added another motive for the necessity of working by making success an evidence of God's favor. As success in New England could not be achieved except by excessive thrift and hard work (unless one was one of a favored few), the inference became obvious. If you did not work hard and were not shrewd, you did not achieve a rising scale of success, and, if you did not do that, you were evidently, for some reason, not in God's favor. To rise meant to leave the wage class and to become a property owner, and property for the most part meant land. So, to rise socially, to be a successful American, and, in New England and where Puritan influence spread, to be one of the elect of God, you had to know the value of property. An odd complex thus developed, of local patriotism, good citizenship, duty towards God, and the wisdom of the serpent, with success and moral virtue measured by money.

Puritanism in the virulent form it took in Massachusetts, in its milder form in the South, and in its later forms among the Baptists, Methodists and other sects on western frontiers, has always been one of the important factors in American mentality. The belief of the Puritan that worldly success was a visible seal of the approval of God as to your life in general was to play many queer tricks in American social ethics. Many a trait and act which appeared to be, and now and then actually was, hypocritical was often not so but could be traced back to this religious idea which worked in the unthinking emotional part of our natures and in deeps of the sub-conscious where successful self-interest became vaguely merged in God's plan for man, and His approval of the individual.

Combined with all this was the fact that the American, in common with the animal kingdom in general, lacked a leisure class. Among animals of all sorts, there is no individual or group which lives on a food supply accumulated in early years or inherited. Every animal scratches for his own living day by day, and is supposed to know how to get it. There is much kindness and "mutual aid" among animals, but, nevertheless, there is no sense of *trusteeship*. In old *human* societies there have been so many individuals, and even whole classes, which have had property but no idea of how to manage it, that a class has grown up to do it for them, and with this kind of relationship, developed the "trustee," with wide social and ethical ramifications. There is dishonesty among individuals in all countries and ages, and there have been plenty of dishonest Americans, but if in selling land or other property the American may be thought by others to lean too heavily on the old maxim of *caveat emptor*, or "let the buyer beware," it is not because he is less honest than others. It is rather that because of the whole history of the country he counts on a high degree of business knowledge and acumen in the buyer. The "root, hog, or die" of the frontier scrabble, the glorification of work by the Puritans, the enormous opportunities to make a competence or garner riches, all made America, to an unprecedented extent, a nation of businessmen who were supposed to know their business.

The interest of the early history of New England for our story is that it is almost like a laboratory experiment in Americanization. We find leaders and followers of different sorts all being subjected to influences of environment, and certain lasting American traits and ideas resulting from the pressures exerted. For example, in Massachusetts we find both the narrowing and the liberalizing tendencies of the frontier at work. Naturally, on any frontier intellectual and aesthetic interests and activities tend to thin out, but the Massachusetts Bay colony was *sui generis*. It was at once a frontier and not a frontier in the ordinary sense. That is, it was a frontier in that it was planted in a wilderness three thousand miles overseas from the cultural and broadening influences of old England, but its comparatively large population, its financial and material resources, and especially its compact form of settlement in towns, made it different from almost any other early frontier in our history. As it expanded northward and westward there were plenty of more genuine frontier posts, with Indian and other dangers, but the little towns around the Boston neighborhood were almost from the start so populous that life in them was about as safe and commonplace as in any remote village in England.

It was, however, even narrower and more provincial. The

twelve or fourteen thousand people who made up the entire colony by about 1642 formed, after all, a very small public. It was easy to be a big frog in so small a puddle, and from the start the leaders had tasted almost untrammelled power, and had relished it. The towns around the Bay, with Boston at their head, continued to be the chief seat of authority, and the leaders, lay and clerical, in them were not so much empire builders in the wilds, at least after the very first, as they were small town persons from England living a smaller town life in America, but with a personal freedom, opportunity and power over others they would never have had in the old country.

Steadily the influence of their American conditions played on them, being what they were to start with. It is true that they had come to America from the desire, among other motives, to worship God as they chose, but they had no high vision of religious liberty. Even in their own religion they were to a great extent taken up with small matters and with an undue sense of their own importance and infallibility. They regarded themselves as the unerring leaders of a people, leaders who had been chosen above all others by God. Among the other motives which had impelled them to leave England had been the economic one, ever-present in American immigration, of hoping to better their lot, and also, as in Winthrop's case, the belief that they might occupy positions of greater public importance than seemed to be within their reach at home under the changing conditions of the times. It is historically as inaccurate to minimize or ignore these and other motives as it is to underrate, on the part of a great number, the genuine if narrow religious one.

From all this complex of ideas and moving forces developed the peculiar Massachusetts of the period of the Theocracy, one of the strongest and most tenacious forms of government, albeit on a small scale, ever organized. So much secrecy had surrounded the plans of the original leaders in England that we are much in the dark as to what they intended, but one thing would seem certain. We have already spoken of it in connection with the care and risks they took in the transfer of the charter. They intended to create if possible a practically independent state, with themselves in control. Obviously such a bold experiment could not have been made anywhere in Europe, where there was no free room for a new state. Nor could it have been undertaken in the American domains claimed by their Catholic Majesties of France or Spain. We have mentioned the climate and other factors in New England as fostering that granite ruggedness in the Puritan Yankee which would probably have been softened or lost in the American South or the islands of the Caribbean. New England was the region marked out for the experiment. What did New England do to it? We may consider first what Massachusetts did for the Theocracy, and then what the revolts against that government, in the free air of America, did for the American.

From the start the leaders paid no attention to either the misused charter or the laws of England, when it suited their purposes not to do so. What they rapidly developed was an oligarchy in which church and state were almost inextricably intertwined. Lay leaders and clergy supported each other and ran the community with the two arms of secular power and religious teaching or terror. It was King and Priest in the closest of old-time combinations, saturated through and through with the spirit of the Old Testament. Occasionally a modern defender of the regime points to a certain proportion of texts from the New Testament quoted by this or that Puritan divine in his sermons, but an unbiased study of the records, laws, judgments and all the acts of the Theocracy indicates beyond question that that government and its philosophy were founded on the rock of the Old Testament. Had Puritan Massachusetts been permeated with the teachings of Christ instead of with those of Moses and the prophets, its whole history would have been different.

This is no place for Biblical discussion but we may note that to a large extent the Old Testament is a hard and harsh, not seldom a cruel, book. But it is strong. Its God, as contrasted with the loving Father of the New Testament, is a God of wrath and war, and it is filled with characters like the prophets, who believed that, whatever the multitude might say or do, they alone knew the views and aims of God. It is to a large extent a stern book, for stern men, "as stern as fate" as Service wrote in his *The Land God Forgot.*

New England was not the land of which the poet was writing but it is one in which man has to fight nature for all he gets. It is one in which he is not granted her largess with open hands but in which he takes life hard because he has to, on its stormy rockbound coast, its stony and glaciated fields, its broken terrain. We must not press the point too far, but it was a land in which such a Theocracy as was intended was planted on congenial soil.

It is interesting to follow the development of the leaders themselves under the new influences to which they were subjected. Little by little we see them degenerate, with their increasing love of unwonted power, their egotism and spiritual pride, and the narrowing frontier life, all of which had their bases in certain American conditions. On the other hand the *reactions* to their *actions* which were produced among the people they ruled and those they drove out were of the greatest importance for the American and also had their bases in American conditions.

We may note first how the narrowing effect of frontier life, which brought New England by the end of the seventeenth century to perhaps the lowest intellectual level it has ever touched, came about. The section had first been settled by the Pilgrims, and although only about a third of their original number had been really religious refugees, the colony was distinctly one of the extreme left wing of the Puritan movement. Then had come the great Puritan migration to Massachusetts. The leaders of that had done their best to cut off as far as possible any political connection with England, and, owing to the transfer of the charter and other causes, there was no

Royal Governor in any of the New England colonies until Massachusetts finally lost its charter in 1690.

The other colonies in the section, even those which were founded as revolts from Massachusetts, were Puritan. After some years, the bad reputation which the actions of the Massachusetts leaders had given New England, even in the eyes of its best friends in old England, combined with the Puritan revolution in the latter country, which left the Puritans, merely as such, no further reason for emigrating, almost wholly dried up the stream of newcomers. English Puritans had no longer any religious reason for crossing the ocean; and the ordinary Englishmen had heard too much of the loss of liberty in Massachusetts and of New England conditions in general to care to go thither if they were to undertake the adventure of emigrating. They went elsewhere in the Empire. New England, so to say, was "left to stew in its juice," which it did very profitably in some ways for our later nation.

New England withdrew into itself. The almost entire lack of fresh blood, its geographic boundaries, its peculiar way of life and preoccupation with religion of a certain type, all tended to make it ingrowing and to set it apart from even the rest of the colonies. For its leaders its educational system also was bad, and the founding of Harvard in 1636 was far from an unmixed blessing. The second generation of them (unlike many of the men of the first, who had been trained at English universities), mostly attended Harvard and got no more experience and broadening than was afforded by that ultra-provincial little institution which was then scarcely more than a grammar school, ranking far below, in breadth and depth of scholarship, several of the universities founded much earlier in Spanish Central and South America.

The people of the section, nevertheless, became generally the most literate of all our colonies. Schools were early started in the South also, but the scattered plantation system of life there made it difficult to gather children together. For this purpose the New England form of settlement in compact towns was admirably adapted, and aside from the fact that settlements were largely made by church congregations as groups, we have again to trace the influence of the meadow and other geographic features on the public school in the American sense.

The mere ability to read, write and cipher, however, does not mean education or breadth of views, and the culture of a people is likely not to rise higher than that of their leaders. In the South many of the latter for long went to England for their education, having no Harvard, and their intellectual preoccupations were rather with the classics and general literature than with narrowly religious thought as in New England. The private libraries in the South well matched in number of volumes those in New England but represented a far wider range of interests.

Literatures are adjusted to both climates and peoples. The culture of the Old Testament is one product; that of classical history and letters another; as that of the Scandinavians is still another. The point is that a society deeply imbued with the spirit of Greece and Rome produces individual minds and a type of thought quite different from one dominated by the Old Testament. I do not mean to say that there was no intellectual inter-action between Old and New England in the seventeenth century. There was much, but it ran largely in narrow channels of religious controversy and preoccupation as contrasted with that of the South, provincial as that may also have been owing to distance and difficulty of transport for both books and persons.

There is, nevertheless, this to be said for New England. If New York was chiefly mercantile and cosmopolitan, and as one went southward an increasingly genial nature dimmed the interest felt in the problems of evil, predestination, infant damnation, the fires of Hell and other matters of Puritan doctrine and discipline, New England, partly for reasons of geographic environment, remained long loyal to them. There, also, government and politics remained so largely in the hands of the lay and clerical leaders that almost all the interests of the entire community were centered in the pulpit and the ministers' sermons. Religion and politics were so closely intertwined that it was as important for a man to be able to judge between heterodox and orthodox religious views, as passed on by the clergy, as it was elsewhere to discuss a question in terms of politics alone.

The New Englander was more than literate or shrewd. He became, partly from innate intellectual and spiritual interest but also from the conditions of life in a Theocracy, a specialist in theology. As his body struggled and toughened itself in clearing and plowing stony fields and fighting against wintry blasts and drifts, so his mind toughened itself in struggling with the hard sayings of Calvinism and the fiery furnace of a threatened Hell.

The leaders of Massachusetts were not men of what we would call liberal or enlightened views, and they became steadily narrower under American conditions. For example, Winthrop had come here not a strong, but rather a gentle and very human, soul. Yet, influenced in part by others and in part yielding to his own ambition and love of power in a remote colony, made semi-independent by the width of ocean, the transfer of the charter, and the interregnum of the Puritan Revolution in England, he was led into committing acts of political usurpation and religious intolerance which he would never have thought of doing or daring in the home country. Governor of the colony for many terms, he worked hand and glove with the clergy, as was the way of the Theocracy, and he himself had said that he so honored a faithful minister that he "could have kissed his feet." It is also reported by the later colonial governor and historian, Hutchinson, that Winthrop when asked on his deathbed to sign a warrant for the banishment of a heretic declined, saying that "he had done too much of that work already." At the time of the Synod of 1646, held to decide certain points of religion, he had complained that too much freedom was being allowed in England, whence orders had been sent to the West Indies and other colonies "that all men should enjoy their liberty of conscience, and had by letters intimated the same to us." Hutchinson also wrote of Winthrop that at first he had been more liberal than some of the other founders "but afterward he grew more contracted, and was disposed to lay too great stress upon indifferent matters."

In his case we find clearly the narrowing influence of the American frontier, and it is equally to be found in that of John Cotton who steadily "contracted" also, and passing beyond his first dislike of democracy tried to write into the laws of the colony the rule that a political office (secured of course with the consent of the clergy) should be for life and like a freehold title to real estate.

After the death of these leaders their places came to be occupied by such men as Endicott and Norton, who were more narrow, bigoted and tyrannical. The faults of the Theocracy, however, had most important results for the American. The leaders in order to maintain their grip on power and to rule the people had to take two lines. They had sternly to oppose any liberalism in Massachusetts itself and, on the other hand, any attempt by the home government to assert authority over its own colony.

In accordance with the first requirement they limited the franchise to members of the Church as they organized it. There was, of course, no such limitation suggested in the charter, but that document gave, as the foundation for a business organization, solely to the stockholders, or "freemen" in the nomenclature of the day, the right to vote in the Company's "General Court," or in modern parlance its stockholders' meetings, which were to be held quarterly. When the charter was brought to America, and suffered the sea-change which was supposed to make it into the constitution of a self-governing state, the stockholders' "General Court" became the legislature of the colony, and as, in the intended business corporation, only the stockholders had the right to elect fellow members, such election was transformed in the view of the leaders, who proceeded to regulate it into the political right of suffrage.

The several thousand immigrants who had been induced to come to America had been influenced, to a large extent, by religious motives, mingled with the usual economic and other ones. They were Puritans, but that does not mean that they were church members. According to law (and in probably the vast majority of cases willingly), they were obliged to attend church, but they could not officially become *members* of the church unless they satisfied the rest of the congregation, and of course the clergy, that they were spiritually fit to do so. The "suffrage law," if it may so be called, limiting the franchise to church members, thus clearly gave the lay and clerical leaders, working in harmony, the opportunity to hand-pick the voters. It was much as though Tammany Hall had the right to decide who should and who should not be allowed to vote in New York City. In fact during the period of the Theocracy only about one-fifth of the adult males had a share in the government of the colony, in spite of protests from even Charles II. It was not until 1691, after the first charter had been annulled and the new one of 1684 had been put in force again after the Revolution in England, that the church membership test was abolished and a small property qualification substituted, under orders from England.

The settlers, even if they were Puritans, were not only Englishmen with their innate love of liberty, but were subject to the influence of the frontier, and attendants, at least, of the Congregational Church, the fundamental basis of which was democratic in tendency and philosophy. These things led them to become more and more opposed to the oligarchic tyranny of the small group of leaders with their followers who formed only a small fraction of the whole population.

In addition to the enormous usurpation at the start by interpreting the charter as the constitution of a state of which they should be the rulers, the leaders also tried to keep its terms from the knowledge of the settlers until popular discontent forced them to produce the document. They had tried to void its requirements. They had suppressed as long as they could any share by the people in law-making. They also, in time, forbade any emigration from the colony without permission. On the other hand they banished citizens, sometimes into the wilderness in winter, at their own pleasure. Among other cases of banishment may be mentioned those of Wheelwright, Roger Williams and Anne Hutchinson. When after her trial Mrs. Hutchinson asked to know why sentence had been thus passed, she was merely told: "Say no more. The Court knows wherefore and is satisfied." Appeals to England, to which citizens were entitled, were denied. It was made illegal to "defame" any Court or Magistrate under penalty of fine, imprisonment, disfranchisement or banishment. A "heretic" could be banished or hanged. (Little wonder that, as we have noted, the people were much occupied with theology and became experts in it!)

In the mid-century came the religious persecutions of the Baptists and Quakers, in which the Theocratic leaders became merciless. They were examples of the stupidity and brutality which seem to be bred by the possession of too great power. Cruel bodily and mental sufferings were inflicted on many, and three Quaker men and a woman were hanged on Boston Common. About the same year another woman was hanged at the same place, as a witch, and this latter phase in the abnormality of the Theocracy and the dominance of the clergy came to a close in 1692 with the famous Salem witchcraft frenzy when many persons were imprisoned, nineteen hanged and one pressed to death between heavy weights, after having been tried and condemned as witches. By that time, however, the end of the Theocracy had come, decreed both by the authorities in England and the plain people of Massachusetts.

One effect of all this was the engraving, deeply and permanently, of the spirit of Calvinism and the Old Testament prophets on the people of Massachusetts, aided by additional factors, geographic and other, which we have also mentioned. I have spoken of the traits and ideas brought over by the early English emigrants in "their knapsacks" (as President Fox phrases it in his illuminating little volume *Ideas in Transit*), and how the earliest English had largely set the mold of American life and thought. Among these ideas "in knapsacks," brought over both North and South, was Puritanism, although in varying degrees of strength and permanency. In our later history, on many successive frontiers, and under guidance of other churches, Puritanism, as we understand that very broad term, continued to be a prime influence in the life of the ordinary American. But Puritanism in its quintessence—the belief that only certain things were right, and that those who preached them were alone in understanding God's commands—stems from the Puritan leaders of early Massachusetts Bay. As Americans we are familiar with such intensely emotional movements as Abolitionism, Prohibition and others, and I think we can trace the narrowness, if you will, and the intensity and fervor of such movements, either started or strongly supported by Massachusetts, to the spiritual climate of the Theocratic period.

The leaders had to suppress all attempts at democratizing the government in America, but also they had to fight off any attempt by the English government to assert its natural and legitimate authority over them. What they did was quite remarkable and would have been impossible except in an American colony of the British Empire at that period. They not only built up a Church-State of peculiar form, which was not in harmony with the ideas held by the government that had granted them their charter, but within the sphere of technical law observance they insisted on an almost complete independence of that government which had unwittingly given them the basis for their own. As a result of the mistake of the Pilgrims in settling outside the bounds of Virginia; of the knowing transfer of the Massachusetts charter to America; and of the always important factor of distance, the settlers of the Bay Colony not only developed a semi-independent state within the Empire, but like the rest of New England kept all royal governors out of the picture for about sixty years. Neither free

Holland nor the bureaucracies of France or Spain would have permitted such a situation for a moment.

Until the British Government finally withdrew the Massachusetts charter in 1684 by the proceeding of *scire facias* the colony had almost wholly succeeded in maintaining a state of practical independence by use of a continuous policy of evasion and procrastination, made possible only by the Atlantic. Investigated by agents and commissions, forced to send representatives to London to defend its actions, frequently ordered to obey the orders of King or Parliament, the colony remained as obdurate as the rocks of its own fields and mountainsides. It refused to conform to the terms of the charter. In part, to repeat what we have said, it refused to broaden the franchise or to give liberty to dissenters from its church. It persecuted, banished and killed those who did not conform. It claimed control over lands and peoples outside its bounds. It coined money in disregard of the laws of England, which it also flouted in many other ways. The King's Writ practically did not run in the Bay Colony, and appeals to England were denied to British subjects. The all-important Navigation Acts were simply not regarded. The authority of Parliament was not recognized. Massachusetts was the Ireland of the first Empire.

This was another of the positive effects and influences of the actions of the Puritan leaders. We need not comment at length on the moral position of those leaders, who had received imperial benefits and protection while flouting all imperial obligations, and not seldom actually prevaricating as well as procrastinating in their communications with the home authorities. For our present purpose it is enough to point to the great influence on the American of their spirit of independence—selfish and narrow as it may have been and compounded of so many mixed motives and vulnerable arguments. Massachusetts was for a while the most populous and powerful of the American colonies. In its dealings with its neighbors it often took more than full advantage of its position, but in its attitude of independence as regards England it served at once as an example and a bulwark to the other New England colonies of which we shall now speak. It also bred in New England, and thence along the seaboard, a feeling that colonies could be independent—which was to be of great influence in the next century in that section and throughout America.

CHAPTER V

REACTION AGAINST THEOCRACY

THE struggle for democracy against the usurpations of the oligarchy began early. In no small degree the fight by the settlers for their local freedom (aided often by the English government and monarchs) brought about not only the success of the people in Massachusetts in their struggle against abuses by their local rulers, but also the loss of the charter and so a closer dependence on Parliament, which meant to a large extent the loss of that independence which the leaders had claimed. So confused frequently are the threads in the skein of history.

From the beginning not even all the freemen were willing to submit without question to whatever was proposed by the inner group. As early as 1631, when the people of Watertown were taxed for the fortifying of Newtown, they submitted, but only after having declared that "it was not safe to pay moneys after that sort, for fear of bringing themselves and their posterity into bondage." Three years later the towns of the Colony deputed two men from each to consider the situation of the local government, and these having made a successful demand to see the charter and having found that its terms were not being followed, proceeded to take matters into their own hands. At a meeting of the General Court it was voted that there should be four such sessions a year, as the charter provided; that they should not be dissolved except by their own consent; that only these quarterly courts would have power to make laws, remove officials, dispose of lands, or raise money by taxation; also that there should be no trial for life or banishment except by a jury summoned by the Court. We cannot recite in detail the long continued struggle from then on between the common man in Massachusetts and the group which wished to retain control. The very year after the incident just mentioned it was decreed that voting should be by secret ballot, and Winthrop, Coddington and others were defeated for office. Winthrop in his invaluable *Journal* noted that in place of himself and the other discarded leaders, those chosen were mostly of the "inferior sort," the popular fear having been that rich men in office would allot to the poor an unjustly small proportion of land. Winthrop himself had secured over 1800 acres, Saltonstall 1600, and Dudley 1700.

During the preceding few months, the leaders had had severe jolts and feared for their control. The chief three factors in the situation, namely the Englishman's inherent love of liberty and his rights, from Magna Carta down; his respect for constituted authority and what we may call the law of the accustomed way; and the influences of distance and the frontier, were as yet in unstable equilibrium.

After Winthrop and the Reverend Mr. Cotton had made speeches, in which the latter pointed out that "among the Israelites" public business was committed to "the elders," the vote was reconsidered and the former magistrates, reëlected. They were, however, still frightened, and it was at this time that Cotton preached sermons in which he advocated possession of office for life instead of a year, as ordered in the charter, but this idea did not receive any public support. During the period here under consideration the forces of the people and the Theocratic leaders swayed back and forth in a tug of war, but the strength of the people, constantly receiving nourishment from the American frontier environment, was finally to win. The ideas of the leaders and of a considerable part of the church members stemmed from the Old Testament, whereas, on the contrary, those of a large proportion of the colonists stemmed from the traditions of English liberty and were growing freely in the American atmosphere. When the people at large won the battles for freedom, democracy and the separation of church and state, it was the victory of the common man over privilege, and, as over and over again in American life, the "inferior sort," as Winthrop called them, proved themselves the superior. It was the solitary farmer or other worker, who struggled with his few stony acres or sailed his little fishing boat, who won the struggle for toleration and personal rights as against Winthrop and his like who, with their one or two thousand acres, wanted public jobs for life, demanded power over the lives, property and thoughts of the people, and had nostalgic longings for the seven or eight servants and the standard of life they had maintained in their comfortable middle-class stations in England.

The details of the story, as it continued for a half century until the loss of the charter and the establishment of a royal government, need not be further rehearsed, and we may now turn to consider Rhode Island and Connecticut, which as offshoots of Massachusetts reacted most strongly against the ideas of religious intolerance and political despotism as practised in the Bay. There were many other settlements, early and late, which contributed their share to tolerance and democracy in the American, but these two illustrate them well at the start and are interesting as showing how the American has been compounded of both the good and bad in his environment. The religious tolerance of Rhode Island and the political tolerance of Connecticut might have been less early and less markedly developed had the reverse traits not been so emphasized in Massachusetts.

The leaders of that colony had to struggle from the beginning, as we have pointed out, to maintain the ascendency of their own ideas and power. The story is long and studded with frequent incidents. One of these was the case of Roger Williams. Williams had arrived at the Bay early in 1631 and had been welcomed as a "godly minister" but gradually fell more and more afoul of the governing authorities. The details are unimportant for us, but they included many boldly expressed criticisms of the American Puritan regime, including such fundamentals as title to the land, which he believed vested in the Indians; the use of civil power to enforce religious conformity; and other points which might perhaps undermine the power of the lay-clerical oligarchy. As a result he was tried and ordered banished from Massachusetts for disseminating "newe & dangerous opinions, against the aucthoritie of magistrates." He escaped in midwinter to friendly Indians at Sowams, and, having gathered a few followers who joined him later, established the first settlement in Rhode Island at Providence in 1636. We need not recite the growth of other villages or the development of "Rhode Island and Providence Plantations" which came to form the colony and later state of Rhode Island. Although Williams received a charter for the Colony in 1644 it never had a royal governor, and its second charter, granted by Charles II, sanctioned the "livelie experiment" in the separation of church and state which Williams had been carrying through.

It had indeed been a "livelie experiment," which threatened the Colony more than once with armed interference by Massachusetts, and which for some three centuries called down on "little Rhody" the sneers and wrath of the Boston clerical historians. Except for a short period of a few years when Roman Catholics, though there were only a very few of them, were denied the franchise, there was complete religious toleration, even for the Quakers, and it is in connection with the persecution of that sect in Massachusetts that we find the most important early statement of our American belief in complete religious freedom at the cost of whatever risk to the state. There was naturally at times some confusion but nothing to justify—except the catching example of liberty—the claims of the Theocracy that Rhode Island was a menace to its neighbors, a hotbed of anarchy, and a nest of unclean birds.

At the time when the Massachusetts government was reaching the height, or depth, of bloody religious persecution of Quakers, a small band of those people landed at Newport and were kindly received. At once Massachusetts sent a letter to Rhode Island demanding that she banish the Quakers already hospitably accepted and prevent any more from coming lest the "contagion" might spread. The letter added, menacingly, that if the little neighbor colony did not take such action Massachusetts would have to consider seriously "what further provision God may call us to make to prevent the aforesaid mischiefe." It was not the voice of the Bay people but of those in control of the Theocracy, and as usual a class in power insisted, and probably believed, that their private interests must coincide with those of the public and the plans of God for the good of the state. That is human nature.

In reply the authorities in Rhode Island wrote, in words which ought to be carved in granite as they are in the minds of all real Americans:

> As concerning these quakers (so called), which are now among us, we have no law among us, whereby to punish any for only declaring by words, &c., theire mindes and understandings concerning the things and ways of God, as to salvation and an eternal condition. And we, moreover, finde, that in those places where these people aforesaid, in this colony, are most of all suffered to declare themselves freely and are only opposed by arguments in discourse, there they least of all desire to come, and we are informed that they begin to loath this place for that they are not opposed by the civill authority, but with all patience and meekness are suffered to say over their pretended revelations and admonitions, nor are they like or able to gain many here to their way; surely we find that they delight to be persecuted by civill powers, and when they are soe, they are like to gain more adherents by the conseyte of their patient sufferings, than by consent to their pernicious sayings: And yet we conceive, that theire doctrines tend to very absolute cuttinge downe and overturninge relations and civill government among men, if generally received.

This document which the almost helpless little colony sent to the Theocratic leaders, who answered with threats, is one of the landmarks in the story of liberty of thought, religion and speech in America, though one nineteenth-century clerical historian in Boston incredibly called it "quaint" and found in it only "naïveté and humor!" Another, Palfrey, in his five volumes on New England history, buries it in a footnote while devoting thirty-five pages to a defense of the Theocratic persecution of the Quakers—so deep a mark did the early Massachusetts leaders leave on that colony and state. It is not to them, however, but to the rebel Williams and the simple and mostly inconspicuous ordinary folk who self-governed themselves in the little towns of Rhode Island to which the American traces back some of the most important strains in his thought and instinctive attitudes. Many events and conditions elsewhere in early and later America tended in the same direction. The American and his Bill of Rights are the product of no one episode or section. Yet the bold answer of Rhode Island to its bullying big neighbor must always remain one of the clearest, as it is one of the earliest, expressions of certain aspects of Americanism.

It was not only American and noble. It was horse sense and worldly wise. Perhaps that also is American. In Massachusetts the common people had almost risen in revolt against the persecuting acts of their ministers and magistrates. When King Charles heard what had been going on as to the Quakers, he vowed he would stop "the vein of innocent blood opened in his dominions, which if it were not stopped would overturn all," and another nail had been driven into the coffin of the old Massachusetts charter. On the other hand, there was no social upheaval in Rhode Island, and although conservative neighbors might fear its contagion and "anarchy," the charter of 1663 remained the only instrument of government of colony and state until the latter adopted a new constitution in 1842. A human society which offered such toleration and personal liberty in the mid-seventeenth century as to be considered dangerous and anarchic by contemporary reactionaries and yet which increased in population, wealth and freedom for a hundred and eighty years without alteration of its written basis of government does not look so bad to the unbiased historian.

Just as we have to leave out innumerable details in writing of the colonies we mention, so we have to leave out some colonies entirely, and ignoring here Maine (then a part of Massachusetts), New Hampshire and New Haven (although each would have something for us), we must turn to Connecticut and there pick up another major item in the making of the American.

About the time Williams had been driven from the Bay, that colony was having plenty of trouble. There was imminent difficulty with the Indians, and in England *quo warranto* proceedings had been instituted against the charter. Wires were being pulled among influential men at home but the Massachusetts leaders were taking no chances and a committee was appointed to "dispose of all military affaires" with power to "make eithr offensiue or defensiue warr." In other words they were preparing to defy the British government by arms. Roger Ludlow, Deputy Governor at the moment, was put in command, but just then the liberal element, as we would call them, were questioning the rights claimed by the leaders under the charter, and the Governor (Dudley), and Ludlow were voted out of office. Ludlow was a leading and extremely able man and not one to take such treatment lying down.

Meanwhile, other things had been happening. Both the Dutch at New Amsterdam and the colonists at Plymouth had established trading-posts near the head of navigation on the Connecticut River. Although these had been designed for the fur trade with the Indians, the rich river meadows had become known and had attracted attention.

The Reverend Thomas Hooker, of Newtown, and many of his congregation, partly perhaps on account of disagreement with the methods of the leaders of the Massachusetts Theocracy and partly on account of the meadows—though I think the former was the real cause—had asked permission to move in a body to the Connecticut, the earliest organized western migration in our history. Meeting with a refusal, they were finally allowed to go, but Ludlow was there in advance. In addition there was an agent and company sent out by Sir Richard Saltonstall who in England claimed a title to the section. Soon there arrived at the mouth of the river, Winthrop's son, John the younger. Having a commission as governor of Connecticut and with orders to take possession of the river and region in the names of Lords Saye, Brooke and others, he built a fort at the mouth of the river, on the Sound, which he called "Saybrook." The situation on the Connecticut was getting decidedly mixed.

Whatever patents or documents might be issued under English seals, this first "western frontier" was considered "God's waste" by the colonists who although they had been in America only a few years had already become Americans. The great empty land beckoned, and the squatter and land grabber had been born. Settlement at Plymouth without legal right had been an accident. Land titles in Maine and New Hampshire were in dispute. Williams and others in Rhode Island were at first solitaries. But those who settled the "three towns" on the Connecticut—Windsor, Hartford, and Wethersfield—simply pre-empted the rich land they coveted, by groups. Practically the whole of the inhabitants of Dorchester, Massachusetts, settled Windsor, those of Newtown (now Cambridge) established Hartford, and those from Watertown, Wethersfield. (Springfield was also settled but proved to be within the undisputed bounds of Massachusetts.) Briefly, the Plymouth people and the Dutch were soon disposed of, and we are for the moment concerned only with the three transferred towns from Massachusetts as forming "Connecticut." By 1638 they were prosperous settlements and their interest for our story lies in the following points:

We have already spoken of the quickening effect of "free land" as given in Virginia and Plymouth when the system of "common stock," or working for the community as a whole instead of for one's self, had proved incompatible with human nature. Ambition, work, the desire to rise and to be independent, at once sprang to life. Now, however, here in the Connecticut Valley there was not merely free land for the individual but for whole communities. That settlers from Dutch New Amsterdam, Pilgrim Plymouth and Puritan Massachusetts began to squabble over it, wholly regardless of any claimants in Holland or England, is part of our story of the American. An American question had arisen to be settled by Americans on the spot and not by foreign governments. America and the Atlantic were exerting their influences.

Distance and the feeling of American independence came out in another quarter. The Dutch and Plymoutheans were disposed of, but some of the Dorchester people—dissatisfied with the first spot chosen—decided they preferred that taken up by the representatives of Saltonstall. Saltonstall was an important man in England. Yet what happened in the beautiful but wild and distant valley of the upper Connecticut? Saltonstall's men were unceremoniously ejected from the spot they claimed, and, not only that, they were slighted "with many unbeseeming words." The wilderness was fair, England was far, and the land of America free.

The emigration to Connecticut has other interesting aspects. The new colony, though perhaps it may as yet be scarcely called that, was the first "west" as contrasted with the settled "east" of the Bay, and in the feelings between them we find the germs of the bitterness between innumerable successive "wests" and "easts" which were to face each other as the nation in the future was gradually to expand across the continent. The migration to the river was hindered by Massachusetts as far as it could be, and for obvious reasons. The strength and power of the Bay, which gave influence to its rulers and permitted the colony to lord it over the rest of New England for a while, came largely from the size of its population and its growing wealth. As in any new and developing country the increase in wealth had been greatly accelerated by the increase in population. As children grew and married and as new immigrants steadily arrived, the prices of land, cattle and other goods rose. Strength and prosperity might wane if large numbers, as in the case of the Connecticut migration, moved out of the colony. In fact, our first panic, that of 1640, proved the Massachusetts leaders right in their economic fears.

The case in Virginia had been a little different. Increases in population had indeed meant increased strength of defense against the savages, as well as enlarged satisfactions, social and other, but without towns or local merchants, and with for the most part only scattered plantations, the chances of profiting financially from growth were by no means commensurable with those in Massachusetts. By 1640 it has been estimated that about $5,000,000 or more, in money value today, had been invested in the latter colony. There were towns—in fact little else—and as immigrants had swarmed in, the prices of desirable town lots and other lands, which were limited in amount within the areas of settlement, had risen fast, as had prices of cattle and everything needed by new settlers. The godly Puritans had learned what an American "boom" means, and they had grasped what the cause was of their own and the future booms which were to occur over and over in later American history: namely, speculation due to the hope of unearned increments owing to increasing demand on account of increasing population. What this could do in contrast to the stability and slow growth of town or country-side in England became obvious, and one of the most characteristic of concepts held by the American had been born, that of "bigger and better."

In Massachusetts, however, the American was to learn another lesson, which three centuries of ups and downs were to impress on him—the unhappy fact that booms are followed by depressions. The westward emigration of the inhabitants of the three towns only just preceded the practically complete stoppage of immigration from England. "Bigger and better" suddenly became "no bigger and worse" as demand, other than that of slow replacement, dwindled in a population now become comparatively stable. The Puritans had bid up prices to a false level in anticipation of continued expansion, when the crash came. "Merchants would sell no wares but for ready money," wrote Winthrop. "Men could not pay their debts though they had enough, prices of lands and cattle fell soon to the one-half, yea to a third and after one-fourth part." The story of the Puritan boom and panic in little Massachusetts of over three hundred years ago may seem unimportant and even antiquarian. If, however, we apply a magnifying glass to all its figures and emotions, and then multiply the incident thousands of times to include all the successive little local or great national booms and crashes, we trace the origin of some of the qualities of the American. Among them are not only the traditional belief that "bigger is better," but the spirit of speculation, instead of the slow plodding and cautiousness of the European who, with the lack of speculative opportunities in a stable and job-filled society, cannot look forward to another boom to lift him out of the hole he may have dug for himself by economic rashness. If the American was to become, in Kipling's lines, a man

> "To shake the iron hand of fate
> Or match with Destiny for beers"

we have just seen the beginning of his training.

In October, 1635, sixty settlers, men, women and children, went from Newtown to the present Hartford and the next May, Hooker followed with the main part of his congregation, driving 160 cattle along the wilderness trail. In a couple of years the river towns were well settled, although not without hardships which were made no easier to bear because Massachusetts, sensing the difficulties in store for itself, placed impediments in the way of settlement.

Although Ludlow may be considered as certainly the chief layman and perhaps the founder of Connecticut, the clergy were usually the spokesmen for governmental policies. Sermons and other pronouncements occupied the place of leading editorials in modern newspapers. When, with Indian and other troubles, the people of this little new Connecticut "west" learned what was being said about their settlement in the Massachusetts "east," it was Hooker who undertook, or was appointed, to give John Winthrop a sound verbal thrashing.

As Hulbert wrote of the letter which Hooker dispatched, "It is the first outcry of an American frontier, the cry of a debtor class to a creditor, or a radical class to a conservative, of a democratic class to an aristocratic." The letter is too long to quote in full and we can give only an extract.

Immediately after the winter [Hooker wrote], because there was likelihood multitudes would come over [to Connecticut], and lest any should desire to come hither, then there is a lamentable cry raised, that all their cows at Connecticut are dead, and that I had lost nine and only one left, and that was not likely to live (when I never had but eight, and they never did better than last winter). We hear still and bear.

And lest haply some men should be encouraged to come because of my subsistence or continuance here, then the rumor is noised that I am weary of my station; or, if I did know whither to go, or my people what way to take, we would never abide, whereas such impudent forgery is scant found in hell; for I profess I know not a member of my congregation but sits down well apayd with his portion, and for myself, I have said what now I write, if I were to choose I would be where I am.

But notwithstanding all this matter is not sure, and there is some fear that some men will come towards Connecticut when ships come over; either some have related the nature of the place, or some friends invited them; and therefore care must be taken, and is by this generation, as soon as any ship arrives, that persons haste presently to board them, and when no occasion is offered or question propounded for Connecticut, then their pity to their countrymen is such that they cannot but speak the truth: Alas, do you think to go to Connecticut? If you do not, bless yourself from thense; their upland will ear no corn, their meadows nothing but weeds, and the people are almost starved. Still we hear and bear.

Here we get for the first time the authentic voice of the American frontier, its independence, pride, hopefulness, and angry disdain of the "effete east" with its failure to see the vision as the pioneer glimpsed it. How strong the feeling was is evidenced by Hooker's expression when he, a minister, wrote to his former fellow ministers, and to Winthrop and the other magistrates, about what was being said by them or others, that "such impudent forgery is scant found in hell."

One more point must be noticed regarding the contributions of early New England to the American. Among the reactions to the Theocracy we have mentioned the religious tolerance developed in Rhode Island. We have also spoken of the reaction in favor of popular government in Massachusetts itself, but that took the form of a long hard struggle. In Connecticut, democracy or popular government sprang into being almost at once. Just as the settlers in America could do certain things untrammelled by the complications of established institutions and customs of the Old World, so over here, as frontiers pushed farther west, the pioneers were in turn freed from even the trammels of the older American settlements. If we could draw lines of Old World and then of successive old and new settlements in the New World, like lines of longitude, we would find in a general way that the complexity of civilization became less with each line as we moved west. We may add that the men who made each farther westward thrust reacted ever more strongly against such hindrances to personal freedom as they had experienced in the society they had just left, and the demands for liberty became ever greater. For three hundred years this influence was at work to emphasize in the American the original English trait of wanting to do just as he pleased.

What the settlers in the River Towns wanted was more freedom from government interference than they had found in Massachusetts. The way they wanted to get it was largely by divorcing church and state, making government more responsive to the freemen regardless of church control, and limiting the arbitrary powers of the rulers. Just what part Hooker, Ludlow or any other settler played in drawing up what are known as the "Fundamental Orders," which served as the constitution of the group of towns which formed early Connecticut, cannot be accurately determined. A few points stand out. It is probable that Hooker and Ludlow had many a talk over it, but there had apparently also been a general assembly of the colonists at which each man might have his say and contribute his bit of wisdom or folly. To Hooker as a leader and clergyman fell the task as usual of publicizing and advocating the ideas which seemed to appeal most to those behind the scenes. Ludlow was the only trained lawyer in the colony. The drafting of the final document bears evidence of his having had first place in the work. Such antiquarian details, however, are of little interest for us here as compared with the general principles enounced.

In his famous sermon in 1638, according to such brief notes as have survived for us, Hooker laid down the doctrines that

> I. The choice of public magistrates belongs unto the people, by God's own allowance.
>
> II. The privilege of election, which belongs unto the people, therefore must not be exercised according to their humors, but according to the blessed will and law of God.
>
> III. They who have power to appoint officers and magistrates, it is in their power, also, to set bounds and limitations of the power and place unto which they call them.

There had also been letters from both Ludlow and Hooker which cast somewhat more light on what the ideas of the Connecticut men were before the "Orders" were "voted" in January 1639.

There are few clean breaks or wholly new departures in history which prove lasting. The Mayflower Compact was a modification of a church covenant to serve as a stop-gap in an awkward situation. The later Constitution of the United States was almost wholly made up of provisions as to ways of doing things which the Americans had already become familiar with in either their charters or their constitutional relations with England. So it was with the Fundamental Orders of Connecticut. There was practically nothing in them which might be said to have been wholly new. Their interest lies in the fact that from former experiments only those things were preserved which conformed to the free and democratic way of life and government as it was beginning in America's first west.

Besides the three principles enunciated by Hooker in his sermon as quoted above, the "Orders" provided, among other things, for a General Court made up of four representatives from each of the towns; for a franchise not dependent on church membership; and declared against the eligibility of any governor to serve a second successive term. In speaking of the governor it may be noted that in this constitution for the new community no mention was made of any external authority whatever, not even the King, and "the governor" was, of course, to be elected by the voters of Connecticut and not to be sent to govern them by the English monarch or government overseas. A group of Americans had founded a state, not by accident as in the case of Plymouth, or legal quibbling as in the case of Massachusetts, but after careful consideration by men who had been living for some years in America. It may be called the first American state, and it was founded on the basic principle that government should be one of laws and not of men.

"Whatsoever sentence the magistrate gives," Winthrop had written from Massachusetts (and the case of Anne Hutchinson, already quoted, was a leading illustration of the doctrine), "the judgment is the Lord's, though he do it not by any rule prescribed by civil authority." Hooker, on the other hand, discussing the office of a judge, had written, that if "The sentence should lie in his breast, or be left to his discretion, according to which he should go, I am afraid it is a course which wants both safety and warrant. I must confess, I ever looked at it as a way which leads directly to tyranny, and so to confusion, and must plainly profess, if it was in my liberty, I should choose neither to live nor leave my posterity under such a government."

In treating of seventeenth-century New England we have made no attempt to rewrite its detailed history. There are many other incidents which had their influence on the character and outlook of the American, such as the two great Indian wars, the attempt at union in the experiment of the New England Confederacy, wholly colonial in origin, or the imperial effort at unification in the Dominion of New England—but I have tried, by selecting certain outstanding episodes and by indicating some of the broader influences of location and environment, to show how by 1700 the Englishmen in America were already on the way to becoming something different from the Englishmen at home.

If I have written thus far only of Virginia and the Puritan colonies it has been because the lines of development are perhaps more distinct in them than in the other settlements which had sprung up and which would properly have their place in a narrative history of the nation as a whole rather than in a mere study of the evolution of the American. By the end of the century with which we have been dealing, the Dutch had absorbed the Swedes who had settled on the Delaware, England had conquered the Dutch, "New Amsterdam" had become "New York," and the whole coast from Canada as far south as Florida had become the home of the English and under their control in spite of some interesting surviving groups of other nationalities. With many local variations, the mold of America had been "set." In the future many alien strains were to add their contributions of brawn and brain, but it was to be the Americans of the old type who were to change and alter *them,* and not *they* who were to change or alter our basic Americanism.

We must now go on to the earlier half or so of the next century when Americans, saved by the frontier and the French and Indian War, were in danger of becoming again mere provincial Englishmen instead of continuing to develop into the "new man" of Crèvecœur's American scene.

CHAPTER VI

THE DANGEROUS PERIOD

I HAVE called the years 1700–1763 the "dangerous period" for the American not because there have not been other periods with their own peculiar dangers, but because the American was in a critical stage in his making during those decades. There were three very special dangers then present which threatened his ever even becoming an "American" at all. The first was that he might become largely continental European instead of English with English political ideas and instincts. On the other hand, the American Englishman was also in danger of becoming merely provincial English instead of "the New Man," "the American." Lastly, with its own important influence on the second point, there was the danger that he might be permanently hemmed in by the French and Spanish, with no chance to expand over that "West" which has done so much to make him what he is.

We spoke at the end of the preceding chapter of the gradual filling up of the seaboard from Maine to Florida by the English. That simple statement has, however, many overtones. We have stressed only Virginia and New England, and have tried to show some of the chief factors in those sections which contributed to the American. The other colonies contributed theirs, though perhaps in less striking fashion. That in itself is a point of some importance. The mere fact that the contrasts were not, and were not to be, so obvious, envisaged to some extent a future merging of points of view which had not yet been realized. The colonies, like the later states, in spite of similarity in forms of government and in the ideas of their peoples, were destined to be experimental stations for different ideas. For example, in speaking of religious toleration and freedom of thought in America, we have mentioned only a few colonies and individuals, but when we consider the many colonies which had developed—such as the New England ones already discussed at some length, cosmopolitan New York with its Dutch Church and many other sects, the Swedes on the Delaware, Quaker West Jersey and Pennsylvania, Roman Catholic Maryland, Church of England Virginia, and so on—we realize what extraordinary lessons were being given and learned by neighbors on our early Atlantic seaboard.

They were lessons in Americanization but the colonies did not yet consciously form an *America.* Each was separate from, and too often jealous of, or hostile to, the others. The connection was not between *them* but between each of them and England. They may be likened in this period, without straining accuracy too much but with perhaps some suggestiveness, to a company of marionettes, each independent of the other but all connected by strings to the hand of the performer—in this case England. The simile breaks down because, unlike unconscious figures in a marionette show, each of the colonies had a throbbing active life of its own, but the comparison holds good in so far as the colonies were each far more closely connected to England and more concerned with their relations to the home country than to one another in America.

This was unfortunate because, as the English government came to realize, and as the colonies themselves should have realized, they had many interests in common on the American side of the ocean which should have drawn them closely together in feelings and policies. We may mention such things as the many sore points in their relations with Parliament and the home government, which were more or less alike, though varying in degree, among all the colonies; problems of trade, particularly under the Navigation Acts, which made friction between all the colonies and the center of empire in the days of the Mercantile Theory; the presence of the Spanish to the south and of the French to the west and north; and above all the Indians on the outskirts of every colony.

But it was all of no avail. If old countries in Europe, even when small, have their thousand years' histories and feuds and settled ways of life which raise far more important barriers between them than mere customhouses on frontiers, no less do young colonies have their local prides and differences. The difficulties which were encountered in trying to unite the colonies in Australia into the present Commonwealth, though the population of all together numbered only a few millions, is one of the many cases which prove the point. The various small Australian provinces even had different gauges for their railways, one of the few methods of intercolonial obstruction not known to our own early colonies. We have spoken of several traits in the English which have bearing on this problem. They had already shown, when they settled America, a remarkably strong instinct for self-government and for political compromise. But they also had a strong instinct of patriotic loyalty to England. And, again, they had equally deep instincts for going their own way, and doing as they pleased as individuals.

All these came into play in the period we are now considering. Early in the seventeenth century, the four New England colonies of Massachusetts, Plymouth, Connecticut and New Haven saw the political logic of union and formed the "United Colonies of New England," on their own and with no reference of the matter to the home government. A few points about this experiment are notable. These four colonies refused to admit Rhode Island and Maine because of their religious and political differences from the others. Also the joint government was made up of two commissioners from each of the four colonies, which was unfair to the most populous and strongest, Massachusetts. It was an early example of the problem of big and little states on which the adoption of the Federal Constitution was later almost to founder. Briefly, the experiment lasted, with Massachusetts often far from acquiescent in her self-denying rôle, for some forty years, the Union dying a lingering death after none too efficient a life.

The next effort at unification came from England. I assuredly hold no brief for the Stuarts, but they did a good deal for religious liberty in New England and had some good ideas as to imperial administration, though with too much of the blueprint in contrast to the human approach. Watching the various small colonies, which had many problems in common, they tried to form a larger unit for administration and common defense. For about three years from 1686, they lumped all the New England colonies together, later adding New York and New Jersey, into one administrative unit. It simply did not work, owing in part to the lack of tact of the administrator, Sir Edmund Andros, but in larger part to the local variations and jealousies among the colonies included. The flight of James II and the Revolution which placed the House of Orange on the throne of England gave the colonists their chance to quash that attempt at unification.

The problem of a welter of quarrelling little colonies, facing united common enemies, such as the Indians and the French, remained. By 1754 it had become acute. The French and Indian War, of which we shall speak later and which was to be of such immense significance to "the American," was just over the horizon. This time the effort to acquire unity was due jointly to the British government and the colonists. The British asked the colonists to form some sort of union in the face of the common Indian danger. We need not here go into all the details of how the colonies had failed to act together, thus immensely increasing the risk of attacks on all by the savages on the borders of each. It was the old story of local jealousies and of the rugged individualism of the frontier. Each colony was afraid it might give a little more in the way of taxes and lives than its neighbors, and individuals in one colony or another feared that their trade with the Indians in arms and liquor might be interfered with.

I was going to say that it was the sort of thing which has happened over and over in the story of American business, but that is too exclusive. It was merely human nature, jealousies, local pride, and acquisitiveness coming to the surface. Benjamin Franklin, originally from Massachusetts, but then, characteristically a citizen of the mediating Keystone State (colony at that time), drew up the plan for Union at the Albany Conference of 1754. It was rejected alike by the British government and the colonists: by the former as abridging too much the prerogative of the Crown and by the latter as limiting too much the independence of each colony. The American, as a citizen of a new nation in a new world, had not yet been born politically.

Meanwhile, certain cleavages other than such as between the approximately 17,000 inhabitants of Rhode Island, 55,000 of Connecticut, 125,000 of Massachusetts, had been growing. There was rivalry between ports. About 1750, Boston still had some 15,000 people, as compared with about 13,000 each in New York and Philadelphia. Virginia had no one great port, but it was wealthy and had a population of some 275,000 as against the 180,000 of Massachusetts. Figures were shifting fast, and one has only to think in terms of current Chambers of Commerce to realize what it all meant. The colonies of New York and Pennsylvania, now as states the most populous and influential in the Union, were then, rather, mediating colonies, and for the extremes of difference we may return to New England and Virginia.

Certain cultural factors—social, religious and other—had tended towards compact settlements in New England, but even in that section there were other factors operating to disperse the population, though the movement was rather by groups than by individual pioneers. In the period we are now to discuss there were various forces at work to change the Englishman or European into something different from what he had been.

Society is not an organism in the biological sense; history is not a science; and to use similes or analogies is not to reason logically. Nevertheless, many things are suggestive which are not accurate, and a few instances from the physical sciences may help us to understand what some of the conditions of the

American environment were to do to the Europeans who were subjected to them.

For example, to turn to physics, we observe that atoms, with unlimited space and no pressure, race in every direction and form only a gas. Under other degrees of pressure and temperature they become liquids, and flow. Again change the degree of pressure and temperature and they become solids, set in permanent shapes. Pressure and temperature can do other odd things. At an elevation of 40,000 feet the temperature is normally 60 to 70 degrees below zero, and one would think that the problem of the aeroplane designer would be that of defrosting the carburetor and not of engine-cooling. However, as the air pressure is only about one-seventh of that at sea level the air has no heat-absorbing value and the problem is exactly the reverse of what one might have expected.

The second example above is taken from a most interesting talk by Charles F. Kettering, head of the research laboratories of General Motors, and I shall give one more by him in the same speech, though he was not talking about history. When he was young, he said, he investigated the boiler room of a new factory which was having difficulty in getting up steam pressure. The theory of the engineers was that the smokestack was not high enough. It would cost several thousand dollars to make it higher. He found, however, that when the tightly closed doors of the engine room were opened, steam immediately got up in the boilers. What was needed was not a costly raising of the height of chimney but a flood of fresh air from openings below.

Now, let us apply these analogies—and that is all they are—to the making of the American. In reverse order we may consider the last example first. The difficulty with getting that boiler room to work was something like the difficulty of old Europe in its social and economic problems. The smokestack may be taken as the symbol of the edifice, rigidly aristocratic, bureaucratic and socially stratified, erected on the remains of the earlier feudal system, but what Europe needed was not more height and cost at the top but more chance of a draft of fresh air from the bottom. That was precisely what the free life of the American frontier provided. The closed doors of that engine room may be taken as symbols of the doors of opportunity. America has always operated under a forced draft, but that draft has been provided far less by the stack rising in the air at large cost than by the innumerable openings at the lowest level. It was the "open doors" which were to attract to our shores throngs of alien races from continental Europe as well as additional immigrants from the British Isles, and to begin one of the complications of American life. Breaking out from the closed doors in the Old World, hordes rushed overseas to pass through the open doors of the New.

Here we come to our other illustrations or similes. For example, we have spoken of Dr. Kettering's mention of the *apparent* problem as contrasted with the *obscure* problem in the cases of the boiler room and the engine of a plane at an elevation of 40,000 feet. That is what happened in America. The plans for a colonization of Virginia were apparently well thought through from the standpoint of an extension of the British Empire, but they did not work out because the *obscure* problem proved much more important than the *apparent* problem. Something uncounted-on happens to engines at seven miles above sea level, and so likewise something happened to emigrants from three thousand miles overseas which had not been counted on.

We have also spoken of unlimited space and lack of pressure on atoms, which make them form a gas instead of a fluid or a solid. That, again, comes into our picture. The French acquired Canada. The Saint Lawrence Valley led them to the West. They spread thence down the Mississippi Valley. They had an empire on the American continent far vaster territorially than that of the English. They hemmed in the English, who were limited to the narrow strip between the Atlantic and the Appalachian Mountains. But, like atoms in unlimited space and without pressure, the French Empire in America was only a gas. The work the atoms did was remarkable and fascinating but they did not combine to found an enduring and *solid* nation.

On the other hand the English and other colonists who were to create the United States, and the American as we speak of him, suffered from pressure. It was not, as we pointed out in the case of New England, the lack of actual acreage but the lack of the right kind and combination of acres and soils and types of terrain. In the South the main staple crop—tobacco—was soil-exhausting, and new lands were steadily needed to take the place of those used up. Moreover the population was increasing rapidly. The claims of the French to the north and west, so long as England remained at peace with France in Europe, served as a sort of Maginot Line to prevent westward expansion. The Atlantic coastal plain had become fairly thickly settled and compact socially. Life in its towns and villages and on its farms was no longer dangerous, and inviting only to the adventurous.

It was rather becoming a field for those who knew how to make their often devious way to modest competence or occasional riches in a well-established social group—politically, financially, commercially or otherwise. Between this "old-settlement" seaboard, of varying width, and the Maginot Line of the French Empire, north and west (and the Spaniards to the extreme south), there was still an American frontier. We must now consider these three factors—the seaboard, the intervening frontier, and the outer wall, partly of mountains and partly of the power of foreign nations, which hemmed the English in.

The seaboard had become settled. The bulk of the English population, which had molded the form of its civilization, were no longer such as those who had come first, the Pilgrim and Puritan religious refugees of New England or those sent out earlier by the Virginia Company to work for a "common stock" and the company at home. Those in the old settlements no longer had to think of wild beasts and still wilder savages or of starvation and other disasters. By about the mid-eighteenth century there were three colleges in America, and numerous lower grade schools of a sort. People were having their portraits painted by such native artists as Copley and others, and in 1757 there was held an exhibition of solely American art in New York City. South of New England, at least, there were theatres, and Charleston was a center for music and the other arts. From 1750 to 1770 the celebrated London actors, Mr. and Mrs. Hallam, with their company performed plays by such English dramatists as Shakespeare, Steele, Congreve and Beaumont and Fletcher, throughout the colonies as far north as New York. There were newspapers with news, essays and book reviews in the style of the contemporary English journals, and the Virginia and Maryland *Gazettes,* in particular, were as good as any similar publications in the mother country. The richer folk imported their books, silver plate, mahogany and other furniture, as well as clothes, from England, which was still spoken of as "home," and there was much correspondence between Americans and their kinfolk or friends in the old land. Many young Americans from the South in particular went to Britain to study at the universities or in the Temple or to learn English fashion at Tunbridge Wells and elsewhere, as immortalized in Thackeray's *Virginians.* The seaboard was in danger of becoming a mere province of England, with the narrowness of English provincial life.

Let us, however, consider some of its problems first, before passing to the frontier.

Without going into historical details at length, we may note that a new world situation developed after the death of Charles the Second of Spain in 1700, and the acceptance of the legacy of the throne of the Spanish Empire by Louis the Fourteenth of France for his grandson, the young Philip of Anjou, in spite of previously given guaranties that the greatest two military powers of Europe should not be controlled by one royal house. The legacy of Charles and the perfidy of Louis changed the world. It is well to recall such instances when inclined to deny the rôle of the individual in history. The immense strength of the practically united Bourbon and Hapsburg monarchies in Europe, and their imperial ramifications over the seas and continents of the rest of the globe, spelled ruin for the hopes and prosperity of the rising trading and colonizing countries of Holland and England unless the menace could be obliterated by war.

War, or rather many wars, broke out for a century or so in all quarters of the earth. So intertwined are the threads of history that thousands of English and other colonists were to die in America because of the overweening ambition of the "Sun King," "le Roi de Soleil," in his palace at Versailles, and the tormented mind of the always half-imbecile ruler of the Spanish Empire in his vast palace of the Escurial. Charles was the son of Philip IV and Philip's niece, born of old age and disease. Constant intermarriages had ruined the Hapsburgs. There is no need to enter into all the historical and biographical details, many of them disgusting, but the interesting point is that all this sordid story of French and Spanish, seemingly so remote from the seaboard towns and unhewn forests of the American frontier, did really help to form the American.

In the wars which resulted, directly and indirectly, from the long dreaded problem of the "Spanish Succession" (the inheritance of the empire of the childless Charles), involvement of the English colonies in America was inevitable. In the first place the English were "cabin'd, cribb'd, confined" in their narrow coastal strip by the claims of French and Spanish. To be sure, the British colonies were far more thickly populated than were those of Spain or France, but the powers in Europe behind the latter two were vast, and in addition the French especially could, and did, unleash their Indian allies on the English frontier settlements. In spite of what we have said about the provincial character of the most densely settled towns and neighborhoods, America in back of those was still wild and primitive. If the French hounded on the savages to attack the English, the godly Puritans and others could offer as high as £50 for the scalps of Indian men, women and children, and threaten the children with slavery in the West Indies.

The Indians were swayed by their desire for the cheaper trading goods of the English, and by the brandy of the French, which they preferred to the British whiskey. Both sides sold them guns and ammunition for profit, caring little for the lives which were endangered. Along the frontier the tale of greed, rapine and murder went on, particularly in the winter of 1703–4, when town after town on the New England border suffered, and in Deerfield over half of the hundred and twenty-five inhabitants were killed or captured. There was nothing of an old English cathedral atmosphere about the border, though the people of Boston, like Samuel Sewall, might be changing from old English Puritans to New England-trading Yankees; and the richer planters of the tidewater South were beginning to adapt English country gentry life to a type of slave aristocracy.

There were other repercussions of the European wars and the problems of the eighteenth century on the making of the American. Influenced by Europe, influencing Europe in turn, and helping to form the American, were our perennial problems of the use of almost illimitable resources by almost illimitable energy and individual ambitions, but with a limited supply of labor for hire. The ramifications of this simply stated situation were endless, and deeply affected the pattern of life and the history of America, as well as America's relations to Europe then and in the two World Wars of the twentieth century.

In the eighteenth, the later industrial revolution, with the vast changes it was to bring about in economic, social and political life, was but obscurely beginning. It is true that certain so-called "manufactures" were starting, and legal prohibition as to the making of nails, hats and other things in the colonies played their part in the growing irritation with the home government as the century advanced. It is noteworthy, however, that in the production of iron, which was becoming more and more important, though the age of steel lay far ahead, the colonies by 1775 produced one-seventh of the world's annual total though they had produced only one-seventieth in 1700. By the later year—a fact of great significance for both psychological and military reasons—they were producing more pig and bar iron than England and Wales combined.

On the whole, however, the wealth to be gained in America was from its natural resources, such as timber, tobacco, furs, fish from the sea, and such things, but above all from land, *land*, LAND, which remained the dominant note in the American economy until the latter half of the nineteenth century. Even after 1800 ninety per cent of Americans were engaged in agriculture of one form or another.

In the period with which we are now dealing, land was the strongest magnet to draw the poor of the Old World to our shores. Many currents in Europe influenced them—economic, social, legal troubles in Ireland; the effects of the wars on the Continent; religious and political oppression in this country or that; the lure of seemingly fabulous wages; the desire for liberty and the chance to rise; what I have constantly called the "American Dream." But all these things were to be achieved by, or to lead to, the ownership of land. Land, *land*, LAND. It throbs through the American symphony like the bass chords in Beethoven. Land—a little home lot in a village, a farm, a clearing in the woods—land in fantastically growing cities with colossal unearned increments—land with surprising things under it—coal, copper, silver, gold, oil—land, cheap or free, and like Aladdin's lamp needing only to be used to bring about personal independence or perhaps the most amazing riches. Land became an obsession for Americans, generation after generation.

But land in differing quantities and under differing conditions meant different things to different people. I am speaking, at this point, of land when it still meant chiefly soil and what could be grown on it.

In the eighteenth century, land for the slave meant something on which he had to toil for the benefit of others with little chance in general to acquire independence and profit by owning any himself. For the "servant," it meant the opportunity to become a freeholder and to rise as high as his talents might permit when he had completed his term of service for his passage. Even the small artisans thought in terms of land rather than of their trades. "I live a simple life," wrote one about 1700, "and hath builded a shop, and doth follow weaving of linen cloth, but I have bought 450 acres of land in the woods." "Land in the woods!" Land anywhere, that was the story, but even for those who were free and who, in one way or another, could acquire land in fee simple by gift, purchase or merely by squatting and pre-empting, a few acres meant liberty and freedom from want for life, given health and the ability to work hard. It meant those things, and contrasted with European conditions meant also the release of boundless energy and ambition, although it might also mean, as it did on many a frontier, a descent into a life of lazy slovenliness. Even that, often carried with it an overweening insistence on doing as one pleased, an opposition to all authority, and a prickly pride and touchiness.

However, the question of land became complicated. A few acres might mean freedom from want for life, on a low scale of living, and by dint of hard work, but *wealth* from land came only from large holdings. Although the factor of unearned increment, due to increase of population in any one community or section, entered into the problem of making money with land as the basis, it was at this time a minor one. In a period when there were no cities but only a few moderately large towns, in the vast American area, to win wealth from the land in the span of one or even two generations meant not obtaining a few acres but thousands of them, and setting them to use by planting them with either crops or people. In all the colonies there were individuals and groups who managed to acquire title to large and sometimes almost fabulous holdings.

The ways of getting them, and also of turning them into quick profits, varied in the several colonies.

For example, we have already seen how in the very beginning almost of the Bay Colony in Massachusetts, the voting to themselves of a thousand and more acres each by some of the leaders, such as Winthrop, disturbed the harmony of the colony group. Later, the legislatures of the New England colonies bestowed grants of ten thousand acres or more on individuals who knew how to "pull the wires." Even in godly and practically independent Connecticut there developed the social landed group known as "Lords of the Valley." However, the topography, variety of soils, and other factors, including the stubborn individualism of the inhabitants, did not in New England allow of establishing large single-crop plantations or of tenant farming. Big landholdings in that region were more likely to be turned into cash or into income-producing property by the planting of whole towns on them. In many cases, under such attempts at exploitation, the greed of the absentee town "proprietors" and the encroachments on the accustomed rights of the settlers created great ill-feeling—class feeling as we would call it—and helped to make a distinction between old and new settlement. Yet, in New England, the big holdings had somehow to be transformed into small holdings to get profit from them, and those who skimmed the cream in the process had to find some other use for those profits to make more wealth. They might set up as shipping merchants or as business men in other lines, but not as great planters or a large landed class. So New England became a section for the most part of small hard scrabble farms which called for all the qualities of Yankee ingenuity to make both ends meet, and of "business" of one sort and another.

In New Hampshire and elsewhere there were some very large timbering operations but lumbering does not create a landed class, and the only exception to what we have been saying was in the South County of Rhode Island where there were some large estates, though not comparable to the great ones developed in the real "South." Those owning these, which were long run by slave labor, called themselves "planters," not "farmers," and the official name of the state is still "Rhode Island and Providence Plantations." It is not strange that in the nineteenth century until the Civil War there was unusually close social connection between the Rhode Islanders and the South Carolinians. The upper class of Charleston and Newport intermingled and intermarried to an extent unknown between any other two northern and southern urban centers. Both were in some degree outside the main stream of the roaring flood which was carrying "the American" to unknown destinies, and it is also notable that South Carolina was to be the first state to secede from the Union, as Rhode Island had been the last of the original colonies to enter it.

Where there were Royal Governors the methods of acquiring land in large grants took a different form. In the Royal colonial Governments the governor was the fount of favors, and the most important of such favors were land grants. Naturally those who had already reached a social or financial position to make them eligible socially or financially for the "Governor's set" stood at the head of the line of these early "Gimmies." There were other methods to be used by individuals in acquiring land—such as a grant from the Proprietors in the proprietary colonies—but, on the whole, titles came from the legislatures or the governors. The eighteenth century was a period of sinecures, of government favors, but in England and on the continent of Europe these took the form rather of gifts, business favors or of lucrative posts in the supposedly public service. For example, Benjamin Franklin wrote from France in 1777 (suggesting that the war against the colonies might not be unpalatable to some in England), that "an auditor of the exchequer had six pense in the pound, or a fortieth part, of all public money expended by the nation, so that, when a war costs forty millions, one million is paid to him." Allowing for some error, this was nevertheless the general way in which government functioned in eighteenth-century England, very different, needless to say, from that of the twentieth.

In America the business man was held down with some fear but no favor by the British government; colonial public offices were not profitable sinecures, except those of some Royal Governors; only one hereditary title, and that merely of Baronet, was ever bestowed on a resident American colonial; and there were no careers open which could lead to such huge gifts as that of between one and two million dollars of public money, in addition to an annuity of £25,000 forever to his heirs to the title, which were lavished on the Churchill who became the first Duke of Marlborough. For the American there was only business on a small scale, crafts of various sorts, merchandising in villages or towns, the fur trade, little mills on streams, the beginnings of very small manufacturing, ocean commerce in steadily increasing amount (legal or illicit, including a lot of smuggling), privateering in war time, and so on—but, above all, *Land.*

We have spoken of the situation in New England where legislatures, properly approached or influenced in the Puritan colonies, might grant 10,000 acres or more to favored individuals or groups. As we look southward we encounter the situation as it was in New York. There, at the beginning of the century, Governor Fletcher had started the ball rolling, by granting one of his favorites, a Captain John Evans, a tract of 356,000 acres, for which Evans said he was offered in England £10,000 (of course a far larger sum in purchasing power then than now). In fact, a later governor, the Earl of Bellomont, asserted that before Fletcher got through he had granted nearly three-quarters of the then available land of the colony to about thirty of his friends as grantees, many of them of bad character. This did not prevent Fletcher's successor, Lord Cornbury, from granting during his term (1702–8) enormous tracts to groups of speculators, such as one of about

100,000 acres, another of 356,000, and the so-called "Great Hardenburgh" patent of 2,000,000 acres.

Continuing down the coast we find similar conditions and practices. In Maryland, Charles Carroll got himself about 60,000 acres, and in spite of indefinite and overlapping boundaries it was said that three or four men held options on all the vacant lands on the Potomac between the Monocacy and the Susquehanna and from the eastern shore settlements of Pennsylvania west to Dorchester County. Of the vast grant to Lord Fairfax of the entire Northern Neck of Virginia extending nominally to the Pacific Ocean, Robert ("King") Carter secured the first sub-grant and survey amounting to 50,000 acres in 1729, which he later managed to expand to 300,000 acres. Speculation continued rife, and almost all the ablest colonial leaders were engaged in it—such as, to mention only a few in the South, George Washington, Richard Henry Lee, the Carrolls, and Benjamin Franklin. Great speculative land companies were formed as, for example, the Mississippi, Vandalia, Loyal, Ohio, Wabash, and others.

Colonials with money and anxious to make greater riches were already looking across the mountain barrier and the French "Maginot Line." The continent seemed to extend indefinitely westward, and so did their desires.

Land and the speculative fever got into the American blood. It was due not merely to the venality of British Royal Governors. As we have seen, even New England Puritan legislatures played their favorites, and one of the worst scandals of all occurred twelve years after American independence was acknowledged when in 1795 the legislature of Georgia "sold" 30,000,000 acres at 1½ cents an acre to a favored group, and started one of the great legal *causes célèbres* in American history, ever since known as the "Yazoo Frauds."

What did this preoccupation with land, and the policies adopted, do for the making of America and the American? In the first place we may note that the situation created was wholly New World. In the Old, the poor man could not usually achieve the ownership in fee of even some scant acres, and there was practically no opportunity for granting, even to the favored few, principalities of hundreds of thousands and even millions of acres. It was the nominally empty continent of America which alone offered the chance for the poor to acquire independence and for the few to gain quick wealth by means of land. The effects were profound and lasting. Let us see what some of these were, running down the colonies from north to south.

CHAPTER VII

NEW RACIAL STRAINS AND SOCIAL STRESSES

LAND, to be translated into wealth, had to be planted with either crops or people. The crops might be either the already standing primeval forests, which made money by cutting the timber, or a staple annual crop, like the tobacco of Maryland and Virginia. The people might be those of a town settlement in New England, tenant farmers, or purchasers of farms for the most part small. But to change the land acquired in large grants into ready cash or income, something had to be done with it, else the owners would have to turn to some other way of making money if they were anxious to have it. In view of the seemingly limitless opportunities in America practically every one who had been here, was on his way here, or who was thinking of coming, wanted all he could get, from simple freedom and independence to as much wealth as his ambition vaulted to.

Considering New England first, the land grants there, in spite of the money made from them, seem almost niggardly as compared with those from Connecticut south. Moreover, immigration had practically stopped, and such new streams as came in driblets were far from welcome, and were made to feel it. When five shiploads of Irish Presbyterians arrived at Boston in 1718 they were met with much surliness. They were considered as Irish, and, therefore, heartily disliked by the New England English. So Irish were they thought to be that, when a group of them in Rockingham County, New Hampshire, popularized the indigenous American potato, already known in the colonies, but hitherto practically not used, it received the name which has always stuck to it of the "Irish potato." The newcomers were not only "Irish" in the minds of the New Englanders, but they were indubitably Presbyterians, and often refused to contribute to the established Congregational Churches. So high did the feeling run that when some of the Scots began to build a church in Worcester the frame was destroyed by a mob which was said to have included "some of the best people in town." Some Germans, who early in the century also drifted in, were no more cordially received than the Scots.

We have already noted the many factors, geographical and others, which tended to set off and narrow the New Englander, and to make the type, economically and otherwise, into which the Yankee developed. In the Scot he met his match, and perhaps, as with the Armenian problem in the Near East, there was an economic base to the dislike, overlaid by religious bigotry and the tendency, which we shall speak of later, of the "old American" to look down upon foreigners. In any case the influences of America, as operating in New England, were having their effects. Not only had fresh English immigration dried up for various reasons, but new immigration of other stocks was discouraged, although such superb frontiersmen as the Scotch-Irish were to prove themselves could have erected a formidable barrier against the French and the Indians. New England was to become more and more ingrowing and inbred, which may account for Emerson's later remark that "from 1780 to 1820 there was not a book, a speech, a conversation, or a thought in" Massachusetts.

Moreover, the vegetable crops to make land valuable were limited, and as the human crop, so to say, which might make land salable and rise rapidly in price, was limited to the natural increase of children of native parents, the tendency to business, thrift and even penuriousness, became greatly emphasized.

Proceeding from the Puritan colonies down the coast, we encounter a new and more or less unique condition in New York. Land might be granted to favorites of the governors by the hundreds of thousands or even millions of acres, but as wilderness it was worthless. It bought no fine clothes, silver plate, nor enabled its owners to live, in an American phrase of a later age of speculation, "high, wide and handsome." Before the end of the century William Cooper, father of James Fenimore Cooper the novelist, was to be able to boast that he had "40,000 souls directly or indirectly under" him, as tenants on part of his huge land ownings in central New York, but, earlier, the effort to people the lands of New York with tenants imported from Germany failed because of the rapacity of the landholders. The new stream of immigration from Europe began to avoid the colony of New York as it did New England, and we have to continue our way south.

Here again we find different conditions. Particularly in Pennsylvania, Maryland, Virginia and the far South, two heavy streams of immigration were used to solve the land and labor problems as factors in the accumulation of wealth and the development of America. One was voluntary, consisting mostly of Germans and Scotch-Irish, with a sprinkling of Swiss, French Huguenots and others. The other was involuntary, the black slaves imported from Africa. Both streams derived from American conditions, and both were to be vast influences in their effect on American history and on the American.

The Quaker settlement of Pennsylvania had early attracted German immigrants of various other pietist sects who came largely from religious motives, similar to those which brought the first Pilgrims to Plymouth. In the eighteenth century, however, the trickling stream increased to an overwhelming flood. The Thirty Years' War in Germany had caused immense suffering and poverty. Then came later struggles, such as that in the Palatinate, causing more misery and hopelessness. America, with its promise of land, high wages, and freedom from oppression, beckoned like the dream of a new Heaven. This dream, of which the poor in Germany caught glimpses from letters from friends or relations already in the New World, was also carefully fostered by business men on this side of the water, working by means of foreign agents and printed propaganda.

These businessmen formed roughly three groups; the shipping men who wanted profit from the lucrative if unholy traffic, as it had become, in transporting immigrants; those who wanted labor for household work, farms or other purposes; and above all those who had received large land grants and wanted tenants or small purchasers to make them profitable. In Maryland, for example, to mention only three of the great developing "realtors" of the first half of the century, Charles Carroll spent large amounts of money in inducing settlers to come over from Ireland and Germany, and built up for a while closely settled tracts of from five to ten thousand acres each. Thomas Brerewood, owing to political influence, received a tract of ten thousand acres in Baltimore County, which he developed in similar fashion. Daniel Dulany had got hold of enormous tracts in Frederick County—a wilderness in 1730—but he followed the same methods, laid out the town of Frederick, and by about the mid-century his county had become the second most populous in Maryland.

Such transactions, which make modern real estate operators look like pikers, called for money and influence. The influence, of course, had to be exerted on governors, proprietors, royal officials or on legislative bodies. The money, to start with, might come in various ways—from agriculture on already acquired large plantations, Indian trade, business, or not seldom (as in the case of Dulany), by marrying rich heiresses. Dulany managed to marry three of them in succession, and we may here merely note how much the Southern tidewater "aristocracy" built itself up in power by intermarriage. All these opportunities were, of course, utterly outside the world of the ordinary man.

Pennsylvania and Maryland were so rapidly becoming Germanized as to cause anxiety. By 1727 there were, perhaps, fifteen to twenty thousand Germans in Pennsylvania alone, and besides the natural increase from these, probably twenty-two thousand more arrived from overseas in the next decade and a half. By the mid-century, of the six newspapers in the colony, three were in German, and the street signs in Philadelphia were painted in both German and English. Even the clear and common-sense mind of Franklin became perturbed, and some years later he wrote to Washington of the Germans, saying:

> In short, unless the stream of their Importation could be turned from this to other Colonies, as you very judiciously propose, they will so soon outnumber us, that all the advantages we have, will not in my opinion be able to preserve our Language, and even our Government will become precarious. The French, who watch all advantages, are now themselves making a German settlement back of us, in the Illinois country, and by means of these Germans they may in time come to an understanding with ours.

Before we discuss the broader aspects of the new labor, land, and racial situations arising, we must speak briefly of the other immigration streams of Scotch-Irish and Negroes.

In the early part of the eighteenth century conditions in Ireland were deplorable owing to many factors, including among others trade restrictions laid by the British government, and exactions from and abominable treatment of the peasants and small farmers by the Irish landlords. In a word, in that "doleful isle" dire poverty and hopeless despair were widespread. Nowhere in Europe or anywhere else on the globe was there a place for these forlorn people to go except America, which was becoming a magic word to lure the stricken of the Old World. The free or cheap land, the high wages, the chance to rise, were as distinctly American products at that time as corn on the cob. America was the giant magnet which attracted to it like iron filings these tens of thousands of otherwise hopeless people. It influenced them; and they in turn were to influence it in a perpetual process of interactions.

Some of the Celtic Catholic Irish came in this period, although it is impossible to estimate their numbers with any approach to accuracy, and, as we have seen, "Irish" was a generic term among the colonists, often used for all those who came from the island. It was, however, the Presbyterian Scotch-Irish from Ulster who formed by far the larger part of the movement in this period. By 1729 there were about 6000 in Pennsylvania alone. Beginning with that year they came in swarms, 6000 more in the next twelve months. Logan, the agent for William Penn, wrote that "it looks as if Ireland is to send all her inhabitants hither; for last week no less than six ships arrived, and every day two or three arrive also." Just as the Germans of this period largely went west of the old seaboard settlements to build up population and townships on the cheaper and wilder lands, so the Scotch-Irish passed beyond both the old seaboard and the Germans to settle a still farther-off and wilder frontier.

Of the horrors of the crossing, of the heartbreaking experiences and failures of hope for many, on the part of Germans, Scots and others, we shall speak presently. At least, however, they came voluntarily, even if all too often only to discover that what they had been promised had been sadly misrepresented. Of all the immigrants to our shores (except a few, kidnapped as indented servants, or those shipped as transported "criminals"), only the Negroes came involuntarily.

Slavery was a coefficient of many other factors, for a part of America. Among these were climate, the Bible, which was considered to sanction slavery, the fact that the Negro was not Christian when brought here, his character and adaptability to certain tasks, the scarcity of labor needful to those who wanted to "get rich quick," and others—above all land, which had to be worked to make it profitable on a large scale. All of the colonies, even the New England Puritan ones, approved of slavery, but owing to climate, and the fact that the Negro, as other than a household servant, proved chiefly adapted to the simple operations of large-scale single-crop production, such as tobacco, and later, cotton, and not to the demands of diversified small farming or business, it came about that slavery became mostly concentrated in the tidewater sections of Maryland, and particularly of Virginia, and of the colonies farther south.

Until after 1700 there were not very many slaves anywhere,

although the first Negroes had been introduced in 1619. Doubt, well substantiated, has been raised by Mathew Page Andrews as to whether these first Negroes were slaves for life, and he points out that in the beginning there were a good many recorded cases of blacks being given their freedom precisely like indented servants, after the customary term of years. However this may be, before long the blacks were unquestionably brought in as slaves and slavery was firmly established. In any case, even if some of the early imported Negroes did legally have the status of indented servants, the fact remains that unlike the vast majority of white "servants" they had not left Africa for America voluntarily but had been forcibly brought here. It may also be noted in passing that the first American slave ship, the *Desire,* sailed from Marblehead, Massachusetts, in the same year that the present Harvard University was founded in that colony.

After 1700, by which date black slavery had to some degree become established in practically every one of the American colonies, the black flood poured in. By 1754 it has been estimated by several authorities, as stated in the *Century of Population Growth,* published by the United States Government, that there were about 500,000 Negro slaves in all the colonies, of whom 116,000 were in Virginia, and 104,000 more in Maryland and the two Carolinas. Although there was no American Dream for these human chattels, nevertheless, apart from the schism created in the nineteenth century and the Civil War between North and South, as well as the colored problem in our own day, the slaves and their descendants were to be of great influence on American life.

We may now turn to consider what these three main streams of non-English immigration between 1700 and the Revolution did to America and what America did to them. Of course, there were other minor alien streams in that period mingling with the main American current—such as the Swiss and Celtic Irish, already mentioned, the Welsh, the Jews, the French Huguenots and others, but for our present purpose we may concentrate our attention upon the Germans, Scots and Negroes.

We may note one point first. Around 1700 the colonies were fairly well united racially. There were of course Jews in Rhode Island; the descendants of old Dutch families in New York; of the Swedes in Delaware; the Negroes; and many other strains; but racially the colonists considered themselves on the whole as English, and their culture and institutions, including literature and language, were English. This did not prevent local jealousies and differences. These were so many and varied as to seem to make the ideal of unity impossible, but there was also an all-pervasive sentiment with regard to one thing, and that was mistrust and dislike of those of other races, "foreigners." "I wish their coming over do not prove fatal in the end" Cotton Mather wrote in New England of the Scotch-Irish, and we hear the same note in all the colonies, whether with reference to the Scots, the Germans or others.

This mistrust became characteristic of the American, and perhaps had no little to do with his later tendency towards isolationism. We may anticipate and note that America is a nation and not a race. America does something to a very large part, though it cannot be said to *all*, of those who come here and throw in their lot with us and make their way. The consequence is that newcomers in time become "American" and begin to look down on later comers, and so, as wave after wave of the same or different races arrives, there has always been a sort of submerged generation or two of "foreigners" who have been given the hardest work for the least remuneration and chance of success. The effect has been that the dislike for the individual who does the work, or who lives in certain districts under certain conditions, has been transferred to the work or to whole sections as such. "The other side of the tracks." In Europe, in the densely populated and old countries, all the work, from top to bottom, from King to ditch-digger, was done by their own nationals, and largely by people of the same race. It was America, with its opportunities for all of all races, but coming in successive "layers," so to say, that brought about changed attitudes, for better and also for worse.

There is no country which has welcomed the foreigner as has America—*up to a point*. The chance afforded him to rise economically and socially has been wonderful—again *up to a point*. As Walter Lippmann once wrote: "Here is no trivial conflict. Here are the new people clamoring to be admitted to America, and there are the older people defending their household gods." This began early in our history, and is one of the major contradictions in our philosophy and outlook, almost comparable to our present contradiction between wanting the old rugged individualism and at the same time the benefits of mass production and a multiplicity of cheap luxuries produced by a system which tends toward regimentation.

Almost all the newcomers suffered on the voyage over similar hardships, though in varying degrees, and even Scots and Germans might be separated from their families and sold—the husband away from the wife, and parents away from their children—as were the Negroes. But there was a difference. The whites were sold for a term of years and the Negroes into life slavery, with scarcely any chance to rise out of it.

As far as the Negro is concerned we have to consider him briefly at this point, from several aspects—what America did to him, and what he did to the Americans, which latter point again splits into two, for the slave did different things to the well-to-do and to the comparatively poor white Americans, in this period.

It is always difficult to appraise, especially after a long period of time, the balance of good and evil wrought by the impact of one race on another of a different stage or type of civilization or barbarism. For example, was it better or worse for the Japanese (and ourselves), that we forced them to open their doors to the Western world and its trade and way of life? Was it better or worse for India—or the welter of races, religions, languages and shifting despotisms which have gone by that name—that the interminable native anarchy and wars were ended by the British and the *Pax Britannica*? Is it better or worse for the world that the American Indian was driven from his hunting grounds and that a sweep of continental area, which once supported only about a half million warring savages or barbarians, now supports 135,000,000 people engaged in peaceful and humanitarian pursuits? There may be many answers, depending on the answerer's racial, emotional and other background.

Considering the problem of the Negro, I may say that assuredly I hold no brief for the slave trade, the institution of slavery, the horrors of the "Middle Passage," and all the rest. Yet one may pause and ask whether America did not benefit the African enormously, just as it did those from other lands. It must be recalled that the terms "African" and "Negro" are generic, as is the term "American" today. The innumerable tribes in Africa which were raided by the slave hunters differed immensely. There were the proud Coromantees; the good-natured easy-going Whydahs, Pawpaws and Nagoes; the almost-good-for-nothing Gaboons; the Mandingoes and Foulahs, with brains and Arab blood, Mohammedan by faith; and many others. But on the whole the Africa of the slave-raiding days was a vast jungle of savagery, with no sign of betterment, in which there were incessant cruel wars involving the enslavement of the conquered. At any moment a Negro might be killed, torn from his family, and even be eaten by his conqueror. Speaking generally, they had no civilization and lived in one of the most ghastly states of savagery the world has known.

Admit all that we must about slavery as practiced by the Americans—and other peoples of the seventeenth and eighteenth centuries—yet, as I have asked elsewhere: "Would the 12,000,000 of Negroes in the United States today prefer that their ancestors had never been enslaved, and that they themselves, if alive, should at this moment be living as savages or barbarians in the African jungle? Would a Du Bois prefer to be headman to an African chief instead of a Harvard graduate, scholar and writer? Would a Paul Robeson prefer beating a tom-tom to thrilling world audiences with his beautiful voice? Would the colored washerwoman I have in the North give up her comfortable house and her car, in which she motors her family to Virginia each summer, for the ancestral grass hut in Africa?"

We could continue the catalogue of questions, but the main point is that America has done an immense lot for the descendants of the original slaves, although obviously not nearly enough as yet. Nevertheless, in spite of the appalling magnitude and difficulty of the Negro problem at present, we cannot consider eighteenth-century ideas and standards from a twentieth-century viewpoint. We have all advanced in our outlooks, but the advance of the Negro in America over most of those remaining under aboriginal conditions in Africa would seem to have been even more rapid than that of the white American. Harlem may not be Heaven but almost no Negro yet who has been offered the chance has wanted to go back to Africa, even to Liberia, which was erected as a civilized Negro state under Negro rule. The population of Liberia is not made up of the twelve or fifteen thousand who can trace themselves back to America but of some millions who never knew America. Even cannibalism is still practiced in that State, or was recently. The African is the only race brought to America against its will, and it is also the only one which does not think of, or want to return to, the "mother land," even for a visit. This indicates something decidedly significant.

Turning from the very problematical question of what America did to the original Negro slave and for the later American Negro citizen under difficult conditions, we must now consider what slavery did to the American in the period particularly under consideration in this chapter. We may note first that it was America which brought about the conditions of American slavery. In Great Britain and the continent of the Old World at that time, there was no need to import slaves as the labor supply was not only abundant but in the opinion of many, superabundant. It was the vast and almost empty lands of the New World—North America, the West Indies, and South America—which called for labor to make them profitable.

We have seen how land was the way to wealth in eighteenth-century America, and to some extent how the problem was handled in the colonies north of tidewater Maryland. Let us take a case in Virginia as typical. The first William Byrd had turned his hand and able brain to all sorts of things in rather Yankee fashion. He had a moderate amount of land on which in 1690 he built a comfortable but very modest house. He had a mill or two, dabbled in iron making, in the importation of indented servants, was quite heavily interested in the Indian fur trade, and so on. He also married the daughter of a great friend of Governor Berkeley, and when the parsimonious but shrewd and far-sighted elder Byrd died in 1704 he left over 23,000 acres to his son, who had been sent to school in England.

The era of American money and English titles, which was to reach its climax around 1900, had begun. The young Virginian heir became friends with the Marquis of Halifax, Lord Oxford, the Duke of Argyle, the Earl of Orrery, Lord Egmont, and others whose portraits he had painted and brought back to the "Old Dominion" to adorn the walls of the beautiful house, "Westover," which he built to replace his father's more simple one. Unlike many a parent in 1900, however, tradition has it that the second Byrd declined to allow his daughter to marry the Earl of Peterborough because of the dissolute character of the noble Lord. Incidentally, although not a good businessman, he had managed to increase his landed inheritance from 23,000 acres to 180,000. The life he led required a fortune, which, also establishing an American tradition, was largely dissipated by his son—the third generation—who committed suicide under a load of mortgages.

The point for us here is the problem which was everywhere

facing the rising capitalists in the colonies, of how to turn their large land grants into cash or income. About the time of the first Byrd, the flood of Negro slaves had begun, and, whether rightly or wrongly, the tobacco planters of the South had decided that black slaves and not white indented servants offered the solution to the labor problem.

This decision, put into practice, brought about two important consequences. Where whites predominated and where white immigration continued, land might be sold in small freeholds or worked by tenant farmers—though with so much free land available the latter method was not very generally successful. It was chiefly so, and for a while only, with the Germans in Maryland west of the tidewater section. For the purpose of transmuting vast land grants into cash or cash income, the Negro slave was of no use *except* as a slave. The very variously assorted Negroes who were brought here had among them many excellent qualities, but, not only were they not the qualities which under the then conditions made good tenant farmers or frontiersmen, but the entire institution precluded them from becoming such. Although a comparatively few were allowed to make a little money for themselves and buy their freedom or were voluntarily freed by their owners, they were chattels—property—bought and paid for for life. To allow too many free Negroes in a slave society would have upset the foundations of the solution to the labor problem which the tidewater South had elected to use. Again, not only were the Negroes as unfitted by their nature from becoming founders of communities on the frontier as, let us say the Scotch-Irish were pre-eminently fitted for it, but they had no chance. They were legally tied—hand and foot—to their master and his plantation.

One result of this situation was that after slavery became an established institution, the southern planter who was trying to get rich quick by the land route had to get more and more land to be worked by more and more slaves, whether efficiently or not. Land *and* slaves spelled social distinction. Social distinction led to political advancement, friendship with those who could bestow more lands, and marriages with those who had lands and money. "To him that hath shall be given." The old spiral.

Those who could build fortunes in this fashion formed but a small part of the population. It is true that there were a good many small farmers who had no slaves or only one or two, and were more or less in the position of small farmers in New England who worked their acres with a little "hired help." It is also true that the Negro was not averse to the idea of slavery. Negroes constantly enslaved each other in Africa and the idea was not alien. When a free Negro in the South could afford it, he bought another Negro as a slave for himself. But the results of all this were far-reaching, and continue to the present day.

Slavery fixed the pattern of high social life in the South into that of the big plantation with a single simple crop, because that was the only way of making money from the big land grants with the available labor supply, the Negro having none of the adaptability of the Yankee or other Americans for becoming a jack of all trades. He could be taught the routine of raising tobacco or cotton, but beyond that stage the intricacies of diversified crops, of manufacturing or a commercial career, were too much for him.

The consequence of this, for American life, was that field work and other purely manual labor came to be rather looked down upon in tidewater Virginia and the South generally because they were so largely performed by black slaves who could acquire no social position or gain any social advancement, however well they might be treated, and even affectionately regarded, by all members of their masters' families. The gulf between merely rich and poor became a yawning social chasm, far wider than anything that existed in New England in spite of the ample snobbishness characteristic of that section on the part of the well-to-do upper middle class, which had nothing above it to serve as a real measure of social distinction, and so became socially conceited, often with little basis.

We have now reached the point where we can touch on the broader effects of all this new immigration of various sorts which America, and above all, the *land* of America, had attracted or brought forcibly to our shores. We may glance first for a moment at what the individuals in these three new streams of immigration brought with them in ideas when they landed on our shores—what, to quote Dixon Fox's phrase again—they "carried in their knapsacks."

Obviously, the mental matters carried in these knapsacks would be made up of the recollections of the newcomers of conditions in their home lands, of their experiences on the crossing over the ocean, of their reactions to what happened to them on arrival and of their hopes for the future. As to the recollections of the home lands we may note how different these were in the case of each of the three streams. The Negro, forcibly torn from the life of the African jungle, which was all that he had known, and separated perhaps from his family, facing an utterly unimaginable future as the captive of a strange race whose language and ways were unintelligible to him, naturally suffered mental anguish. His situation, however, was quite different from that of the Germans or Scotch-Irish. On the one hand, he did not come to America voluntarily to escape from conditions at home. He did not come with the American Dream in his heart or brain—the desire for freedom and to rise. On the other hand, his memories of his tribe or locality had no such influence on him in relation to the America then taking form as did the recollections of the Germans and Scotch-Irish. All three groups of immigrants suffered grievously on the ocean voyage and on their arrival here, but the reactions from, and repercussions of, their experiences were to be wholly different.

The contributions to America by the Negro, over some three centuries and more, have been great but they have been different, as regards the making of the American, from those of the other two races we are now considering. In the period here being discussed his influence was powerful, but by indirection. Of course, his status as a slave had much to do with it but there are other points to be considered. One of the most remarkable things in our history is the relation of the Negro to the white. It is difficult to appraise the balance of good and evil for the Negro himself in the long run of the whole story of slavery, and of the post Civil War period. Obviously we cannot judge one era by the ethical or humanitarian standards of a later one, though it is an extraordinarily common mistake. For example, writing in his Journal in May 1851 of the Fugitive Slave Law, Emerson, vituperating against a speech by Rufus Choate, said he must have known that "the stern old fathers of Massachusetts . . . would have died at the stake before soiling themselves with this damnation." Of course the fact was that the "stern old fathers," including the clergymen among them, bought, used and traded in slaves, and were as particular about their rights in them as in any other form of property. Many a stern old father founded the family fortunes on the triangular trade in rum and slaves, though the descendants may prefer to dwell on the period of Abolitionism a century later.

In considering slavery before, say, the middle of the nineteenth century, we have to transvalue our values and take the then and not the present contemporary standards, else the Rev. John Cotton, the Rev. Cotton Mather and many other historic lay and clerical saints and heroes of early Boston would fare badly at the bar of judgment. The point we are concerned with here, however, is not what the New England reformers of the 1850's or the public opinion of today thought or thinks of slavery but what America did to the Negroes who were brought here as slaves, and to their descendants. I have spoken of the remarkable relation which has existed between the Negroes and the whites, and I make that statement with full knowledge of the difficult social, economic and political situation in our own time.

Certain facts, however, stand out literally in black and white.

In the entire period of slavery there was only a negligible number of slave insurrections or even plots. On the other hand, all through the South for a century and a half, white families, heavily outnumbered by the blacks, lived in safety on widely scattered plantations. As a culmination, we shall find the slaves during the Civil War, without a single noteworthy exception, guarding the women and children, and the family jewels and silver, of the masters who owned them as slaves while those masters and owners were away at the front fighting the Northerners who were promising these same slaves their freedom. So far as I know, there is nothing like this in all history.

The Negro did not protest as did the other new races against the social, economic or political conditions which he encountered. I think there are several reasons. As I have said, although we use Negro as a generic term, there were many tribes brought here, with greatly varying characteristics, but in general the Negroes were a fairly easy-going race with many qualities, such as even temper, affection, great loyalty, and others, which helped to fit them into their new and strange world. Its complete strangeness, added to the character of the Negro, enabled him to accept and adjust himself to his new environment with a minimum of opposition or resentment. The Germans, Scots and poorer white Southerners, all knew enough about the general system to react vigorously and effectively against what galled them in it.

The things which gall the Negro of today are all things which he has learned about in America. He would have known nothing about democracy, the chance to rise, or equal social position had he remained with his primitive tribe in Africa. They came here with their minds blank as to western European ideas regarding property, personal liberty, the political state or social gradations. They had no literature and could not read or write. With their imitativeness, even temper, willingness to follow a leader or master, and their fatalism, they quickly accepted the new life of which they formed a part. (Of course I am generalizing, but I think the generalizations justified.)

Attempts to enslave the native Indians had proved always a complete failure, but the Indian slaves were living on or near what had once been their own land. They had different traits from the African but also everything around them reminded them of their former free state. On the other hand, Africa, the jungle, the old tribal life and all the rest quickly faded from the minds of the Negroes, certainly after the first generation. I recall a concrete instance. An old aunt of mine, long since dead, an American but one who had lived much in Cuba and Europe, had a personal Negro maid named Christina, originally bought as a slave. The maid went everywhere, travelled widely with my aunt, visiting with her at all sorts of great houses in England and on the Continent, intelligent, a perfect maid but also the sort of family friend and retainer whom all the family and friends (statesmen, and such singers as Adelina Patti, and so on), always asked to see. Yet her mother had been an African "princess," so-called, who had been brought to Cuba straight from the jungle, with her face slashed with the scars which denoted her tribal rank. Christina knew nothing of Africa. She was a wholly civilized woman, interested in the life she lived, and as devoted to the family and their circle as they were to her. The little incident has bearing on what we said before as to the eventual results of slavery for the Negro. Would Christina have been happier and more of a human being if her mother had not been barbarously captured and brought to the New World, and she herself had grown up among the original tribe? There is no answer, but the incident also illustrates how easily the Negro was assimilated to our form of life.

The Negro accepted it and became part of it with amazing rapidity. Not only that but an interesting point is that in a nation slowly getting geared to a revolutionary movement, the Negro individually, in spite of all the ills he suffered, was for the most part a conservative factor. He identified himself with the whole system as he found it, in spite of the rare plots we have mentioned. Perhaps one of the curses of the old romantic South was the extreme stress laid on family position, but nobody stood by that more instinctively (or perhaps imitatively) than the slaves, and even today, to a great extent, nobody insists more on knowing who's "quality" and "who ain't" than the Negroes who have some recollection of the old days and ways.

We have dwelt at perhaps somewhat undue length on this particular racial strain added to America in the eighteenth century because it entails peculiar problems in the making of the American. Not only did the descendants of the original Negroes form in 1940 about ten per cent, 13,000,000, of the total population of about 135,000,000 but their influence on American history has been tremendous.

The Negro and slavery helped to set the mold of the old tidewater South and its tradition of the "big house," the big plantation, society and "the family," the acquiring, by means we have mentioned, of big landed estates, helped by the English customs of entail and primogeniture which had been mostly abandoned in New England and on the frontier everywhere. We have spoken of the New England Yankee farmer or trader as typifying "Uncle Sam" and the American, but the Americans are much more complex beings than even they themselves realize. We have to set, for example, David Harum opposite Colonel Carter of Cartersville, and so on through an almost endless list of antitheses which could be made up from thumbing the pages of the twenty volumes of the *Dictionary of American Biography*. If there is a lot of buncombe about the romance of the Old South, there is also a lot about the Babbittry of the North. The American is a romantic and a dreamer, and the romance of American life has come from North and South and West. Perhaps the most heavily scented romance—like the odor of jasmine—came from the South, still alluring many a successful Northern Babbitt to try to savor it and flavor his life by buying an estate there. That particular romance was created largely by the Negro and the slave.

But while they were contributing to that romance they were

also helping indirectly to bring into being the more virile if less charming and cultured romance of the southern frontier and the advancing lines of settlement and later of "the West." The tidewater South in the seventeenth century had been democratic—economically, politically and to a great extent socially. With increasing wealth for some individuals, class cleavages developed in all the colonies, but this was particularly emphasized in the South because of the Negro. It was not only that large-scale landholdings made wealth and social position, and that slaves and the money to buy them kept the ball rolling; there was another factor.

We have suggested that there has always been a tendency on the part of "old Americans" to look down upon the newer immigrants, even if they were no more racially different from the English than the Scotch-Irish, the Germans or the later Celtic Irish of the nineteenth century, and to confound the dislike or contempt for the newcomer and "foreigner" with the work he was set to do or had to do. In the case of the Negro, however, there was not only a much greater racial difference, there was also his submerged status as a slave. White indented servants might be brought over to do all sorts of work from manual labor up to tutoring in wealthy families, or what not, but they had the chance to rise socially and otherwise in the scale in a few years. The situation of the black slave was wholly different. The consequence was that in those sections where he formed a large part of the population the taint which attached to his race, as well as to his status and social position as a slave, was transferred more indelibly than in other cases to the *work* he did.

The free white who did the manual labor which the slaves performed, such as cultivating fields, carpentering, bricklaying and all the rest, began to feel himself sinking not merely in the *economic* scale but also in the *socio-political.* As compared with a man of the same sort in the seventeenth century, he felt that the democracy, the chance, the American Dream, which had all been open to him in the earlier period, were disappearing. As a result of these factors and the increasing concentration of landholdings, he saw less opportunity for himself and almost none for his many children. The gorgeously multicolored rainbow of hope was fading into the cold white light of Old World reality from which he had fled on his romantic adventure.

For these reasons thousands of small but very independent people began to pass southward to North Carolina or west to the higher and freer lands of the Piedmont and the Blue Ridge. The Negro himself, because he was not free to do so, and also because he was unfitted for the life of a frontiersman, never individually and willingly did anything to build up the frontier. But because of the many pressures created by him on the poorer whites he did do so *indirectly*.

It is now time to turn to those who were building up the new western frontier, which America alone afforded in that period, and see what it did to the American. The settlements which built up this country were all "frontier" of one sort or another from the beginning, but the typical American frontier may be considered as greatly increasing its influence on the American after it moved well back from the seaboard and away from the ocean and the streams and rivers which gave easy and direct access to it. The background of the coast frontiers was the Old World, chiefly of course England, whereas that of the new frontier was the social, political and economic society of the seaboard where Americanization had already partly made its effects felt. This new frontier developing from what may be called the "westward march," so immensely important in the making of the American, may be considered as getting into its real stride after 1713.

In the period we are now discussing it originated largely in Pennsylvania and Virginia. The Roman Catholic French Empire bordered immediately on northern New England, and on that account and because of climate and other conditions, the New England farmer was not tempted to try to settle across the boundary. Canada was then considered both by the

British Government and the New England colonists as a cold and barren land from which the French and Indians made forays on our settlements but otherwise as an unimportant Arctic waste, much as, later, we were to regard a large part of our now valuable and populous Southwest as the "Great American Desert."

Those who believe in tracing the course of history from some one controlling factor, geographic, economic, or other, would probably have predicted as a certainty that the westward advance would begin from New York, as that colony was the only one on the entire Atlantic seaboard which possessed an easy water route, by way of the Hudson-Mohawk River system, into the interior of the continent and the magnificent Mississippi Valley. But, as often, the unpredictable human factor entered, and not only were the French and their Indian allies at the western end of the colony but the grasping nature of the great New York landowners of the period did much to prevent the increase of population in the province and to cause the diversion of the streams of immigration to the south.

Behind the seaboard settlements of Pennsylvania and Virginia there was a fairly broad stretch of fine frontier lands, before the main range of the Appalachians, with the French on the western side of them, was met, and that vast back-country section became the cradle of the western advance. It is notable that the two "fathers of the West," Washington and Jefferson, were both Virginians. We may therefore concentrate for the moment on what the Germans, Scotch-Irish and discontented tidewater Virginians were doing to build up our great westward expansion.

We may cast one backward glance at the Old World or old settlement environments they had left. The Scots, as we have noted, came here smarting under the wrongs they had suffered in Ireland. They hated the English government for its unjust trade laws, and the Irish landlords for their harsh treatment which had made starving peasants out of men who belonged to one of the most independent, strong-minded and stalwart racial breeds of the time. They were staunch Presbyterians with the strength of individual character which, at its best, Calvinism bred. They hated the Celtic Catholic Irish of the southern part of the island (Ireland) which they themselves had been led to colonize in Ulster. They hated most of what they had encountered and endured in the Old World. Unlike the earlier English, especially the prosperous and successful English colonists of the American seaboard, England was never thought of by them as "home." What they brought with them was not a new tie of America to England as a home country but a new strain in "the American." This is clearly indicated by the epitaph on the gravestone of one of their leaders who in the van of these born pioneers penetrated far into the Shenandoah Valley. The stone as I saw it, more or less unknown today even to the citizens of the town he founded, off the highway and with its untended though fenced plot overgrown with tall grass and weeds, has on it: "Here lies the remaines of John Lewis, who slew the Irish Lord, settled Augusta County, located the town of Staunton, and furnished five sons to fight the battles of the American Revolution." There you have, graved on stone, evidence of the beginning of a new strand in our story. What the rusted iron fence, the weeds and unmown grass may indicate, is another point.

The Germans, unlike the Scotch-Irish, had no hatred of England, but, on the other hand, they certainly had no affection for it, as well as almost no knowledge of it. For them the word "home" as applied to England held no meaning. Yet they were to become a very important element in pre-revolutionary America. In 1766 Franklin estimated that there were about 110,000 to 125,000 in Pennsylvania, forming one-third of the population of that pivotal colony. Besides those of the Scotch-Irish who had already settled here, John Finley estimated that 12,000 came yearly for the thirty years preceding the outbreak of the war with England. It is obvious that in these two streams we have something to consider in the light of international relations, and the making of the American.

Both strains also contributed much to the fundamental Puritanism and religious character of America. The Calvinism of the Scots added tremendously to the original Puritanism of the South and the Calvinism of New England which continued dominant until the optimistic period of the nineteenth century. On the other hand, aside from other Protestant Non-Conformist sects, the Methodists in particular, who with the Baptists were to do so much to spread Puritanism of a slightly different sort in the later South and West, owed much to the Germans of this general period. Charles Wesley had attended Moravian services in London where he was influenced by Count Zinzendorf, while his brother John stated that his own "religious experience" was largely due to Peter Böhler, and both the brothers were in America where they were closely connected with the many German Pietist sects and colonies from Georgia to Pennsylvania. "The American" was clearly becoming more complex.

CHAPTER VIII

NEW MEN IN A NEW WORLD

WE must now turn from what the newcomers brought to the new country to consider what the transit did to them, how it influenced them and how in turn, as a consequence, they influenced America and the American.

First, there was the voyage over the ocean. Ships had become a little larger but conditions for immigrants had not improved. They were, if anything, worse. We need not detail the oft-told horrors of the "Middle Passage" for the slaves, who were herded on vessels in holds with ceiling room from only eighteen inches to five feet, sleeping "spoonwise," men and women, sick and well, even dead and living. They were often brutally treated, allowed on deck only for fresh air and exercise, and died in large numbers, the hopelessly sick often being thrown overboard with the corpses. For the various reasons mentioned above, however, these horrors seem to have made more impress on the imaginations of the whites of a later humanitarian age than upon the memories or actions of the slaves themselves, for the most part of the earlier generations, and did not to any marked extent affect the relations of the slaves to their new masters or to the structure of colonial society and law.

It was different with the Germans and the Scots. Both these groups of voluntary immigrants suffered hardships on the voyage certainly comparable to, if not quite as bad as, those borne by the Negroes. Packed into ships "like herrings" they often feared to die of starvation or thirst. Food was sometimes so full of worms and other vermin as to be eaten only in the face of famine. Cannibalism was sometimes threatened and was practiced in at least one authenticated case. On one voyage hunger-maddened Scots ate six dead bodies and were cutting up a seventh when rescued. Smallpox and other diseases swept through whole vessels. As a sample of voyages, among many for which we have statistics, we may note that in one case two hundred and fifty passengers died, out of three hundred and twelve. Children under seven rarely survived the passage, and child-birth was almost inevitably fatal to mother and child. Sanitary arrangements were indescribable.

Then there was the arrival in the "promised land." Misled by false reports and the glowing pictures painted by land agents and printed propaganda, many passengers brought out little money, thinking to be able to make their way at once. The shippers piled up costs. Those who reached America alive had to pay the passage money for the dead of their families. When they could not they were sold for a term of service, and husbands found themselves separated from their wives, children were sold away from their parents. In myriads of cases the American Dream turned for a while into a nightmare of human misery. Sometimes an entire shipload would be held responsible for the passage money of all the dead, so that even those with some money left would be sold also.

America had lured them with a rainbow of hope. They had dreamed the dream, and they would not yield it for God or man. God and freedom and a chance to rise were in their hearts, but man, as they had encountered him on sea and land, was to be fought or disregarded. And now we come to the impact of America.

Those of the newcomers who could do so in one way or another got away from the settled seaboard as fast as possible. Had it not been for America they would have remained huddled in the crowded and hopeless countries of the Old World. There would have been no unspeakable voyage with such heartrending experiences. Had the seaboard not already been fairly thickly settled and the lands pre-empted the newcomers might have remained near the coast. But there were the empty lands beyond until one came to the French, and rumors of a vast continent beyond *them.* Land was what all the newcomers craved, the hard-working steady German farmers and the less painstaking but more adventurous and pioneering Scots. The effect of the hardships of the voyage and the conditions encountered on arrival, made all these people bent on wresting what they could for themselves out of what they found. As they went west to break fresh land beyond the old settlements it is not strange, but nevertheless very significant for our story, that they should have cared little about the niceties of legal titles or the claims of favored individuals to vast areas of wilderness while they lived luxuriously in elegant tidewater mansions with their slaves, both of which had been largely acquired not by suffering and hard work but by what came to be known and hated in America as "privilege."

Logan, who was the agent in Pennsylvania for the interests of the Penn family, complained bitterly that both the Germans and the Scots (or "Irish" as he called them) were coming in swarms and that "both these sets frequently sit down on any spot of vacant land they can find, without asking question, [and] pretend they will pay but not one in twenty has anything to pay with." Again, speaking more specifically of the Scots, he makes them sound a genuine American and frontier note when he quotes them as saying that they had no regard for land titles and that "it was against the laws of God and nature that so much land should be idle while so many Christians wanted it to labor on and to raise bread." It was perhaps equally natural that those firmly entrenched in their financial and political positions on the seaboard should be loath to surrender any of their privileges to these uncouth "foreigners" who were squatting on lands to which the seaboard gentry held paper titles while the frontier was talking about the laws of God and nature as being above those of paper grants, by governors and others, to favorites.

Among the consequences were the partial failure of the seaboard to protect the new settlements from the Indians, and insistence on steadily lessened representation in the legislature as new counties were formed westward, so that political power might be retained among the old settlers by limiting the rights of the new. As settlers passed into western Pennsylvania counties, down into the Shenandoah Valley, and as the discontented poorer whites of the Virginia seaboard also pressed westward towards the beautiful lands of Augusta and Albemarle Counties and the Blue Ridge, a new American was forming, with new ideas. The Germans did not care about England and the Scotch-Irish hated it.

After arrival here, however, their grievances were less against the "mother country" than against what they had had to suffer at the hands of the shipowners, immigrant importers, landowners and others of the propertied and exploiting classes of the seaboard in America itself. The vast expanse of land was producing new Americans who were not thinking so much in terms of opposition to England as in those of opposition to *privilege* wherever found and exercised, and who were demanding freedom in every quarter to do as they wished. The "West" in general, as it was then understood, and particularly the Shenandoah Valley, which seemed almost as remote from Old World complications as the later Mississippi Valley has considered itself, was beginning to think in terms of the rights of man rather than in those of opposition to British Parliamentary policies. In other words an America was beginning which was to bring about before long not only a war with England but a "Revolution" in America itself.

The Shenandoah Valley, or rather the parallel valleys which go by that name, quickly filled up. That section became a sort of sluiceway which in time was to drain population through it to the real West, to Tennessee, Kentucky, across the plains to the Pacific. There were some large land grants made to such men as the Alsatian Baron Joist Heydt, the Dutch Indian trader Jon Van Metre who had drifted down from the Hudson Valley, the Scot John Lewis, who was to become a "Lord of the Hills," and others, on condition that they would settle other families on their large holdings. This new frontier which was to build up in a veritable rush was rough and democratic but not irreligious. It was characteristic that under the natural molding forces of all our frontiers, the rich Baron Heydt should soon become plain Joist Hite, a later leader in the western advance. It was briefly noted in a sheriff's report that a certain writ could not be served "because of an axe," but when a new road was opened eastward into old Virginia it was done with prayers, and the court records show a Puritan outlook which almost outdid New England.

If the frontier had its influence so did also the mere size of America. When great sub-grants of land were made by Fairfax and other earlier grantees to develop their properties by settling them, the usual terms were that each of the sub-grantees had to settle one family for each thousand acres! The old fifty-acre "head rights" of the seaboard began to look small indeed and the hugeness of opportunity in land for even the ordinary man if he went west was beginning to dawn on the minds of settlers. The rich limestone and other soils of the Valley with a thousand acres to a family became fabulous. As the movement continued, there went with it rapidly increasing herds of cattle and the celebrated razor-back hogs. The hog was the only animal which could put on a hundred and fifty pounds of weight in eight months, and both hogs and cows could "walk to market" on their own legs. The picturesque figure of the later Western "cowboy" on horseback had been born, and men and herds were on the move.

Some years later, in the war with England, the battle of "Cowpens" with its brilliant victory for the Americans, is a reminder of the part which cows played in the advance to the West. Mild as Bossie usually is now, she was then often wild and was hunted down in the woods as game. That section of the western South was the first real "cow country," though the term was to be more precisely used in the nineteenth century of the long range region of the Far West. Cows, steers, hogs, buffalo and other animals have never been "Americans" but they have played an extremely important and often picturesque part in American history and romantic tradition. From the time when Hooker and his followers drove their cattle along the narrow wooded trail from "the Bay" to the Connecticut River settlements, down through the colorful period of the "Wild West," and the later growth of the meat barons and packing houses, to now when we are helping to feed the world, these animals deserve a niche in America's story. We have mentioned the early phrase of "root, hog, or die." If that lowly animal now figures chiefly in the newer term of the "pork barrel" of every successive session of Congress, that is the fault of the American and not of the hog.

To return to the western trek of settlers, we may say that America had always been on the move, first across the ocean and then through the wilderness to beyond the outskirts of old settlements. Again we come back to *land,* which was altering *the American* profoundly from the *Old World Man* he had formerly been. In England and Europe, whether attached to the soil as serf or free to move, the farmer or peasant was deeply attached to the particular locality or bit of soil where his family might have lived for generations. It has been said that for the French peasant, for example, "France" means fundamentally his own precious though few acres which he and his ancestors have tilled and nourished with loving care and the utmost frugality. Although in France a Breton might differ widely from a Provençal, as in England a Yorkshireman from a Cornishman, yet they were all of one race and nationality. This homogeneity of race combined with the deep affection for long-known localities and landscapes did much to fuse their ideas of nationality.

America changed this. It did so least of all in New England, where landholdings were small, people were "sot," and thrifty, and in this period there was almost no infiltration of foreign strains. Even in that section, however, there were those who were known as "goers" and "stayers." The goers broke old ties and went to the frontier, and in time a Portland, Maine, was to be balanced three thousand miles across the continent by a

Portland, Oregon, with a broad band of New England villages and greens in between. It was chiefly the American frontier, one after another, that made the change in the American from the European, and we may take the westward advance through the Shenandoah as an example.

In that valley, shut off by its mountain ramparts, there was no racial unity. Although Scots, Germans, and discontented English from the southern tidewater, made up the bulk of the population, there were also Dutch, Huguenots and others. Moreover, these people were all "goers." They had all left old homes, overseas or in our own older settlements, and kept going. They or their descendants were to keep going, as so many other Americans were to do, for another century and a half and more. The land kept beckoning them ever onward. They appear to have been on the whole devoid of local attachments to any farm of a hundred or a thousand acres if they got word of better land beyond. Moreover, they did not practice thrift. Life called for hard work and endurance but not for that particular virtue, once out "beyond." Lord Fairfax, inspecting his lands in the Shenandoah on one occasion, was horrified to find that people with hundreds of cows did not take the trouble to milk more than was needed for the table of the household. He did not seem to consider the fact that milk, even in cans—and there were none—did not "walk to market," and that there was no milk market. As in the case of the magnificent forests which he burned down to make clearings, the frontiersman got used to waste and prodigality. Above all, it was nobody's business but his own. That was one of the main sources of satisfaction in being an American.

So, we see again certain traits in the American emerging or becoming emphasized. "Baron Heydt" becomes naturally just plain "Joist Hite." The men who were carving out a wilderness and settling it felt oppressed by the rich on the seaboard who claimed privileges for themselves, political and other. Religion, in increasingly simple and emotional form, but strongly Puritanical, remained a dominant factor. Love of home and locality largely evaporated. Restlessness developed. Homes were not something to love and nurture and to hand down to remote descendants but temporary shelters, means to make money and to use only until something better offered, on beyond. There was no tradition. History begins wherever the pioneer starts a new clearing or settlement. The pioneer did not think of all that had happened to his ancestors on that bit of ground or in that locality. He had never had any there. There was only the hard-working present moment, the land, and the future. The *future* here or after another trek to cheaper, larger, better land "on beyond." The nation itself became not a racial concept, or something rooted in old memories, long loved localities, or tradition, but a Dream of the future, a Dream not of what has been but of what is to be, a rainbow, a glimpse of what never was on land or sea, a Dream woven of hopes of personal success, of the chance to get ahead, to be unhampered, a Dream of happiness and freedom in which each willingly takes his chance of rising or falling but demands that he be not interfered with while struggling.

Nor were the dreams which proved false false because of lying and cheating, as Dickens claimed in *Martin Chuzzlewit* a century later. But in many cases they were the dreams of dreamers who dreamed too far into the future. The dream was often true. The rainbow was often real, but often also many lives and lifetimes were lost in reaching its end, and finding the pot of gold, though that likewise was real. How fantastically impossible would the America of today seem to those who lived on the frontier in the period we are now discussing, or even to the Americans who lost money for Dickens in his ill-advised investments! To many an onlooker the American was a liar and a cheat. To himself he was the dreamer, the prophet and the seer, and it was in the end to be his dream, his prophecy and his vision which were to prove the realities. At the end of myriads of toilsome journeyings, the pot of gold was found to be no wraith of fond imagining but true and tangible, enriching both the material and spiritual lives of millions who sought it, unhampered and with a courage and stubbornness which nothing could subdue or conquer. That was America. It was the dream, the dauntless struggle, the ultimate success or failure, but the glory of *Opportunity* and of one's chance to make the most of it.

We have seen how the first adventurous settlers had had *their* dreams, but we have also seen how in time the seaboard settlers began to develop classes and privilege, and came to feel confined. We have seen how the effect of climate, and soil and the meadow made the New Englander what he was; how the small white independent farmer in the tidewater South began to feel the effect of slave labor; and how all along the seaboard the artisan and laboring classes were also beginning to be restive. The Shenandoah Valley was to become the gateway to the West and was a veritable land of Goshen, but back of all the colonies from Canada to Georgia there was a frontier to which the ambitious, the discontented and the pioneering Americans were drifting. We have also spoken of the variations and jealousies among the original colonial settlements, but conditions all along the frontier were much alike, and the "back settlements" were much more unified in feeling than the seaboard ones. The frontier was what I have called it elsewhere a "selvedge edge," the edge which binds a fabric together and prevents its ravelling. Of all the frontier, however, the Shenandoah Valley had given the developing Americans the grandest glimpse of what lay beyond. But what lay there was in the possession of the French. We must now turn to the war which drove out the French and to a large extent determined the destiny of America and definitely made the American.

In accord with the theme of this book we are interested not in a narrative of events but rather in a summary of their effects. We may select three of these as of special importance. One was the change in the attitude of the colonists towards Britain; another was a change in American conditions; and a third was a change in outlook on the future.

To understand the first we must glance backward very briefly. We have spoken of how the English colonists regarded England as "home" and even took some interest in the Empire as such. They were willing to cooperate to a considerable extent, but the result of cooperation was finally to be separation. There were unlucky elements in the situation. On our side of the water there was the ever-recurrent strain of jealousy. Each of the dozen—later thirteen—little states, as they almost considered themselves, could not unite for any length of time on any general policy or movement. Moreover none of them were warlike or organized for military activity, though the colonists here and there could meet a purely local emergency, such as raids by the French, Spaniards or Indians, with skill and bravery. They knew well how to beat off forays on the borders but were incapable of organizing and sustaining large-scale expeditions.

On the other hand, during this period the government in England reached a very low level of stupidity, venality and inefficiency. The American, who was satisfied with himself and believed he knew his own business, was touchy and critical; while the English, especially the officers of the armed forces, had developed that sense of superiority to all colonials which characterized them for too long. Coalitions in war are always clumsy and usually breed ill-feeling even when necessary for ultimate victory. History supplies innumerable instances. The colonies, with their strong sense of semi-independence and their individualism, were willing to help at their own will and when and as they saw fit. In America a family attacked would fight as a unit to the death against Indians or other foes, but the Empire was not a unit in spite of the simile of a "mother country" and its offspring. In war, England and the colonies formed only the loosest sort of alliance, with especial dangers of misunderstanding and bad blood. Each partner would naturally minimize or entirely overlook its own shortcomings and over-emphasize those of the others. Moreover, England, fighting all over the world, would place Empire first and separate colonies second, whereas the colonies, while willing to think of the Empire, nevertheless would place that second and the interest of their special colony first.

The colonists felt the impact of the Anglo-French struggle of 1689–1697, known to us over here as "King William's War," but although the French and Indians harried the New England frontier, and Massachusetts made an unsuccessful attempt to capture Quebec, there was no joint expedition of English and colonials. With the next war, one of the many of the "Spanish Succession," and by us called "Queen Anne's War" (1701–13), England and the colonies did try to join.

In the beginning there was an English naval expedition to the West Indies and there was enough imperial sentiment to permit the Royal Governor, Dudley, of Massachusetts to raise a company in that colony and another in New Hampshire although both colonies were themselves hard-pressed at home. The other New England colonies would not contribute but these two did. Dudley felt so strongly the significance of the event and the chance to draw imperial ties closer as to cause him to write the governor of Jamaica, whither the two companies were being transported, that "They are the first men in armes that ever went out of this province, or from the shoar of America, and if at first they meet with discouragement I am sure I shall never send hence one file of Volunteers more." The expedition was an almost criminal failure due to English mismanagement and blundering. Disease, poor food and complete lack of efficiency resulted in the return to America of only about fifty ill, starving and unpaid men of the two companies which had volunteered.

In the same war we may mention two other incidents. The New Englanders and some of the other northern colonists offered to cooperate with the British fleet in a joint attack on Canada. In 1709 there was again gross mismanagement on the part of the British, and although colonial preparations had been made and heavy expenses incurred, the fleet did not arrive at Boston until the middle of October, too late to do anything, and after the colonials learned that all their work and waiting had been in vain, the ships sailed to the Bahamas. The following year there was, however, another joint effort made, but again the British fleet was late and plans as made had to be abandoned, except for the capture of Port Royal. Again, in 1710 came the final effort at cooperation of this war, which was the greatest fiasco of all, tinged with scandal which reached even to the Throne. The fleet was once more late, the commanders incompetent, and when the ships finally reached the St. Lawrence the latter part of August, a wrong course was steered and eight transports were cast on the rocks with the loss of a thousand men. The expedition was abandoned and the ships ignominiously sailed for England.

Nevertheless, once more in the "War of Jenkins' Ear," so-called, the colonists again tried to assume a share in imperial defense, and over 3700 volunteers, mostly from New England, but also a goodly share from Virginia and other colonies, were raised to take part in the Cartagena expedition. The British naval and military officers again showed themselves wholly inefficient, and of the Americans two-thirds died, and the survivors brought home accounts which would naturally spread. One more joint effort may be mentioned before we come to the more decisive event of the French and Indian War in the mid-century. In 1745 a joint expedition under Commander Warren of the British Navy and colonials, mostly from Maine, made a successful, and for once, harmonious attack on the supposedly impregnable French fortress of Louisbourg, and captured it. The Americans did good work, and Warren (who had an American wife), understood them, knew how to work with them, and was a competent officer. The happy event might have done much to restore good feeling but unfortunately because of now understandable imperial reasons, the British Government felt obliged to restore the fort, so important to colonial commerce and safety, to the French when a temporary peace was made in 1748. So, instead of creating a new tie between English and Americans, their common victory merely acted as a fresh wedge to split them apart.

This was the state of mutual feeling to which the efforts at cooperation by the English on the two sides of the ocean had brought them after a half century of mutual aid but also mutual recrimination. In 1754 the struggle between France and England, only nominally relinquished in the years between, began again, the American phase of the world conflict being known as the French and Indian War. This did nothing, to say the least, to improve relations, but this time the effects of the final peace, 1763, were to be very far-reaching.

The details of the nine years of war do not concern us. We are interested only in what more than sixty years of trying to work together had done to the Americans in the Empire. In the French and Indian War the British sent aid on a large scale to the colonies. Forty-one British warships and eleven thousand British troops took part in the recapture of Louisbourg alone, and there were troops fighting in other parts of America. Largely due to the genius of Pitt, Britain won victories in all parts of the world, and we shall speak later of the effects on the American of the terms of the resounding Treaty of Peace. Here we must note that the old friction between British and Americans continued. Leaving out the failure of such men as General Loudon to understand or get on with the colonials we may merely mention the classic example of General Braddock, with his two regiments of red coats, who, as every school child has been taught, refused the advice of Washington and lost his own life and the battle by insisting on fighting Indians behind trees in the Pennsylvania forest as he would have met European regulars on the open fields of Flanders.

It is true that Washington himself had been defeated the year before and had been obliged to surrender at Fort Necessity. The point is, however, that two generations of fighting in company with the English had left the indelible impression on the minds of the colonials that the English were inefficient, often impertinently condescending, and incapable of understanding American conditions and needs. These impressions were naturally far more vivid to the colonial than his own lack of understanding of the needs and problems of a world empire. He knew how to look after himself in America, or certainly believed that he did. The defeat of Washington was overlooked as due to the superior force of the enemy. The defeat of Braddock, a brave man, was set down to British stupidity and refusal to learn. The fact was that that unfortunate if somewhat typical eighteenth-century British officer was destined to become a sort of symbol of everything British in relation to America.

The result of these sixty years of contacts of the sort noted was to create a certain cockiness in the American, a sureness of himself in relation to American conditions, and to give him a sense of superiority to the English, well lined with a good deal of irritation and resentment. In regard to all this we come back once more to the continual influences of the general American environment—that of the frontier—and of the distance from England. Had these Americans who were acquiring these new feelings as to the English, and a new consciousness of themselves as somehow different, been merely Devonshire or Yorkshire men or soldiers from other English counties, with no experience except that of life in the old country, they might have cursed their officers under their breath, and talked of the rottenness in food or in high political places, but they would not have thought of themselves as particularly different or superior. They were all of the same breed and knew of nothing else. In small England the threads of personal interests of all classes and groups were almost inextricably intertwined, but these were in a multitude of ways severed by the three thousand miles of sea. Experience gained from economic and political legislation, from attempted military cooperation, and in other ways was steadily making the American conscious of having a land of his own which was his to run and develop and get the benefit from as he alone saw fit.

There were other important effects of the wars of the mid-century in particular which were due to the usual economic and political consequences of war rather than to the American environment but which had so great an influence in the making of the American and on the events which were to continue to mold him that they must be mentioned.

One of the effects was the very rapid rise in wages, a phenomenon to which modern wars have accustomed us, just as the great plagues of the Middle Ages made employers all too familiar with it centuries ago. We have already spoken of the peculiarly independent position of labor, due to American conditions as compared with those of the Old World. These were emphasized by the wars with their drain on the scant existing supply of man power for hire. During these years the same complaint in different terms is heard in all the colonies. Workmen, we read in one paper, "are very difficult to be met with even at the most extravagant wages." In another are advertisements for workmen at "high wages" and with liberal cash extras every week. Labor, always in a position to be cocky in a new country where resources and opportunities are far out of balance with the number of those who feel the need of working for others instead of for themselves, was becoming far more cocky. In one colony the governor complained that wages had become so high that men would do only about a half day's work for a full day's pay and that it had become almost impossible to build or to do business. In another, an opponent of slavery feared that that institution would spread because for the equivalent of sixteen months' wages paid to a "bungling free laborer" one could buy a slave for life. Labor from the start had been in the saddle but was now coming to ride the horse hard.

The farmer, too, had been enjoying the high prices and ample markets which wars provide for a while, with the usual result that he overextended himself, thinking the fictitious prosperity would continue forever. High wages and high prices for food would have tended to raise other prices all along the line even had this process not been aided by inflation due to excessive issues of colonial paper money and by speculation on the part of those men with money who knew how to take advantage of the situation—"forestallers," as they were then called. As the ends of these successive wars came, there was a series of crises such as always occur. Each time when the forced draft of war demands ended, war incomes declined. But the cost of living had each time gone up, and those who had been profiting had grown used to extravagance and a too rapid advance in the scale of personal expense. As one complainer wrote from Virginia in 1763: "Things wear but a gloomy aspect, for the country is so excessively poor, that even the industrious, frugal man can scarcely live, and the least slip in economy would be fatal." Labor lost high-priced jobs, farmers were losing their lands by foreclosure, and all the usual symptoms of post-war economic crises were found. In fact, wars and subsequent depressions had been now occurring at intervals for about two generations, and all the unhappiness and resentments engendered by such episodes had been emphasized by frequent repetitions of the ups and downs.

Although many of the war results would have been common to any country under modern conditions, there were certain factors in the American situation which gave a particular turn to these normal post-war influences.

America at that time was well over ninety per cent agricultural. Of this large proportion of the population only a small fraction had great estates. Those who had them loomed large in the social picture of the period then and in the later romantic tradition of the country, as well as in its political history. Yet the typical American then, all the way from the Canadian boundary to the far South, was not a landed and social aristocrat, but a small man, socially and economically, with a big family biologically, scrabbling along to make a living and to get ahead. In various sections and different ways, he was becoming antagonized by the rich and "privileged." The little man did not like to see the few big ones, by merely being in the governor's set or in other ways, get big slices from the cake of "privilege," especially in that all-important commodity *land*, and by that road, slaves to work the land and to provide the social and political means of getting more land, and more slaves, and so on up the spiral.

We have seen in the South the smaller people going out into the wilderness of the frontier because of lack of land and on account of the competition of the black. We have noted the conditions in New York and New England, where also small people and their children, as they grew, went to the outskirts of civilization to get land and start again. We have seen how Germans, with no knowledge of England or interest in it, the Scotch-Irish with a hatred for it, were treated on landing here, and their flight to the frontier. We have seen how the frontier was considered by conservatives in finance and politics in the "old settlements" of the seaboard. We have moreover seen how colonials, still feeling themselves somehow part of the English race and Empire, tried, with a conflict of colonial and imperial emotions, to keep themselves a part of the Empire and to play that part, only to come, by an unfortunate combination of time and circumstance, to dislike and to look down on the particular Englishmen with whom in joint operations they had come into contact.

The result of these and other strands in our story was to be a complicated set of relations, American and Anglo-American, by the time that peace came at the end of the French and Indian War in 1763.

Owing to American extravagance the burden of debt owed in England by Northern merchants and Southern planters alike added its share to the mistrust of the Old Country due to contacts in the wars; objections to many laws passed by Parliament as to trade; and the instinctive dislike of a large part of the most virile men of the frontier for the English overseas.

Also, there was the growing dislike of the small man for the privileged rich, and of the American frontier for the American seaboard. The "small man" (excluding the slave) was the small farmer everywhere, the artisan or laborer, and the frontiersman. So we find interesting new patterns forming in the American scene. We see presaged, for example, that union, both natural and unnatural economically, between the laboring class and the farmers which was to play a part in the Revolution; a union which some forty years later was to be seized on by Jefferson to form his "Democratic Party"; and which was to remain the somewhat unstable and uneasy basis of that party ever after.

These two groups had a natural affiliation with the frontier, for all three had certain grievances against the same upper class in the East. Although we cannot understand the combined Civil War in the Empire, soon to loom, and the local Revolution in America, without understanding clearly all these stresses and strains and complex alignments in American social organization, on the other hand we must guard against considering them from the modern Marxian point of view. The upper class might talk of "the mob," and the mob might dislike many of the upper class and resent their too easy share in the good things of America, but there was practically no one in America who did not believe in its opportunities and in the general system which gave them their chance even if they had to fight individuals or groups to "get theirs," as the later slang expression picturesquely described it.

The frontiersmen and the poorer classes of the seaboard, however, drew towards one another, helping to bind the East and West of those days together in spite of the resentment of the one-class West against the upper classes of the East. Also, although seaboard conditions differed widely in the colonies, those on all the frontiers were much the same, so the frontier, the "selvedge edge" as I called it, helped to bind America north and south. It may be noted that all these ties binding Americans together in a criss-cross of geographically horizontal and vertical lines, developed among the common people of all sections rather than among the distinguished men, who for example at the Albany Conference of 1754 had been unable to make a united America. What *they,* with all their political experience, could not do, was being done almost unconsciously by the ordinary folk who were considered uneducated and radical.

But if they were radical they were not so in the modern sense of wanting to overthrow the whole system which they were used to and which they wanted in order to exploit it to their own advantage as did such favorites of fortune as the bigger landowners and capitalists. In America as it was developing almost every one was hoping to be a favorite of fortune himself in the sense that somehow the future would give him more of the kinds of things he cared for than he had yet acquired. And here we begin to get on the trail of that apparent but not real contradiction in the American which seems to puzzle not only many foreigners but many of our native reformers. These do not appear to be able to understand why the American, who is so radical and opposed to privilege in so many ways, still reverences the Constitution and the Supreme Court. This contradiction has run consistently through much of our history. Americans of all sorts and grades wanted to have every aid given them to "get theirs," but having got it, by luck or hard work, they wanted to be sure that the same safeguards would be afforded them as were enjoyed by those who had got there first.

In considering the America which was getting ripe for considerable changes that were to emphasize the differences from Europe, we may note one last point. The leadership was beginning to be shifted, both in old settlement and frontier, and America was doing it. In general the early leadership had been by the conservatives, the men of substance who backed the first settlements, the clergy who kept a firm grip spiritually, intellectually and politically over communities. It is possibly too great a contrast to be considered universal but we may compare Ludlow, and the clergyman Hooker who led the first western trek from Massachusetts to Connecticut, with the quite different types who became the leaders of the greater western advance in the Shenandoah, men like Heydt and John Lewis and the fiery Presbyterian clergy who ministered to the new groups.

Even in New England the influence of the earlier clergy was fast waning. The clergyman in his pulpit was no longer the only, or leading, mouthpiece of the civil authorities. The class of lawyers was rising as business and life became more complex. With the increase in newspapers, laymen over their own names or more often classical pseudonyms, contributed articles or long letters which to a great extent took the place of the old sermons as topics for discussion. Moreover, as communities grew and opportunities for social and public gatherings became more numerous, the church began to lose its unique position as the one gathering-place for the people. Another factor was the extent of the land itself and its riches. As life grew safer and easier, and people realized they could carve out a good life for themselves, much of the old Calvinistic theology and preaching of the extreme Jonathan Edwards type lost its appeal and its hold. This, of course, was more true of old settlements than of the frontier, where life was still hard and lonely, where books, newspapers and social gatherings were rare.

America by 1763 was already becoming quite different from the Old World, and was growing away from it in many ways which the colonists themselves hardly realized. Except for comparatively few among the well-to-do, there was little travel from America to Europe. Practically no immigrants who had staked, and perhaps lost all, enduring incredible hardship and loss, to build a new life over here, ever went back. They had come, after a final decision, to make America and to have America make them. They looked only to America, the future, and their dream.

But if America and they were to grow, both must be free

to expand. They could not remain a long narrow strip of a nation, like Chile, running up and down the coast, and hemmed in by the mountains and the frontier of another power. They had glimpsed the riches and the vastness of the continent. Washington and others in the last war had seen the marvelous lands of the Ohio Valley, claimed by the French. Companies across the mountains had been formed by the rich to take up huge tracts. Poorer frontiersmen were pressing forward. The gateways to the West seemed to be doors to unlimited opportunity in an America which was surpassing all the dreams yet dreamed.

Then came the end of the war and the making of the peace. The British Empire had vanquished France in all quarters. After much balancing of the comparative advantages of Canada and the Mississippi Valley as against the rich sugar islands of Guadeloupe and Martinique or other possessions to be acquired, the British statesmen decided for Canada. When the treaty was signed all the lands north of the colonies and west of them to the Mississippi were ceded by France and became part of the British Empire in North America. For Americans of all kinds and grades the continent appeared to have expanded to supply every want and ambition for untold generations to come.

No more could the French dispute their advance. No more would the enemy unleash savage allies to harry their outlying settlements and murder their wives and children. America and the future took on a new meaning which was staggering in the immensity of its opportunity. The sense of unlimited energy face to face with unlimited resources, of which we spoke earlier, fired the whole people. Land, land, land, stretching on with incredible richness, was theirs to exploit. The French were gone, and England was no longer much thought of as a serious enemy. Had not Americans during the whole century up to then measured themselves with the British and come to consider themselves superior? Now, released from the French pressure, they could expand to a great power. Not only the workmen had grown cocky. Not only were the frontiersmen cocky and ready to rush to the richest Land of Goshen ever glimpsed. All America was cocky. A new conception of the destiny of America and the cause of it—Land—had come to it. One of the greatest American poets, Robert Frost,[1] who has kindly given me permission to quote a recent poem of his, also saw the vision of what the western land would mean, and has meant.

> The land was ours before we were the land's.
> She was our land more than a hundred years
> Before we were her people. She was ours
> In Massachusetts, in Virginia,
> But we were England's, still colonials,
> Possessing what we still were unpossessed by,
> Possessed by what we now no more possessed.
> Something we were withholding made us weak
> Until we found it was ourselves
> We were withholding from our land of living,
> And forthwith found salvation in surrender.
> Such as we were we gave ourselves outright
> (The deed of gift was many deeds of war)
> To the land vaguely realizing westward,
> But still unstoried, artless, unenhanced,
> Such as she was, such as she would become.

The endless tossing waves between the Old World and the New. The endless land stretching to the western sun. The future. America and the American, and the hope of an endless march across all the known horizons of the past.

[1] Robert Frost, *A Witness Tree,* 1942, Henry Holt & Co.

CHAPTER IX

FROM DASHED HOPES TO THE BOLD STROKE

THE treaty between Britain and France which so thrilled the colonists and seemed to offer them almost unbounded expansion was signed in Paris, February 10, 1763. Not only for the colonists but for all the British still overseas in the mother country the event appeared to presage infinite possibilities. The conquest of the French possessions on the mainland of North America was the most magnificent addition to the Empire of "white man's country" England has ever made, before or since, by war. Yet, almost exactly twenty years later, on September 3, 1783, another treaty, also signed in Paris, broke the Empire in two and divided the English-speaking peoples into two hostile groups for many years after. In 1763 there was a united people vibrant with hope. The colonists glimpsed that "manifest destiny" which was eventually to lead them to the Pacific and to give them control of the richest and fairest portion of the two continents of the New World. British merchants could look forward to ever-increasing markets among people of their own race. Capitalists, courtiers, "younger sons," the poor and ambitious, all saw a new sun rising in the west across the tossing waves which Britannia claimed to rule.

Yet those two short decades, 1763–83, dispelled the dream. The Empire broke, and a free America was born. If the struggle ending with the peace of 1763 had made the colonial "cocky," as we have said, the struggles which followed and led to the peace of twenty years later added an enormous impetus to the belief of the American in himself and in his destiny. The American colonial, even while nominally a "British subject," had more and more been "feeling his oats," as the saying is, but this was to be nothing to what the American citizen of a free and independent United States was to come to feel. The years of those two decades were indeed fateful both for the American and the world. What happened?

The period included a social revolution in America and a civil war between two parts of the Empire. Such things do not occur overnight among the English-speaking peoples. In matters of fundamental government they are not subject to impulse. They tend to be slow-moving, cautious and compromising. What happened on both sides of the water in these two decades must, therefore, have been due to deep and slowly developing underlying causes, unusually virulent sudden ones, or a combination of both. The last of the three is, I think, the true explanation.

History moves steadily although sometimes with a seeming slow dullness to those who care less about its processes than about the sudden brilliant fireworks observable at intervals. With a nation as with an individual, we cannot understand the sudden romantic flare-ups if we have ignored the more or less obscure influences and the slow process of development between them.

As the strands of history used to be considered almost wholly military and political, and as "the American" was considered chiefly in his relation to the English government, overseas or through its local representatives, the only reason for sudden change from comparative dullness in 1700 to growing rebellion sixty-odd years later had to be considered political, and as the causes suggested were neither altogether sound nor altogether to the credit of the colonists, they had to be made to appear so. Thus recourse was had to the simplifying but satisfying formula of the scapegoat. The shining mark, in the absence of laborious research in other directions, was obviously King George III, who, if he could be shown to have been exercising a tyranny of an utterly unbearable sort, would account for everything. Even the Declaration of Independence, drawn up by such able men as Thomas Jefferson, John Adams and others and approved by the leaders of American thought, consists for the most part of an indictment against that rather stupid, and at times actually mad, monarch, much in the way in which an ambitious district attorney might draw up his case against an accused criminal. There is much more to the Declaration than those long passages, and there was also much more than the dull old Hanoverian King that led to the drawing up of a Declaration at all.

I have spoken of slowly developing underlying causes, unusually virulent sudden ones, and the combination of both. The first, in my opinion, were that the American, of several races, had already when the Peace Treaty of 1763 was signed become that "new man," the American, instead of a mere colonial Englishman. Unlike a crisis in England the impacts and reactions would not in America concern a thoroughgoing Englishman of one home county or another, but a new type of English-speaking people (even some who did not speak English and had no English traditions whatever), who had come into being in America. This change had been in process for a half century and to a considerable degree even through the century before that. This was an enormously important underlying, slowly developing cause.

Then came the sudden ones. First among these I put the terrific disappointment created by the announcement of the line to the west, beyond which settlers would not be allowed to pass, by the so-called Proclamation of 1763. There were other sudden, or seemingly so, causes, such as the Stamp Act, Boston Port Bill and others, but the great jolt to that new man, the American—capitalist and pioneer alike—had been given by the apparent closing of that West which they had glimpsed when they believed that they and the British together had driven the French from the continent and opened it to become, on a far vaster scale than Sir Walter Raleigh had foreseen, a new "Englysshe nation." But even all these causes were not enough. There was still needed the most skillful revolutionary propaganda. This was provided, as we shall see. The achievement of independence was of such importance in the creation of the American that we must consider these various causes and to some extent the course of the struggle itself without trespassing on the field of factual narration.

At the beginning of this book, in speaking of "the American" I noted that his American quality does not stem from birth, citizenship or even a prominent place in American history. I mentioned George Washington, who although assuredly one of the greatest of Americans was not on account of that especially typical of *the* American. *The* American has developed from what America has done to the common man. *The* American is all the John Does and Richard Roes who have found their opportunity in the American environment to become just uppish and fresh or to expand to the full and noble stature of a worthy human being.

The French boy of whom I spoke earlier and who found the most characteristic trait in America to be the way that "every one looked you straight in the eye," would not have been surprised if a United States Senator or a bank president or the head of the Steel Company had done so. What he noted was that the elevator boy, the bootblack, the subway guard, and all the rest, did so with no sense of difference or inferiority or effort to be insolent but just as naturally as breathing. This is right. This is America. It has not been the comparatively small number, in proportion to the whole population, of leading statesmen, business leaders, clergymen or others who have made the American. It has been America itself, acting on all the ordinary folk who have come to her, that has done so. The American, I repeat, is John Doe and Richard Roe, occasionally rising far beyond the ordinary stature of Does and Roes to become world figures. He is the American, the "New Man." It is difficult to write history in terms of the often too similar and humdrum lives of the Roes and Does. Yet to understand America and the American, and why they are different from other parts and peoples of the world, we have to keep these in mind.

To understand why America got into a ferment after 1763 and in another dozen years was preparing for open revolt and the momentous step which was to lead to a free America and the complete development of the American, we have to think in terms of leaders—yes—but even more in those of the Roes and Does. We have never had complete democracy in America as seen from every possible angle. It may be well that we have not, but we have on the whole got nearer to democracy than any other people. I do not think it is necessary here even to try to define the word. "Equality" is a much misused term, but a real equality, which is the basis of any real democracy, must spring from many sources. Basically it should spring from character, and a common attitude towards the most important things in life, and what they are. Basically we can be equal if we have as far as possible equal opportunity to develop such ability as we may possess; equal justice before the law; equal desire to serve as citizens and to build up a real "commonweal" in the old English phrase. For the realization of this ideal America gave an opportunity which the human race had never known before. We have not used it to the full. We have abused it in part, but that ideal *is* America.

And now we must place ourselves again in 1763. What happened, and why did what happened have such a repercussion on the world of then and of today?

We have spoken of certain influences at work on all who came here, practically all with the spirit of revolt, ambition or adventure in their hearts. There were the hardships of breaking old ties in the home lands to start fresh in a new and unknown world; those of the voyage over, and those which unexpectedly awaited them here. There were the distance from old established authority; the sense of space in America; the unlimited opportunities to gain a competence or wealth; the high wages; the lack, not of all class distinctions, but of class barriers which could not be broken through. As the late Vernon L. Parrington well said, in his *Colonial Mind,* of the period we have been considering: "It is plain that those unremembered years were engaged in clearing away encumbrances more significant than the great oaks and maples of the virgin wilderness: they were uprooting ancient habits of thought, destroying social customs that had grown old and dignified in class-ridden Europe. A new psychology was being created in the wide spaces that was to be enormously significant when it came to self-consciousness. If this middle eighteenth century wrote little literature, it created and spread among a vigorous people something of far greater importance to America, the psychology of democratic individualism." And as he added "the stir of achievement filled the land." It is perhaps in this sense of the "stir of achievement" that we find most the growing American. Rich and poor, capital and labor, could each feel the true meaning of Shakespeare's words

> There is a tide in the affairs of men,
> Which, taken at the flood, leads on to fortune.

The land of opportunity had been reached, and if it was not yet that of equal opportunity for all, it was so much more so than any other land its settlers had ever lived in that it caused them to thrill to its chances and to glimpse the dream of a perfect equality.

There were, indeed, rich and poor, and some class feeling. In 1704 the witty and delightful Madame Knight of Boston undertook the long and tiring journey to New York by road, and left us an account of it in her *Journal.* She described some very poor families she encountered, but for our purpose one paragraph is particularly worth quoting. Speaking of the country people along the way, she wrote: "They Generally lived very well and comfortable in their famelies. But too Indulgent (especially ye farmers) to their slaves: suffering too great familiarity from them, permitting them to sit at Table and eat with them (as they say to save time), and into the dish goes the black hoof as freely as the white hand. They told me that there was a farmer lived near the Town where I lodged who had some difference with his slave, concerning something the master had promised him and did not punctually perform; wch caused some hard words between them; But at length they put the matter to Arbitration and Bound themselves to stand to the award of such as they named—wch done, the Arbitrators Having heard the Allegations of both parties, Order the master to pay 40s to black face, and acknowledge his fault. And so the matter ended; the poor master very honestly standing to the award." If we ponder the many facets of that little story we can glimpse how different life in America was compared with that in still feudal Europe.

We have just glanced at one aspect of New England. About twenty-five years later, one of the great Virginia magnates, Colonel Byrd, wrote an account of his expedition, to establish the colonial boundary line between his colony and that of North Carolina. After descanting at some length on what appeared to him the laziness and slovenliness of the backwoods settlers he made some observations which fit into our theme. Complaining that the Carolinians preferred not to be included in the Virginian colonial bounds, he wrote: "Wherever we passed we constantly found the Borderers laid it to Heart if their Land was taken into Virginia; they chose rather belong to Carolina, where they pay no Tribute, either to God or to Cæsar. . . . Another reason was, that the Government there is so loose and the Laws so feebly executed, that, like those in the Neighborhood of Sydon formerly, everyone does just what seems good in his own Eyes. . . . They are rarely guilty of Flattering or making any Court to their governours, but treat them with all the Excesses of Freedom and Familiarity. They are of Opinion their rulers would be apt to grow insolent, if they grew Rich, and for that reason they take care to keep them poorer, and more dependent, if possible, than the Saints of New England used to do their Governours."

Speaking of governors, we have already mentioned what happened to one in Virginia and may note here the incident related by Samuel Sewall of what happened to Governor Dudley on an occasion. Driving by high snowdrifts, he met two farmers carting loads of wood, and ordered them to get out of his way and let him pass. After some altercation one of the farmers flung at the Governor that he was as good flesh and blood as the Governor and *he* could get out of the farmer's way. When Dudley drew his sword the farmer snatched it and broke it. To make a long story short, the Governor had the men put in jail, but they were promptly released and finally won their case in court. Dudley—like other royal functionaries—was to complain of how mere countrymen stood on their rights and would not even pull off their hats in the presence of their Excellencies.

We may give a few short quotations from Crèvecœur before going on with our story, because he gives us another slant on the American as he was developing in the years which led to 1776. Speaking of America as having been formed mostly from the poor of the Old World, he wrote that these newcomers could hardly be said to have a country overseas. How could any of them call that land "his country," he asks, "that had no bread for him, whose fields procured him no harvests, who met nothing but the frowns of the rich, the severity of the laws, with jails and punishments; who owned not a single foot of the extensive surface of this planet?" In America, he says, "Everything tended to regenerate them; new laws, a new mode of living, a new social system; here they are become men. . . . Formerly they were not numbered in any civil list of their country, except in those of the poor; here they rank as citizens."

Again, he wrote: "An European, when he first arrives, seems limited in his intentions, as well as in his views; but he very suddenly alters his scale . . . he no longer breathes our air than he forms new schemes, and embarks in designs he never would have thought of in his own country. . . . He begins to forget his former servitude and dependence, his heart involuntarily swells and glows. . . . From nothing to start into being, to become a free man, invested with lands, to which every municipal blessing is annexed. . . . *He* is an American, who leaving behind him all his ancient prejudices and manners, receives new ones from the mode of life he has embraced, the new government he obeys, the new rank he holds."

These various quotations, all from well-known books of the eighteenth century, afford us a good many brush strokes for our picture of the American. We glimpse at first hand again many of the traits we have earlier mentioned as slowly in the making—the growth of a democracy, the dislike of authority, the wish to get ahead, and to do it in one's own way, above all to manage one's own life as one chooses with an absolute minimum of interference from anybody else. The American in the making would have had scant use for blueprints, bureaucrats or regimentation. Some were ambitious and some shiftless, some were successful and some not, but in every case they had found a world in which they could be either, as they chose or as the luck fell. The frontier bred up wastrels and loafers as well as heroes and "he-men," but all of America bred people who wanted to do as they "jolly well" pleased, and in time the only government they wanted, if they wanted *any*, was one which would leave them free to do it or help them to do it. Any government which would tie their hands or thwart their chances could expect short shrift.

Of course, all Americans were not alike in all these points, any more than all individuals are alike in any considerable group, but on the whole, what we have gradually indicated was what was becoming "the American." Various individuals, various classes, all had their own contributions—for good or bad—to make to the growing American specialized type of culture. We would not now have, for example, those beautiful collectors' items of early American furniture, silver or glass, had there not been the rich to give orders to Revere and Phyfe and others, or had there not been craftsmen such as those just named to make them. We needed the explorers, frontiersmen, pioneers, to extend the bounds and population of the nascent nation, but such pursuits leave little opportunity for the cultivation of learning or the arts, and we needed these also to become a civilized country. The men, for example, who were to form that remarkable group who would rescue the emancipated nation from anarchy and at the Convention in Philadelphia draw up our Constitution, could not have been picked from hard-scrabble farmers, Indian traders in furs, or many other types who were forming the American democracy and making their own contributions to the America of the future.

Nevertheless, the upper social group, which in one colony and another added so much not only to the romance and beauty which we have inherited from the past but who were important leaders in establishing our new government, were being influenced even in fundamental political ideas by the very democracy—the "mob" as many of them liked to call the common folk—in a great diversity of ways. Later we shall have to mention some of these when we shall discuss briefly the propaganda necessary to awaken the people to revolt, but we may cite one here in passing.

Religion has always been an extremely important factor in American life and is yet, although in spite of, or perhaps on account of, the extraordinary number of creeds, sects and church organizations, I doubt if more than an infinitesimal number of attendants of any one congregation could give an intelligible account of how their creed differs from those of others. Unlike, say, the early New Englanders, no congregation today would listen for hours while the clergyman discussed fine-spun theological points. We are here, fortunately, interested in only one or two of the broader aspects of the problem. The chief ones are those of religious freedom and the absence in the United States of a state church, with all that these two things involve.

We may first clear our picture of two old-time errors. One is that Protestantism at once brought about religious liberty. The "race for empire" period of the seventeenth century was characterized by strong religious as well as national animosities, and it is hard to say whether the English hated the French and Spanish more on account of their nationality or on account of their being Roman Catholics. At any rate the constantly stressed and reiterated stories of the horrors of the Spanish Inquisition and other Catholic persecutions, true or bad enough as many of them in reality were, came to overshadow what happened under Protestantism. The truth was that the Protestant Reformation brought not peace but a sword, as any one familiar with history can recognize if he will recall the long religious wars, and not merely the persecutions of Catholics by Protestants but the persecutions of some sects of Protestants by others or by the established churches when Protestant.

The other ancient but popular error is the belief, now pretty thoroughly dispelled, that such early immigrants as came to America with the religious motive predominant came to establish religious liberty. This idea was especially fostered with regard to New England, and this error, like many others, crept into our history because it was for long written to a great extent by Massachusetts writers, lay or clerical, more bent on defending their Puritan forebears through thick and thin than in presenting unbiased truth. This is an old story now to modern historians but the folk lore lingers. The fact is that in Massachusetts, founded by the Pilgrims and Puritans, there was every intention on the part of the leaders of worshiping as they chose and of establishing their own church but not the slightest intention of allowing the same freedom to those who might disagree with them. The worst religious persecutions this nation has known were perpetrated in the colony which long prided itself as having been founded to secure religious liberty.

Neither Protestantism nor the acts or attitudes of the earliest religious refugee immigrants explain why America became the first country to enjoy complete religious freedom with no established church. The real explanation is America itself, that new environment which started so many strands of influence at work to make the new world of character, outlook and institutions which we call "America" and that new man, the American. Although Rhode Island and Maryland had made notable advances towards religious liberty, nevertheless for most of the seventeenth century there was nothing marked about religion in America as essentially different from that in Europe. America was not merely a cross-section of the many European sects but the Old World ideas as to the necessary relationship of church and state had also been brought over. It is true that in proportion to population there was an extraordinarily diverse collection of creeds and churches in the American colonies as compared with any one country overseas, and we have already spoken of this. In New York and Pennsylvania, for example, we may cite among others Church of Englanders, Dutch Calvinists, French Calvinists, a few Roman Catholics, all sorts of Quakers, Ana-Baptists, Jews, several types of Presbyterians, Lutherans, German and Dutch Reformed, Dunkers, Mennonites, Moravians, Schwenkfelders and others. The mere fact that all these could get along in neighboring colonies with a fair degree of toleration and a minimum of legal interference and practically no persecution, was a lesson in itself. *Experientia docet,* and as in so many other ways it was the actual *experience of life* under American conditions and not the spinning of intellectual theory, which molded the mind and outlook of the American. America has always been action rather than thought.

In spite of the interest in religion and the extent of its influence, there were at the end of the eighteenth century probably more "unchurched people" in proportion to population than anywhere else in Christendom, as has been recently pointed out by the leading authority, Dr. W. W. Sweet. This was due to a number of causes, including absence of state churches in many colonies, and, even where there were such, the difficulties in the way of becoming full-fledged church members.

Several factors tended towards fluidity in the entire religious situation. There was the experience of a great variety of creeds and beliefs, just touched upon. There was also, among the upper classes, an increase of a somewhat loose Deism and a decrease in old-time dogmas. Many of the leaders of this period, such as Washington, Jefferson, Franklin, Madison and others, though not irreligious men, were not definitely connected with any one church or denomination. Lastly, the amazing freedom allowed and the lack, for the most part, of heavily enforced central control permitted individuals so much latitude that they could embrace any sect they chose.

America was becoming the land of the small man who decided all his life for himself. Many glimpsed not only a new world but a new Heaven. More and more the appeal welcomed by them was made by the more emotional and Evangelical groups, most of them in a minority at first, the Methodists, Baptists and others. As Dr. Sweet has said, "The eighteenth century saw American religions more and more democratized, and, in the Great Colonial Revivals, for the first time religion reached down to the masses. In the process the old European Church-State relationship was gradually changed, and with independence came the opportunity to bring to a successful completion the century-and-a-half struggle for religious freedom and the separation of Church and State."

The relations, however, were close between religious and political liberty. John Locke, the English philosopher whose writings on political freedom so greatly influenced the leaders in America and whose ideas became common coin in the discussions among even those colonists who had never read his books, wrote as strongly in favor of religious liberty for all dissenters as for political, and Madison, one of his followers and the father of the American Constitution, had absorbed Locke's writings, as well as those of Voltaire. Madison used to quote from the latter the statement that "If one religion were allowed in England, the government would possibly become arbitrary; if there were two, the people would cut each other's throats; but as there are a multitude they all live happy and in peace." Madison himself said that "Security for civil rights must be the same as that for religious rights; it consists in the one case in a multiplicity of interests and in the other in a multiplicity of sects."

The close relation between freedom, democracy, and religious and political liberty may be illustrated by the famous quarrel at the beginning of the century between Cotton Mather and John Wise. In the too much neglected life of the latter we find a perfect example of what the American was becoming at the beginning of the eighteenth century, and also one which ties together the threads of the story we have just been telling.

Wise's father came to Massachusetts as an indented servant and worked his time. The son, without money or social standing, made his way through Harvard. Boston was snobbish as far as the leaders could make it so. Harvard was also, and students were listed according to the social position of their parents. The clergy formed largely a closed group, jealous of its social, intellectual and political standing. The "Mather Dynasty" considered itself about "tops," yet the redoubtable Cotton Mather was to be worsted in controversy with this son of a servant, who, after Harvard, became a clergyman at Ipswich and fought with pen and sword for democracy, liberty and liberalism.

Before publishing his celebrated book in 1710, he had gone to jail for defying the illegal imposition of taxes by the Andros regime and had taken part in the Phips expedition to Canada, not only praying as chaplain but joining the storming party in the effort to capture Quebec. He was a good fighter. He was also, what practically no other Massachusetts clergyman was, or had been, a student of profane as well as sacred history, and of political philosophy. We early spoke of the attitude of the leaders, lay and clerical, towards democracy, and how they drew their laws and political ideas almost wholly from the Old Testament. They wanted also a centralized control of all community life, a control naturally to be centralized in themselves and not in England. The strongly democratic tendency of Congregationalism had been fought by them, and, upholding the tradition, the Mathers in 1705, attempted to introduce the Presbyterian rather than the Congregational way and organization.

Wise entered the arena with his book called *The Churches' Quarrel Espoused,* followed by another work seven years later in 1717. It was a critical time, and it is interesting to note that Wise's books, although unread by the present generation, were republished at two other crises in our history, in 1772 and 1860. His works treated primarily of "the Churches' Quarrel" but they show the close connection, as seen by Madison, between religious and political liberty and forms of control. "The very name of an arbitrary government is ready to put an Englishman's blood into a fermentation," wrote this doughty American, "but when it comes and shakes its whip over their ears, and tells them it is their master, it makes them stark mad."

He pleaded for democracy in church government, but also demanded it in state as well as church. "To abbreviate," he wrote, "it seems most agreeable with the light of nature, that if there be any of the regular forms of government settled in the church of God, it must needs be . . . a democracy. This is the form of government which the light of nature does highly value, and often directs to as most agreeable to the just and natural prerogatives of human beings. . . . It is certainly a great truth, namely, that man's original liberty after it is resigned . . . ought to be cherished in all wise governments; or otherwise in making himself a subject, he alters himself from a freeman into a slave, which is repugnant to the law of nature. Also the natural equality of men amongst men must be duly favoured; in that government was never established by God or nature, to give one man a prerogative to insult over another. . . . Honor all men. The end of all good government is to cultivate humanity, and promote the happiness of all, and the good of every man in his rights, his life, liberty, estate, honor, etc., without injury or abuse to any."

There we pick up again the authentic American note, in what Mather called "a foolish Libel" by "a furious Man," though Wise's two small volumes are worth more than almost all the shelves of volumes by Mather, who, incidentally if he had been born in Texas instead of Massachusetts would probably not have had the Bostonian and Cambridge incense steadily burning before him. Wise was a very religious man but we begin to find the law of nature set beside the law of God. Unlike John Cotton and John Winthrop he does not damn democracy because "there was no such law in Israel" but turns to all history to discover the ways of God to man. If Old World Calvinism was falling before the free life of America, so was Old World opposition to democracy crumbling before the conditions of the American environment.

In Wise, the circumstances and developing traits which were making the American become extremely vocal, and we encounter even those phrases which in slightly different form were to ring round the world: "Honor all men"; "the natural equality of men"; "the light of nature"; "the end of all good government"; the right to "life, liberty, estate." These were to become more familiar in the works of Locke, but from the days of Wise what they portended had been steadily germinating on American soil, as it had less consciously from the first landing at Jamestown. Much had happened since little Virginia Dare had been born and disappeared, and John Rolfe had married the Indian chieftain's daughter. Now the American had been born, had not disappeared, but had vowed to wed the broad land of America. The French had fled and it was the American, the New Man, who stood on the summits of the Appalachians gazing on the abandoned empire which had become his. Or so he thought.

The eastern seaboard was settled and won. The clashes there were now less between whites and redskins than between the rising democracy and the so-called aristocrats or Tories. In Massachusetts Peggy Hutchinson, the proud daughter of the Royal Governor of Massachusetts, was soon to be complaining that "The dirty mob was all about me as I drove into town," but along the whole line of frontier was a democracy that relied on itself and cared for no man. Beyond that frontier was something that again bound the classes of the East together in ambitions and hopes if not in understanding and kindly feeling—the Land, the land now gained and waiting to be exploited.

For decades the richness of its possibilities had been extolled by French and English travellers and second-hand popularizers of other people's facts or fancies. From the Peace of Paris on, the flood of literature and interest about what lay over the mountains increased. Even in England it became a mania. In 1766 it was said that a large part of the people of that island were "New Land mad." We have spoken of the great land companies formed by the rich both overseas and in the colonies, but the dreams became vaster. The "Walpole Company," for example, as the Grand Ohio Company was popularly called, had been content at first to limit its requests for a grant to 2,500,000 acres but later expanded its demand to 20,000,000. It is not often that we are able to express historical forces or tendencies in mathematical terms, but the two figures just mentioned afford us a chance, and indicate how the American had been altered by the French and Indian War.

The new land lured not merely Anglo-American nabobs and capitalists. They were important and were to remain so, but the driving force was provided by those ordinary folk we have already talked about—the disgruntled and discontented in the old seaboard colonies; the sturdy land-loving and land-grabbing Germans who had swarmed out from Pennsylvania; the Scotch-Irish who had complained to Logan some fifty years earlier that "It was against the laws of God and nature that so much land should be idle while so many Christians wanted it to labor on and to raise bread." There was also, in the very van of the advance, that fringe of roughnecks, "outcasts," as even America-loving Crèvecœur called them, who formed, as he said, "the forlorn hope, preceding by ten or twelve years the more respectable army of veterans which came after them," and who, as he added, would retreat farther and farther, "making room for more industrious people, who will finish their improvements, convert the loghouse into a comfortable habitation, and rejoicing that the first heavy labors are finished, will change in a few years that hitherto barbarous country into a fine, fertile, well regulated district. Such is our progress, such is the march of the Europeans towards the interior parts of this continent."

But there was another factor to be considered, the Indian. Let us listen to one of them. "Wherever we turned about," he said, "we saw our Blood, and when our Young men wanted to go ahunting the Wild Beasts in our Country, they found it covered with fences, so that they were weary crossing them, neither can they get Venison to eat, or Bark to make huts, for the Beasts are run away and the Trees cut down."

The Indian problem had troubled the British government for many years, and we have noted how, after the colonies had long shown their incapacity to unite on any common Indian policy, it had asked them to hold the conference at Albany in 1754 in order in part that they should do so. They had failed, owing to jealousies, selfishness and lack of interest. With the end of the war, and the enormous increase in territory and Indian tribes to be handled somehow, the problem had become acute for the government in England, which was the only one which could handle it if the colonists themselves refused to do so. Then came the new settlements pouring into the former French country, the reaction of the Indians, and the beginning of the Pontiac War. Within a few weeks all but three forts scattered over an extent of a thousand miles had been captured by the savages. Something had to be done, and the blow fatal to the hopes of the colonists was struck.

Although the Proclamation of October 1763 was issued hurriedly to counter the emergency, Indian regulation had long been considered. There could be no question as to either its need or the fact that it would have to be handled by the imperial government. Although the arrangement then made was intended to be only a temporary makeshift it was not altered for over ten years. The Proclamation provided for the establishment of an Indian reservation south of the Hudson Bay-Quebec territories, west of the watershed of the Appalachian Mountains, south to Florida. Settlement on the vast Indian territory thus designated was forbidden; settlers already over the mountains were ordered to go back and give up their lands and houses; private purchases made from the Indians were declared void; no new purchases were to be allowed except by British officials for the Crown; and the Indian traders were to be licensed and placed under strict regulation.

In an expanding Empire the British Government, trying to balance all factors, has often had to antagonize settlers on the spot in order to try to be fair to native populations of a lower stage of society. Whatever may be said as to either the need or wisdom of the Proclamation of 1763 as a stop-gap, there could be no doubt what its effect would be in America, especially when it was to remain so long without modification. The Americans, rich and poor, who had just glimpsed the vision of a glorious future felt that it had been snatched from them by a tyrannical power when they had already had it within their grasp. Squabbles with governors, quarrels with Parliament, there had been in plenty, but this was something more. This was the fiat of an English King and government directed against manifest American destiny, and innumerable personal property rights and dreams of wealth. It was the beginning of what was to follow in the next dozen years.

It is true that it did not wholly halt the western advance, though it made it illegal. The large land companies were hampered, harried and made sore. The big men who had been counting on making money from huge grants had to have their papers in order. They were risking much, and only the power of an organized and approving society and government could ensure their investment.

This was not true of the little man who could take land with the vaguest title or none at all; who had nothing to lose but his skin and scalp and was willing to risk those; and whose weapons of defense were not sealed grants but an axe and a rifle. Such men as these poured over the mountains, despite the Proclamation. How many can never be known but they trekked steadily, and in 1770 George Croghan, the Indian trader and land speculator, wrote that "What number of families has settled, since the congress, to the westward of the high ridge, I cannot pretend to say positively; but last year, I am sure, there were between four and five thousand, and all this spring and summer the roads have been lined with waggons moving to the Ohio." Croghan himself, who was a member of the Grand Ohio Company, and also tried in vain to secure legal recognition of his claims to 2,500,000 acres on the upper Ohio and 1,200,000 on the Mississippi, died in poverty.

Meanwhile the West was filling up with hardy men determined to defend their new homes at every risk and cost. In thinking back over the many factors we have touched upon as making for democracy: personal liberty, dislike of authority, and, in a word, that New Man the American, we must again stress one fundamental point. It was *America* which made him. There had been scarcely a new idea born in the new country. The history of the Old World was strewn with ideas, with rebels, reformers, idealists, dreamers. Democracy, the rights of man, religious liberty, resistance to tyranny, and all the rest, had long been discussed there. Matters of theory, they had only very slowly, here and there, at intervals, and with much danger and suffering to individuals and groups, been translated into terms of actual life. Never before in history had a people, and particularly all the *common people,* had such a chance to start fresh and make facts out of ideas. It was not only that there was desire to do so, not merely that the opportunity had come, but that all the conditions of their new life and environment almost forced them to do so. It was not that the American was a superman, intellectually, spiritually or politically, who was consciously drawing up a blueprint for a planned society. It was simply that in a land where numberless barriers—old customs, habits, inhibitions, pressures of all sorts—had suddenly disappeared, human nature let itself go in an upward surge and found itself possessed of things long longed for—freedom, property, the chance to rise and grow, the sense of being somebody and just as good as, or a little better than, any one else. The process which had released the energies of Englishmen under Queen Elizabeth was at work in America on a vaster scale.

The Proclamation of 1763, drawn up, it has been claimed, in six days, had been a terrific shock, but there were now to be others.

The Indian problem was not the only one with which the British Government was confronted at the end of the war. As a consequence of the struggle the debt of England had risen to the then almost unthinkable sum of $650,000,000, and the annual cost of the army and navy from $350,000 pre-war to $1,750,000 post-war. True, Britain had defeated her rival and won, among other things her American possessions, while the relief from the pressure of danger on the Americans was great, and their opportunities had been enormously increased, for the Proclamation settlement was intended to be only temporary. On the other hand, the English felt that the colonists had not done their fair share in the work though they were greatly to benefit by the results. Although the duel with France had extended all over the globe, even on the mainland of America, in which Americans were most interested and where they were expected to share the spoils, England had provided even in the New World more than half the armed forces, as well as a large part of the expense of the colonials, and all the cost of the navy. She also estimated that it would take ten thousand troops to garrison the forts and territory acquired from France, and was assuming the cost of that.

It was therefore not unnatural, though perhaps unwise, that war-weary and tax-weary Englishmen should count, without thinking much about it, on contributions from the colonists.

Unfortunately at this critical moment the bureaucratic-minded George Grenville became Chancellor of the Exchequer. The Americans had always nominally acquiesced in the doctrine that England could lay taxes in the form of duties for the regulation of trade, but Grenville, nosing about, made the interesting but extremely unfortunate discovery that owing to widespread smuggling indulged in by American merchants, and connived at by local British officials, it was costing the British Government $35,000 a year to maintain customhouses in the colonies which yielded a revenue of only $10,000. Grenville was dull but honest. The statistical discovery horrified him.

The result was inevitable, even though Grenville is still classified as a "statesman" in the English *Dictionary of National Biography.* To remedy the condition he had unexpectedly uncovered he touched the match to an already inflammable imperial structure.

In 1764 he secured the passage, through an otherwise busy and more or less non-understanding Parliament, of the Sugar Act, which calls for brief comment, not as factual history but as casting another ray of light on the growth of the American.

The colonies, like most new countries, were short of capital, of hard cash (so they believed they *must* have paper money), and of foreign exchange with which to pay their overseas debts, incurred for capital loans, manufactured goods, wines, silver plate, clothes, furniture and other luxuries. The southern colonies had staple crops—notably, of course, tobacco—but even so it is estimated that the southerners were in debt to the merchants in London, Bristol and other ports, to the tune of about £3,000,000 Sterling at the outbreak of the Revolution, and in studying the American we must never forget the debtor-creditor, frontier-old settlement complex which we saw beginning when Hooker wrote from Connecticut to John Winthrop in Massachusetts.

New England was in far worse case than the South. According to the old Mercantile Theory of empire, colonies were supposed not to compete with but to supplement the Mother Country. In general they were expected to provide the raw materials for the manufactures of England, which, in turn, they were expected to buy, or those for her foreign commerce. The sugar islands of the West Indies and the staple crop colonies of the South fitted into this blueprint. New England never did. In order to secure the foreign exchange which enabled her to buy British goods, she had to turn to trade in a great variety of ways, which mussed up the blueprint, as national-planning blueprints have a way of getting mussed up, and also mixed the plans laid for inter-Empire trade in general.

For example, the most lucrative trade which the shrewd and holy New Englanders developed was the triangular one of distilling the molasses, bought in the sugar islands (French and British), into rum, selling the rum for slaves in Africa, selling the slaves and other things in the West Indies again, and so on round and round. (This is a rather generalized description of a somewhat complicated trading cycle, but it will serve our purpose here.) The British islands could not produce enough molasses to provide New England with enough rum for enough trade in slaves to buy enough goods in England, hence the trade with the French, to which the British West Indians, with a powerful lobby in Parliament, like the silver and other lobbies in our own Congress today, strongly objected.

Parliament was in a quandary. It had to decide between the extremely vocal demands of two different sections of the Empire in trying to put into practice a blue-printed and complex scheme of imperial planning. In Parliament itself, naturally, the powerful and rich planter lobby, largely resident in London, won out against the disliked Saints of New England, but in fact it was New England which won, by the simple method of disregarding the duties levied. To have paid them would have ruined all New England trade, as well as many London merchants. New Englanders became a race of smugglers, bought molasses where they wished, and continued to have money enough to buy goods from England. The original law, known as the "Molasses Act," had been passed in 1733. Parliament, with the three pressure groups of the sugar island planters, the London merchants and exporters, and the tough

New England colonials, on its hands, had, for a generation, looked the other way.

Smuggling, proving both profitable and unpunished, naturally spread to other products, from the sugar islands to the wine islands, and so on, and we may insert here a comment on the attitude of the American towards law, which the English, perhaps the most law-abiding nation in the world, by choice and not by compulsion, had much to do in muddying. If we had slaves after England freed hers, and if we are less careful of laws than the English, the tangled causes go back to England rather than America.

We come back again to distance, misunderstanding, and attempted planning on a world scale. The British sugar island planter, whose profits enabled him to live lavishly in the West Indies or London, saw no reason why he, as a Britisher, should allow a New Englander, also a Britisher, to trade with the French. The New Englander, striving to get enough money in any way, from his stony acres, fishing off the banks, and by any other means possible—which was making the character of the Yankee—did not see why he should not be allowed to trade where and how he could. The harassed London merchant, wanting profits and sound bills of exchange from anywhere and anybody, was perplexed. Parliament, thinking in terms of eighteenth-century mercantile imperialism, drew its blueprint, and then, when things got hot, looked away and let them take their course.

But there was more to it all than that. Parliament had a way of passing laws affecting trade, and theoretically this was accepted in the colonies. However, distance and the lack of a locally effective centralized authority gave the colonists the opportunity to ignore such laws, by smuggling or otherwise. The English government also claimed the right to disallow laws passed by the local colonial legislatures, but again distance came into the picture. It usually took a couple of years or more, owing to two trips across the ocean and the slowness of official red-tape, for a law which had been passed and rejected to be returned as void. Meanwhile it would be valid, and if the colonists smelled that it would be disallowed they could pass another.

Thus in one way or another—smuggling, lawmaking chicanery, or just absolute non-observance with no penalty—the American developed the deep instinctive belief that he need not obey any laws he did not approve of or which might be deemed unprofitable to him. What developed this trait in him, and it is a trait, was America—its distance, its new conditions so different from those of eighteenth-century Europe, and the lack of control. It was not an outcropping of original sin nor the lawlessness of a criminal mind or of one who has lost contact with the ways of an ordered society. It was the result, in such cases as, for example, that of the rich John Hancock, of American conditions, of distance and of trying to run a far-flung empire, under the circumstances of time and space in that period, from one central point.

CHAPTER X

THE AMERICAN COMES OF AGE

THE English colonial, for better or worse, was becoming the American. And why shouldn't he? England had claimed America largely on the basis of Cabot's voyage and discovery, which was rewarded by the niggardly Henry VII with a few dollars. English merchants and adventurers had put up money for some of the earliest settlements, but as the Americans, now coming to number well on to three millions, including races other than English, thought things over, in spite of loyalty to the Empire—and there was much of it as we shall see—they thought of what they themselves had contributed to the building of this new "Englysshe Nation," and they were determined to be themselves.

There were many who were still loyal to imperial rather than local interests. There were, as always, many who were lukewarm and wanted only to be let alone and not to have to think or decide, but I am speaking of those who were what we consider now as American and who so wrought on events that they did much to create the American.

There are one or two other points, which were to be of importance when the American was to start Constitution building. He had come to think of law observance as something suiting his own convenience or profit. Besides the aid which time, distance and the notorious dilatoriness of eighteenth-century bureaucrats and politicians overseas afforded him, he was also helped in his dangerous and far from laudable trait by the fact that for the most part the local judicial system was much under his control through the purse strings and the jury system. Distance again meant that this would be administered by his own friends and neighbors, who would usually take his side. Moreover the local American controlled the election of members to the Assemblies, or lower houses of the colonial legislatures. The Royal Governor, in such colonies as had one, was often a hated official at the head of the local government but representing one from far away, and which to many was coming to appear almost foreign. Governor Nicholson of Virginia noted in 1701 that "The Country consists now most of Natives, [native-born] few of which have read much or been abroad in the world" and, again, that the natives "begin to have a sort of aversion to others, calling them strangers." I well recall that in a village where I once made my home, those who might have lived there for long years, but whose ancestors had not, were spoken of as "from away" and even as "furriners."

On the other hand, it is an odd trait in Americans that although they were to become roamers and develop little or nothing of deep local attachment to a bit of ground or a landscape, yet they have their own sense of local pride and locality. Set a Floridian and a Californian, though each may have lived in their respective states for only a few years, discussing their respective merits and you will see what I mean. So the American who was beginning to think of himself as a New Englander, a Virginian or what not, rather than an Englishman, objected to the overseas appointed governor and often to those members of the Councils, or upper houses of the legislatures, who owed their positions to his appointment. The consequence of all these things was that the American, who held himself aloof from such "foreigners" as Scotch-Irish, Germans and others, had come not only to fear but to resent interference from England, thus developing a feeling that his own safety and liberty depended upon a popularly elected legislature and the Courts—both American—and to be afraid of the power of the Executive, who for the most part had appeared to him in the rôle of a "foreign"-appointed and hostile governor. Of these points we shall have occasion to speak again later, and we may now mention merely one more before we turn again to Mr. Grenville and his Sugar Act.

Crèvecœur mentioned it, as necessarily all must notice it

who trace the course of the American. The observing Frenchman wrote of all the immigrants who came here, "*Ubi panis ibi patria,*" and "Here the rewards of his industry follow with equal step in the progress of his labor, his labor is founded on the basis of nature, *self-interest*; can it want a stronger allurement?" No, it could not, and in spite of all the winds of doctrine since, it has remained a dominant American trait, though it has not spelled selfishness but rather a princely generosity in later times. The American, however, has insisted on the right to "get his," and then to scatter or hoard it as he will. It is not without significance for our theme that Benjamin Franklin, one of the most American of Americans, managed to absorb and propagate as a young man the doctrine, which was not originally his, that "labor is the measure of value." The American had become a thorough-going individualist, sure of himself and where he was headed for, and was getting to be a tough nut to crack. The British Government decided to try to crack it. Rather, perhaps, it more or less slid into the effort without sufficient consideration of the problem and of possible consequences.

The few years following the passage of the Sugar Act were to be notable for a series of other measures, ending with what came to be known as the "Intolerable Acts." In the earlier ones, at least, it now appears in the calm reflection afforded by nearly a century and three-quarters that there was no intentional malice or attempt to tyrannize. The Americans had acquiesced in the Molasses Act in theory though not in practice for over thirty years. The Sugar Act reduced the duty by fifty per cent, from 6d to 3d, and the new duties on additional commodities, such as wine, coffee and others, were moderate and even if paid would have left a good profit on the imports. The difficulty was that instead of looking the other way as when the old 6d duty on molasses had been evaded, the British Government intended that the new ones should be collected. Warships were sent to American ports, naval officers given the right to collect the duties, and prosecutions for smuggling were taken over by British Admiralty Courts and out of the hands of the local American judicial system. All this raised a storm of protest in the colonies. In the effort to rationalize the colonial position—which effort played so great a part in the next decade—new theories of taxation and representation were brought forward.

Grenville looked about for additional taxation which might be borne by the colonists, though it must not be forgot that he still intended that England should pay a large share of the cost of maintaining and defending the newly acquired possessions won from the French. A stamp tax was customary and easily collected. Some of the colonies had themselves used this method of raising revenue. When such a tax was imposed by Parliament in March 1765 only a few Englishmen, such as Isaac Barré—whose name with that of the radical Wilkes was to live on in Wilkes-Barre, thought that it would make any difficulty. The British Government had always been badly advised by the local Royal Governors and other royal officials who did not understand what the American was becoming but even Americans themselves did not wholly understand either, nor did so good an American as Benjamin Franklin think the act would breed any difficulties. He even advised two of his friends to accept office as Stamp Collectors. However, a storm broke, largely under the leadership of Patrick Henry of the frontier section of Virginia, and the "Virginia Resolves," of which he secured the passage in the Virginia Assembly, ran up and down the seaboard like a prairie fire. Grenville, who had asked colonial advice before he proposed the tax, had been badly misled, not only by government functionaries but even by patriotic colonials themselves.

Another act, declaring colonial paper money not to be legal tender, added fuel to the flame. America, struggling to create sources of exchange with which to buy its necessary British goods, saw the complete draining away from itself of its small stock of precious metals. The Stamp Act, however, was repealed the year after its passage, largely due to American pressure on

British merchants and the efforts of leading English statesmen, who sensed that the struggle was not merely one between the mother country and its colonies but an extremely important episode in the always continuing defense of the subjects' liberties in England itself. The ill-feeling aroused in America gave place to rejoicing, after the repeal, for most Americans paid little attention to the accompanying Declaratory Act asserting the right of Parliament to bind the colonies in all cases whatsoever. In spite of growing tenseness there was a widespread inclination to let sleeping dogs lie, and to trust as usual to distance and lax central enforcement of laws. America had been angry over many things but, after some rioting, was not in any mood to stage a revolt just for the fun of it. In spite of the Proclamation Line, ordinary folk, if not the great land speculators, were somehow getting over the mountains to the rich and promised land beyond. The Stamp Act was licked, and as for the Declaratory Act, the English at least have never bothered their heads much about political theories or mere logic until they feel the pinch in the denial of specific individual and accustomed rights.

Then the British Government put its foot into it again, with Charles Townshend as Chancellor of the Exchequer, and with an ill Prime Minister, William Pitt, who should have known better. In 1767 a new tariff act was passed levying duties on a number of articles, such as tea, lead, glass, and painters' colors. It was supposed to raise about £40,000 a year. Intense opposition was again aroused. Next came the death of Townshend and the repeal of all the new duties except that on tea. Once more there was an immense feeling of relief in America, especially among the local merchant class, who had been hit by the Townshend duties as the lawyer and the newspaper group had been hit by the Stamp Tax. The British had struck in successive acts at the capitalist and small man in America interested in western lands; at the rising lawyers and developing newspapers; and at the merchants. Despite good intentions they could hardly have done worse.

There was plenty of trouble brewing but even so, if it had not been for a comparatively small group of extremely able agitators and propagandists, things might yet have been smoothed over. Between these, however, and the continued stupidity, rather than tyranny of the British, the fat was soon to be in the fire. The tax on tea, and the conditions under which it was laid, were used by the propagandists to bring about the celebrated "Boston Tea Party." This in turn enraged the British Government, and led to the passage of what came to be known as the Intolerable Acts, namely the Act closing the port of Boston to all commerce; that changing the government of Massachusetts by strengthening Royal authority at the expense of popular liberty; the act changing the administration of colonial justice; and that providing for the quartering of troops. These were distinctly punitive measures, passed because of the destruction of the $50,000 worth or so of tea which had been thrown into the harbor of Boston. Another act, which did not belong in the same class, although it was so included by the propagandists, was the Quebec Act, designed to conserve the rights of the Catholic inhabitants of the conquered French province. With the ultra-strong anti-Catholic feeling of New England and many of the other colonies, this, of course, added fuel to the flame.

The Proclamation Act of 1763 had dealt a terrific blow at the friendly relations between England and her American colonies, regardless of how justified it may have been as a hastily drawn and presumably temporary measure. Then the other acts followed at intervals for about a decade, yet as one or another of some of them were withdrawn or modified, feeling in America against England declined. The line was somewhat like that of a fever chart. I think it must be admitted that what brought about the final result was due, directly and indirectly, to extremely able propaganda by a past-master in that art, Samuel Adams, and others. Propaganda has had innumerable definitions but in its most generalized one—the effort to win other persons to accept your point of view—it is certainly as old as the human race after it had acquired the ability to communicate between individuals.

A most important difference must be drawn between propaganda and the various techniques employed in its use. There is nothing wrong in propaganda itself, although there may be in the technique, and it is the abuse of the latter which has given the term the extremely bad odor which it now carries with it. To appeal to calm intelligence by the presentation of cold and accurate facts is certainly wholly justifiable; when facts are selected so as to appeal to emotion and not to mind, we are crossing a border line; and when facts are misrepresented or absolute lies are told, we have plainly gone a long way over the line to the evil side. Sam Adams and the other propagandists—and even George Washington was fully aware of the need of influencing the mind of the public at critical moments—ran the whole gamut—facts appealing to the cold intellect, those appealing to the emotions, and false statements intended to appeal to both.

The American had been slowly evolving into something different from the Englishman and from the Old World peoples of other races which had contributed their emigrants also. Perhaps the three points which we have had occasion to stress most were the increase in democratic feeling, in strong individualism, and in the insistence on the right of every individual to go as far and as fast as he wished and could. But all this was more or less generalized. It was what we speak of as the intellectual or moral climate of an age. Like the physical climate of large parts of the American continent, with its brilliant sunshine, clear, sparkling air, its dazzling light and black shadows rather than modulations of "tone," its electrically charged air which makes people walk faster, act more emphatically, and perhaps think less or differently than in Europe, this "climate" enveloped and molded the American unconsciously. Democracy and individualism were not results of committees, organizations or "movements."

Nevertheless, the American had become a different animal

from what he had been in youth in the Old World, or from what his ancestors of one or three generations back had been. Again, all Americans were not alike. Even as today, if there were then exaggerated Anglophobes, there were also Anglophiles or even Anglomaniacs. It would also be a mistake to think that all the latter, as the propaganda which we shall discuss presently tried to make it appear, were of the rich and propertied classes. Assured economic security in the framework of a given society is likely to breed conservatism, but far from inevitably, as our millionaire Communists and "parlor pinks" indicate. On the other hand poverty by no means equally inevitably breeds a revolutionary radical. Although no statistics can be cited to prove my point, it has been my experience that the so-called working class tends very strongly towards conservatism. The Negro slaves, who were certainly "underprivileged," were, on the whole, conservative, and I have found the same to be true of many of the similarly named groups in all sorts of occupations or races, in many countries. Loyalty, fear of the effects of too rapid change, love of tradition and of the accustomed ways of living and getting a living, are extremely powerful. It is well that they are, for although there would be no advance without radicalism, unhampered radicalism, with no ballast of conservatism, could easily become anarchy and retrogression. Perhaps one of the best jobs God ever did was to make the difference in temperament between youth and age.

This was true of the America of the fermenting period between the end of the war of 1763 and the beginning of what is variously called, with ample meaning in both terms, the American Revolution and the Civil War with England on the part of the colonies. The spiritual and emotional climate of the colonies had become as different from that of England as the physical one, but if the people of England, including their statesmen, did not realize it, neither did the Americans think of imperial relations in that way. It takes more than change of atmosphere to induce men to enter on a bloody war and to take immense risks. The acts passed by Parliament, as cited briefly above, meant one thing in England, and another in America, but, even so, war would probably not have resulted from them at that time—and if not at that time who can say when or how or under what conditions?—had it not been that, as always happens in such crises, a comparatively few men pulled the wires and influenced public opinion. Thus we return to the propagandists and the work they did. Our main interest is in the wires they pulled, as indicating what appeals they thought most important to make to the American, and consequently what, in their opinion, the American had become, wanted, and was thinking about.

We may notice two general points at the start. One is that the methods of propaganda were almost as completely organized in the eighteenth century as they have been since, except for new methods of communication, such as the radio, and so on. These constitute media rather than method, and the method has not much altered. The appeal has always been to certain emotions and ideas. The other point is that even when the appeal is emotional it must be made to fit the emotions of the particular people to whom it is directed. The type of propaganda appeal made to any people by those supposed to know their reactions best will tell us much about the kind of people they are.

As almost invariably happens, the leaders organizing the new social and revolutionary movement made up but a small group, but the pretense of large numbers and unanimity of general public opinion was put before the public as conspicuously as possible. There were as yet no radios or "big circulation" magazines, but there were newspapers with a considerable number of readers, the pulpit—more influential then than now, —addresses on public occasions by leading citizens, often fairly widespread in pamphlet form, and other ways of reaching the public. There were no syndicated columns (by one writer), which could give the impression of the unanimous opinion of perhaps a hundred writers in a hundred different papers, praising or damning one book or one course of action, but the same effect was easily achieved in another way.

Sam Adams, for example, who was the leading propagandist of the movement, wrote for the Boston newspaper, the *Independent Advertiser,* hundreds of articles, signed by at least twenty-five different names. This made one man speak as a multitude. This trick was explicitly referred to during the war by William Livingston of New York, who wrote in answer to a letter from George Washington asking his help to oppose the proffered peace from England in 1778, "I have sent Collins [a news editor] a number of letters, as if by different hands, not even excluding the tribe of petticoats, [one letter was signed "Belinda"] all calculated to caution America against the insidious arts of enemies. This mode of rendering a measure unpopular, I have frequently experienced in my political days to be of surprising efficacy, as the common people collect from it that everybody is against it, and for that reason those who are really for it grow discouraged, from magnifying in their own imagination the strength of their adversaries beyond its true amount."

The newspapers were invaluable media. In the twelve years from 1763 to 1775 their number exactly doubled, rising from twenty-one to forty-two, or about the same in relation to population as the number now existing, and the press marched almost like a drilled and disciplined army. There was endless repetition of ideas, phrases and even articles. John Dickinson's influential *Letters From A Pennsylvania Farmer,* for example, appeared in every colonial newspaper but three up and down the entire seaboard. During the years of agitation the press was practically unanimously anti-British. This was due in part to threats of violence and other forms of intimidation; in part to the activity and ability of the propagandists; and in part to the fact that the British Government itself by the Stamp Act, with its heavy duties on news sheets and legal documents, had managed to range against itself the large majority of American editors and lawyers, two groups eminently capable of influencing opinion through the press.

Although there were leaders in many colonies, such as Dickinson in Pennsylvania, Patrick Henry in Virginia, and Christopher Gadsden in South Carolina, who spoke and wrote and also operated quietly behind the scenes, the master of them all as an agitator and organizer without being either an orator or a great writer, was Samuel, or as he is usually called, "Sam," Adams of Boston. For a brief interval in a long life, marked in its earlier and later years by inefficiency and lack of success, he found the precise niche for which his talents fitted him. He understood, during that period, although not later, what motivated the common man in America, and even on occasion could bring into his fold such an uncertain and vain but highly useful money-bag as John Hancock, the richest man in New England.

Adams destroyed great masses of his private papers covering the crucial years, but it is evident that for a period he was the arch manipulator behind the scenes, whether letting out or pulling in the violence of the "Boston Mob," managing public meetings, organizing Committees of Correspondence, in fact manipulating all the wires. Any agitator or advertiser knows the value of constant reiteration and that seeming unanimity of opinion of which we spoke above. If public resolutions of towns, parishes or what not, as we go along the coast, were often the result of propaganda, they were themselves propaganda, and when, as in one case among innumerable, we find, for example, forty towns in Massachusetts all adopting the same resolution, drawn by John Adams, we can see the fine hand of his cousin Sam at work, and the citizens of Massachusetts and those of other colonies were made to feel that all the people of the Bay Colony were a unit. Of course, even in that fairly unified colony, they were not, but the effect was given according to Livingston's formula.

In those dozen years or so, public opinion and emotion ebbed and flowed. We may distinguish in all, from the standpoint of propaganda, three distinct periods, those from 1763 to 1774,

1774 to 1776, and the purely war propaganda after the Declaration of Independence.

There can be, I think, no question of the profound influence on the American of achieved political independence from the Empire. In that task, whatever else we may say of Sam Adams, his rôle was pre-eminent and of a peculiar sort. In the period before 1774 he was the only one of the propagandists who counted, or perhaps one of an unknown and uncertain very few, who looked forward to absolute independence for the colonies. There were plenty of anti-British, plenty of angry merchants, land speculators, pioneers and good patriots, but they were mostly appeasers and, in the best English tradition, compromisers.

Sam Adams practically alone kept his eye on one thing, complete severance of all ties with Britain. He was wise enough not to state his goal, or to seem to set a pace, and yet kept the pot boiling. When Britain made concessions, such as the repeal of the Stamp Act, and the Imperial barometer might begin to point to "fair" again, Sam Adams saw to it that new grievances should be found and emotion whipped up. I think the so-called "Boston Massacre" can be laid to him, and at any rate it was a godsend to him, with its ensuing succession of annual addresses of the most inflammatory sort. In the Boston Tea Party he would have overreached himself and made a bad blunder had not the British Government come to his aid by promptly making a far worse one. Such patriots as Benjamin Franklin and John Dickinson heartily disapproved of the destruction of the tea, and John Adams reported much popular feeling against it.

However, we need not go into the factual details of the events of those hectic years. The point is that, in spite of all the grievances of the past and the then present, it required every resource of propaganda, especially from 1774 to 1776, to work both people and many of the leaders such as Washington, up to the point of declaring their complete independence of the Empire instead of merely fighting for their rights, legally or physically, as loyal citizens within it. Admitting that the split in the English-speaking people came about as a result of the stupidity of the British administration and the influence of American propaganda, what can we find in the latter which sheds any light on our particular topic, which is that of the *American*? Propaganda, well directed by those who know, will tell us much about those to whom it is directed. To what did the Americans of that time react favorably?

All those features of propaganda to which we have long become accustomed appear. For example, there is the claim that God or the supernatural powers are in favor of the nation. Addressing England, one propagandist writes: "Why do you suffer your fleets and armies again to be sent against America? Are ye not yet convinced that the Great Jehovah is on her side? and that God helping, the Gates of Hell shall never prevail against her?" Over and over this note is sounded, and it is one to which the New Englanders especially had been accustomed from the beginning when Stoughton announced in the early Massachusetts Bay that "God hath sifted a whole nation, that he might send choice grain into this wilderness." It was all in the tradition leading up to the American phrase "God's Country." America had its bad lands, dust bowls and Death Valleys, but the sense of superiority, moral or physical, plays its part in molding the character and reactions of a people. It occurs only among certain peoples and under certain conditions, but reiteration engraves it deeply on a national consciousness and the Americans have reiterated it about themselves for over three centuries.

The churches played a large part. By 1775 there were approximately thirty-two hundred of them, of at least eighteen well-established denominations. In different colonies, different approaches had to be made, but the pulpit still ranked with the newspapers and public meetings as one of the means of influence. In some colonies the intimated threat of the appointment of Anglican Bishops could be used to excite fear. Throughout practically all of them, the Quebec Act, intended in large part merely to protect the rights of the French Catholics in Canada, could be made to appear as a threat of Rome and the Inquisition to all American Protestants, and the "Pope of Rome" and the "Whore of Babylon" were good stage properties. Not only in the field of religion but in others, loose generalizations were constantly used which could be made to seem to apply to the conditions and prejudices in very varying localities.

After the war had begun, there were all the usual "hate" stories. The English were described as all licentious and immoral. They had determined to make all Americans slaves. There were the customary tales of atrocities, of wanton attacks on private homes (incidentally the Boston Mob had destroyed Governor Hutchinson's beautiful house and scattered all his manuscripts and books, invaluable for the history of the colony, and stolen or burned his silver, family portraits and furniture). Tales were told of the British or Hessians raping innocent young girls, of babies barbarously killed, of women assaulted when they were in pains of childbirth, of corpses dug up from graveyards (as in Newport), and treated with indignity. Even germ stories appeared, of wells being poisoned and smallpox and other infectious diseases being spread. We need not continue the now all-too-familiar catalogue. The point is that war propaganda and hate leave scars, and the war of the American Revolution, and every detail of it, was especially important and was played up for some generations because it was not just an ordinary war but one from the travail of which came the birth of the nation.

There were other points about the propaganda, or method of playing on the minds of Americans, which are important for our main theme. For one we may note the constant insistence upon personal liberty. So incessant were the thumbings on this one string that it is not necessary to quote. Over and over and over, Americans were told in print and speech that they would be SLAVES if they did not revolt and fight, and that they would lose all freedom. The stress laid on this point indicates that those fingering the keys of the organ of popular opinion felt that the Vox Populi was, as some organists use the Vox Humana, the most appealing to pull out. Here, then, we get a note in propaganda which tells us something specifically about the American of this period.

Land and property also figured in the picture. One propagandist, typical of many, wrote that if the British conquered, "which God forbid, slavery would be the consequence, this good land would be divided into lordships, and instead of being masters, we should be servants to as abandoned a set of men as ever the earth produced." The topics of pensions, other forms of privilege, titles, etc., bureaucracy with its threat of interfering with every one doing as he pleased, also were used with strong effect. Taxation without representation, of which we shall speak again, and which we have conferred on Alaska, Porto Rico and other territories, was dinned into the people during the legalistic period before actual war. Civil freedom was closely tied up to religion, as we have noted in a quotation from James Madison. Long before Madison wrote, Sam Adams was preaching that "The religion and public liberty of a people are intimately connected. Their interests are interwoven, they cannot exist separately; therefore they rise and fall together."

We get another slant on the American when we find the whole problem, after all legal rationalizing, coming down to individual happiness. John Dickinson in his *Farmer's Letters* (and again it must be recalled that such statements as were supposed to fit the American's hopes and fears were repeated everywhere), wrote: "Let these truths be indelibly on our minds—That we cannot be happy without being free—that we cannot be free, without being secure in our property—that we cannot be secure in our property, if without our consent, others may, as by right, take it away."

Public resolutions and documents largely sprang from propaganda and became themselves the most effective propaganda.

The freedom of the individual and his happiness perhaps dominated all the rest, and no public document has been so influential as the Declaration of Independence.

That was made up of two parts—a long indictment of the supposedly tyrannical acts of the King, George the Third, and of certain general clauses. Nobody today could repeat the paragraphs of the indictment, but the general clauses are still of the bone and sinew of the American, such as: "We hold these truths to be self-evident, that all men are created equal, that they are endowed by their Creator with certain inalienable Rights, that among these are life, liberty and the pursuit of happiness. That to secure these rights, Governments are instituted among Men, deriving their just powers from the consent of the governed."

Here we have the American emerging from a long period of development. In the gradual change in ideas and words, the phrase concerning the inalienable rights had been altered from "life, liberty and property" to "life, liberty and the pursuit of happiness." The choice of these three rights is enormously significant. All the American asked was life, freedom to do as he wanted and to pursue happiness in his own way. He had come to feel that if he were sure of these he could take care of all the rest. He did not ask government to feed or clothe him or to do anything except keep out of his way and keep its hands off him, as far as was consistent with the barest fundamentals of maintaining order. Like the oft-quoted Cape Cod fishing captain we may say that all he asked was "civility, just civility, and that of the plainest and Goddamnedest kind."

The significant fact about his dropping the word "property" was not that he believed in Socialism or Communism or had any dislike of property. It was exactly the reverse. I recall that some years ago, that charming woman and historian, the late Miss Ruth Putnam, speaking of a friend of hers, made the comment that "she had that peculiar form of human happiness known as '*money-of-your-own*'," slurring the phrase as if it were a term of one word. The Americans, men or women, have always considered "money-of-their-own" as a form of happiness. We have seen, both at Jamestown and Plymouth, how society almost broke down when the colonists were not allowed to acquire it. They had emigrated from the Old World, and pioneered and worked and suffered to gain it, and had fought local governments, Royal Governors and the imperial government on questions of taxation to retain it. They would not have understood the current political slang of "human rights vs. property rights." In their eyes the right to win, hold and use property *was* a "human right," and so essentially a factor in happiness that when that word was used to denominate one of the three inalienable rights it could not fail to include the right to own property.

When Sam Adams and the other propagandists—writers and orators—kept reiterating that Americans might become SLAVES, what the average American understood was, aside from religious and other slants to the situation, that he might be prevented from making his own way *in* his own way. He wanted to be, in a stock American expression, "as independent as a hog on ice," which in meaning and wording is typically American. Later in our story we shall see that altered conditions, and in some cases population, caused certain mental changes, but with all the limitations which even the old American feels he may have to place on his old-fashioned outlook, that is the way he still instinctively reacts. The other evening an old New Englander was talking with a man who was telling how public spirited he had been in the village in which he had formerly lived, and how he had got ordinances passed to make the citizens do this or that and to create a modern and model community. The New Englander listened patiently and then said: "Well, from all you say, it seems to me that you must have spent a hell of a lot of time sticking your nose into other people's business." They were both Americans, and their types may be found anywhere among us, but I think there is little question as to which would be taken as the American we are mainly writing about.

The American, that "New Man," had come into being but there was as yet no American nation. The colonies for the most part were not well acquainted with one another, and extremely jealous as always, even though Patrick Henry, Christopher Gadsden and others here or there might call for an all-American and not a local spirit to prevail. The fact that the same propaganda flowed up and down the whole seaboard, that difficulties with Britain became more and more common to all, that leaders met, under the Stamp Act, in Continental Congresses, and under the welding pressure of the war, helped, but sectionalism and local prides and dislikes were to continue. We glimpse it as long lasting in a letter of John Adams written in 1817, and published in full only a few months ago, in which he states that the three main pillars of the entire Revolutionary movement and the chief factors in its success were all Massachusetts men, Otis, Hancock and Sam Adams. To these he probably in his own mind added himself, and says that both Washington and Franklin were only "moons" illuminated by these "suns." Both, he adds, were "not only superficial but ignorant" and often "terrible Embarrassments." We glimpse in this letter of old age some of the disunity, dislike and localism which for generations were to preclude an America, as contrasted with the American, from coming into full being.

There were more than colonial differences. We have already touched on the social and economic cleavages and must recur to them in connection with propaganda and its more permanent effects. The Whigs and Tories were divided by political beliefs and loyalties but not by classes. It is true that when finally some sixty to a hundred thousand colonists loyal to the Empire left the colonies, the loss of the rich, conservative and cultured was felt more than that of the much larger number of ordinary folk. There were plenty of the latter left but the upper class, in the best sense of that term, had always been small in America and, ignoring a certain amount of bitterness left as a residue from those days when men had to take sides, there can be no doubt that America, not as a new country in the throes of war, but as a permanently going "cultural concern," lost a good deal in the exodus, even though it may be an exaggeration to compare it with the loss to France through the similar exodus of the Huguenots.

Allowing for much misunderstanding of the colonies and for misinformation sent to the British Government by Loyalists, official or other, they had been right as to one point. That was that they could not win against the might of the Empire unless, in what might become a world war, they had the help of France. Even in the midst of the struggle Washington himself admitted that. France pretty nearly did not come in, and we pretty nearly lost.

What measures were taken to unite the Americans, and how did they behave? As to the first point, John Adams once wrote, in a statement quoted time and again, that when independence was declared one-third of the people were for it, one-third against, and one-third passive and uncaring. It was all right for Franklin to declare, as it is said he did, when he signed the Declaration of Independence, that if the leaders did not hang together they would hang separately, but if the colonists were successfully to defy the British Empire every man-Jack possible of the three one-thirds mentioned, would have to be whipped into action in some way. That was a job for propaganda.

The social and economic class discontents of which we have spoken had been growing, and during the turbulent period of dispute with Britain from 1763 to the Declaration of Independence they had been steadily increasing. Such groups as the Sons of Liberty, built up first as patriotic clubs in connection with the imperial quarrel, began to have a way of turning into labor organizations. In a word, if the conservative and other leaders who prepared the way to fight Britain and who brought on the struggle, were to succeed, they had to bring all the three one-thirds together, and in order to do that they had to disseminate ideas and make promises as to what all of the discontented elements in the various colonies might expect for themselves in the post-war period.

The consequence was that propaganda was turned on full blast, not to get votes but followers, soldiers and helpers to win the war. The ordinary man had become an American but he had been largely inarticulate, and had *felt* what he wanted rather than thought it out. Now he became provided almost daily (although all the newspapers were weekly) with high-sounding arguments, a political philosophy, and promises that he would get—and was entitled to them as a human being—those things he had merely *wanted* before and often largely got. It is impossible perhaps to overestimate the influence on the then and future American of this rationalizing and verbal popularizing of everything which the factors we have mentioned from time to time—distance, freedom of the wilderness, land, and all the rest—had done to him more or less irrationally and unconsciously. All the arguments used against Britain became arguments against "slavery" and for freedom at home, in the seaboard towns, in the outlying counties of every colony, on the frontier—arguments not against property but against privilege; arguments and ringing slogans for the common man and his rights. These have rung down the generations since, and the pioneer chopping his trees to make a clearing could hear echo from his axe Jefferson's words: "All men are created equal . . . they are endowed with certain inalienable rights . . . life, liberty, and the pursuit of happiness . . ." SLAVES, SLAVES, SLAVES, Sam Adams and others had thundered, their comparatively few voices multiplied as by a loud-speaker through thousands of issues of papers, speeches, resolutions. The American had become articulate. What had been conceived in his guts had been born in his brain.

But before passing on to the end of the Revolution, the military course of which we need not here follow at all, we must touch on some other points in connection with the American, as brought out by the struggle. America, with its environment, its opportunities, and its doctrines of freedom and individualism, was a heady wine. It was both strengthening and demoralizing. Like the frontier it could make the human material on which it operated into virile upstanding men and women or into lazy, shiftless, idle wastrels. There is no escaping the fact that men in organized societies must either submit to discipline or discipline themselves. A minimum of the former and a maximum of the latter was obviously called for by the American Dream and philosophy, but it has not by any means always worked out in the right balance. In other words America has found, as God did in Eden, that the human beings He created were somehow oddly imperfect. We have spoken several times—and may again because it is of the essence of America—of what may happen when unlimited energy and ambition meet unlimited opportunity. The situation may work out for an enormous accumulation of goods, and, in the Greek sense, of *the* Good, but it may also produce some very unpleasant by-products.

When Washington wrote to Governor Trumbull of Connecticut of the trouble he was having with his troops, the Governor of that little State, which from its start had been one of the most independent, democratic and American of all, replied that it was hard "to support liberty, to exercise government, to maintain subordination, and at the same time to prevent the operation of licentious and levelling principles."

Again, when Washington took charge of the troops besieging Boston he was almost in despair. He found one of the bad fruits of democracy in the election of regimental officers by the privates. As he wrote: "I have made a pretty good slam among such officers as the Massachusetts Government abound in since I came to this camp." Many of them, he added, were "nearly the same kidney as the privates," and he could not get "officers of this stamp to exert themselves in carrying orders into execution—to curry favor with the men (by whom they were chosen and on whose smiles possibly they may think they may rely again) seems to be one of the principal objects of their attention." Here we glimpse not only Washington's difficulties with officers in such a "democratic" system but the future difficulties of the nation with its politicians.

Washington also encountered some of the by-products of individualistic exploitation of opportunity. He found everybody profiteering—the farmers, army officers, all. "Such a dearth of public spirit," he wrote in another letter, "and want of virtue, such stock-jobbing and fertility in all the low arts to obtain advantages of one kind and another . . . I never saw before, and pray God I may never be witness to again." In yet another letter he added, "Such a dirty mercenary spirit pervades the whole, that I should not be at all surprised at any disaster that may happen." Officers walked off, A.W.O.L., and took privates with them to get in crops. Washington wrote to the Governor of Rhode Island of this difficulty of rampant individualism which was to plague and hamper him through all the hard years of the war. The militia, he said, "are not to be depended on for more than a few days; as they soon get tired, grow impatient, ungovernable, and of course leave the service."

So much stress has been laid by the singers of our national story on the Minute Men rushing to fight at Lexington Green and Concord Bridge and on picturesque incidents here and there, such as the noble valor of the few who stood by Washington at Valley Forge in that winter of suffering, that Americans have been taught not only a wrong but a somewhat dangerous view of an America at war. It is the kind of thing that breeds the false confidence which led Bryan to say, more than a century later, that if America should go to war a million men would spring to arms between dawn and sunset.

We have already noted that only one-third of the passengers on the *Mayflower* were religious Pilgrims, and that the rest, who made the trouble and necessitated the drawing up of the Mayflower Compact, were a very mixed lot, largely from the streets of London, so that a "Mayflower Descendant" may have come down from a highly respectable religious refugee from Leyden or from an ordinary plain son-of-a-gun who had to be taught his place by the Leydenites. In the same way a Son or Daughter of the Revolution, whose sole claim is descent from somebody who fought in that war for a few weeks or months, may have a very worthy ancestor or may not. It is all interesting because to some extent it reveals a sort of nostalgia on the part of Americans and their instinctive feeling of a lack in their past.

It is well if, by a candid view of all the effects of what made the American, we realize that some of those effects were bad, and were to remain so in the next century. To understand the success or failure of the American Dream or of America we must understand human nature and that some of it can rise and some cannot. Democracy, if it succeeds, is the most satisfying of all forms of government, the only one which affords scope for all men to rise to their full stature and to make the most of their talents for the good of themselves and of society as a whole. On the other hand, it is the most difficult, both in peace and war. It is not for all peoples. One thing is certain, that if we do not face its difficulties, drawbacks and shortcomings, we cannot work intelligently and wholeheartedly for its success.

At long last the war was over. It had been six and a half years from Lexington and Concord to Yorktown, and eight years from the time when the Minute Men swarmed out to turn back the invading British from Boston to the date when peace was signed in Paris, and the United States of America was acknowledged by the British Empire to be a free and independent nation. They had been years of gruelling hardship. War was war. There was as yet no thoroughly organized central government in America to conduct it. The national finances, if so they could be called, were in confusion. The currency with which, in place of adequate taxation, the war had to be fought was practically worthless. Inflation had worked its horrors on all. The Continental currency bills had become a joke and a curse. Americans still use the phrase, often without realizing its origin, "not worth a Continental," just as in some neighborhoods, long ago occupied by the British, children still swear at their small friends as "You damned Hessian," in unknowing reminder of the hatred their great-grandfathers had felt for the soldiers whose services were bought from their German princeling masters and quartered with the British army here and there. The war was over. America had cut loose from the Old World. The New World was free. Yet it was in economic, social and political chaos. There was a huge surge of relief and hope, but what next? The American had demanded his right to do as he pleased, and had won it. What would he do with it?

CHAPTER XI

AMERICA BUILDS HER SHIP OF STATE

IN considering the post-war period we may note first the enormous difference between the consequences of the Peace of 1763 and that of twenty years later, 1783. The hopes raised by the first had been dashed; those raised by the second could be made good but only by the Americans themselves. There were two changes of the first magnitude. In 1763 the West had been won from the French and had become part of the Empire, of which the colonies themselves were part, but British Imperial policy took a mistaken course and the colonists found themselves barred from that "West" of imagination and actuality which they had glimpsed unconsciously but truly as making the future of America and the American. They themselves were also still subjects of the Empire. The situation at the time of the peace twenty years later was different. Not only had the most important part of the West become the domain of the freed colonies instead of being controlled from Britain, but the colonies themselves were free. If ousting the French and apparently opening the way to expansion as part of the Empire had given a tremendous fillip to the energy and ambition of the colonials, this was multiplied many-fold by finding the promised land their own and themselves free to use it as they would.

The boy had indeed become a man and left the old home to begin a gay and successful life, as he thought, on his own. As not seldom happens, however, he felt, without thinking it out very clearly, that he could somehow have the new freedom combined with the old safety and advantages. "Dad would stick by him." Well, Dad didn't, and morally, at least, there was then no reason why he should. The boy had slammed the home door in anger, and after a grand row. There were many difficulties and dangers ahead of him, but before we discuss those we may outline sketchily what he did with some of the property into which he had unexpectedly come by the help of friends.

There was, first, "the West," always a tremendous influence in the making of the American, from the first trek of Ludlow and Hooker from Massachusetts Bay to found Connecticut, all through the innumerable successive westward migrations, some of which we have mentioned, down to the "land rushes," such as in Oklahoma, well within my own lifetime, and which occurred here and there even for some twenty years after the "frontier" was officially declared closed in 1890.

From the standpoint of the American there are four important points to be mentioned as to the new lands. First there was the inrush of settlers. We have already spoken of those who had begun to pour over the mountains, and of the large land companies and the small individual pioneers. Both continued, aided by the lands granted to the ex-soldiers of the Revolution. Numerous as the pioneers had been even before 1775, they were as nothing compared with the flood which followed. Books by travellers, advertising by land companies, and, perhaps even more important, the news of what the pioneers found as handed back to the restless in the older settlements, started multitudes pouring through the Cumberland Gap and other passes. The "Ohio Country," but particularly Kentucky with its rich blue grass lands, drew tens of thousands of settlers to plant themselves on the new and free domain which had become theirs. There was no limit to the rapturous accounts given of Kentucky in particular, rising in crescendo to the celebrated peroration of a sermon some years later, that "Heaven is a Kentuck of a place!" In 1776 that section became a county of Virginia, and by 1790 there were perhaps 150,000 people living over the mountains. In one year, 1788, it is said that about 18,000 men, women and children floated down the Ohio River on rafts, and perhaps an equal number tramped or rode over the southern mountain passes.

The second point is that not only did all these people, who were fast forming a nation of their own, have the magnificent domain of the eastern half of the vast Mississippi Valley, from the mountains to the river itself, to exploit and develop, but both their geographical orientation and their psychological outlook changed. Their outlet for surplus production, and so the way to wealth, was not up the rivers they had come down, and back over the mountains, to eastern seaboard cities and ports, such as Boston, New York, Philadelphia and Charleston, but down the great Mississippi to Spanish New Orleans, and from there over the seas of the world.

What the Spaniards might do became of life-and-death importance to the new Westerners, and they became bound to the South instead of the East by the Father of Waters.

It was to be the building of the railroads, binding the East and West, in the 1850's, after such earlier links as the Cumberland Road and the Erie Canal, which were to break the West-South combination, and, at the expense of a great financial panic, save the non-slave Northwest to the Union in the critical period of the Civil War. The expansion of America was by chance to coincide with the machine age, and if American democracy owes an infinite debt to the West, the West itself owes its rapid development, and the preservation of the Union, to the machine. Had the West been permanently molded by geographical features only, notably the mountain barrier to the east and the great river draining the whole western basin southward, American history would have been different, and perhaps also, the American.

We have mentioned that Kentucky in 1776 was erected into a county of Virginia, which brings us to our third point as to the influence of the western lands. The bounds of the colonies under the old charters had been vaguely drawn, covering territory in a then unknown continent. Some of them ran from the Atlantic to the "South Sea," which turned out to be the Pacific Ocean 3000 miles away. Bounds overlapped, and some colonies had western claims, of very varying extent. Others had none at all. After independence was declared it became a burning question as to how big some of the future states might become. The claims of Virginia, for example, covered an empire. Maryland refused to sign the Articles of Confederation because she feared the possible extent and might of her neighbor when they should both be independent states. Finally, by a happy and unusual display of cooperation and self-abnegation, it came about in 1781 and the next year that Massachusetts, Connecticut, New York, and in part Virginia, ceded their western claims to the Confederation, so that when the war was finally won, the West had almost ceased to be a bone of contention and had become the property of the *United* and not the *several* States. Before long the southern part of the West also passed into the possession and control of the Confederation.

This gave to the West a peculiarly national character. The similar cultural conditions prevailing along almost all the old frontier had served as a sort of selvedge edge, as I have called it, to bind the old colonies together. So, even more, did this contribution of the several colonies or states to the Union of a territory, as large as or larger than the old colonies combined, to be held as a common possession. There were no longer merely thirteen colonies but a nation made up of them and, in addition, of a vast empire which they all owned together.

As such the West was truly national and American in a new sense. The emigrants moving over the mountains would no longer be building up new counties to add to the strength, population and prestige of this or that state, but would be building up *new* states. A settler who engaged in the grand westward movement, whether he started from New England, Virginia, South Carolina or elsewhere, would not feel he was losing his identity as a citizen of the state from which he had started. He became something different, bigger and more significant. He became a Westerner, a "man of the Western Waters," as it was called—an *American*. On the seaboard, a man like Patrick Henry might declaim that he was not a Virginian but an American, yet still in the old bounds the old local traditions and jealousies clung to most of them. As of old the sundering ocean had been a powerful factor in making the American something different from the man of the Old World, so now again, a new barrier crossed, the Appalachian range of mountains, was again emphasizing the American with heavy underscorings of the qualities and character so many of them had already acquired. If the Atlantic seaboard had been no place for the Dukes or "belted Earls" or any others of the highly placed and successful in the old home, so neither was the West any place for the rich and comfortable upper-middle class which had "got theirs" in the counting-rooms, plantations and handsome Georgian mansions of the East.

Once more the frontier was at work, a work which has been so well recognized by western historians, such as the late Professor Turner, but which now and then seems wholly incomprehensible to an occasional scholar who thinks the "frontier" is really not closed because there are still abandoned farms in New England on which a city man can go and raise chickens, or try to. Raising chickens, with electric light, taxes, telephones, and all the rest is one thing. Fighting your way against hardships and savages across an empty and unknown continent, building an empire and knowing yourself to be an empire builder with every possibility open to you, is another. It is very different from just going out early in the morning in a well-policed community with a box of corn and calling "cluck, cluck, cluck." If the fact that there are such or such a number of acres of abandoned land in New England indicates to some people that the geographical frontier is still open, this merely shows what the comforts and gadgets of today have done to them and how incapable they are of feeling the thrill of building a nation out of a wilderness and becoming a leader in a new society.

Those were the thrills which came to the Westerners, and which made the vast Mississippi Valley the cradle of a new democracy. In that cradle a new type of American was to kick lustily for the next few decades, kick against the hampering

Spaniards at New Orleans, the East which would not help, and against everything else in the way of developing the new land as the settlers wished. He was the old American we have been watching grow, only more so. He was so different from the man who today may find an outlet for all his vigor, energy, adventurous spirit and ambition in running an abandoned New England farm—admirable in many ways as such a person may be—as to make it almost incredible that even an occasional historian cannot appreciate the difference.

There was a fourth point about the western lands which had been wrested from the Empire and had become American and national. The states had, almost by a miracle, considering their former inability to unite on anything, given their western claims to the new nation. What would be done with them? The Continental Congress and the Confederation, always weak, were fast approaching the *rigor mortis.* Could any statesmanlike settlement of the government and fate of, say, a quarter of the present United States, without government, be reached? In dealing with peoples capable of self-government, the British race has shown itself incomparably the master of all, and our political, even if not our racial, inheritance is still overwhelmingly British—our system of law, our institutions and ways of looking at things. The mold early set was the British mold. America has now many times had to face political problems which were new and of extreme difficulty, but it should be an encouragement to us today, as we are facing still more difficult ones, that we have always solved them in the past to the extent at least of workable plans.

John Doe and Richard Roe have always been of immense importance in this New World, but there have also been leaders, and among the early statesmen none had a greater influence on the West and on America than the liberal-minded aristocrat and democrat, Thomas Jefferson of Virginia, one of the most hated men in the New England of his day. We need not enter into the historical details of the two Ordinances, those of 1785 and 1787, passed by the dying Continental Congress and for which Jefferson was mainly responsible. The earlier one provided for a survey of the entire Northwest, and its division into townships six miles square, made up of sections (the term and the size continue today) of 640 acres each, one section in each town being reserved for a school fund and four for the Federal Government. Land was to be sold to settlers at a dollar an acre, but this proved too high a figure. Moreover large speculative companies, like the Ohio, which bought 1,500,000 acres, competed with settlers by getting a discount on such wholesale purchases. For more than a century there was to be free or fairly cheap land to be had by any one. What is of more importance for us at the moment is the revised Ordinance of 1787.

This embodied a genuinely American contribution to the science of government, and was a combination of British ideas of self-government with the peculiar conditions of American expansion. This expansion, wholly unlike that of the Empire, was to be for a century and a quarter over a contiguous continental area instead of over far-separated areas in all parts of the globe. The second Ordinance provided that the Northwest should be divided into districts administered by Congress but that when the free male inhabitants over twenty years of age numbered over 5000 in any one district they could elect an Assembly of their own choosing and send a delegate, without vote, to Congress. The Governor was to be appointed by the Federal Congress, and the upper house of the legislature was also to be appointed by Congress but only from a list of names sent in by the lower. This in its set-up was much like the old form of a Royal Colony but there was a tremendously important addition to the old form, which was to change the structure from that of a colonial empire into a permanent federal union of equal states, so far, at least, as the contiguous continental area was concerned.

The districts, with their form of colonial governments, were not to be colonies of the Federal Union, but by a simple plan, the simplicity of which, however, was evidence of political genius, the colonial districts, as we may call them, would in time become part of the nation. It was provided that the whole of the Northwest Territory should eventually be divided into not less than three or more than five states, and when any one of these attained to a population of 60,000, it was to be admitted to the Union "on an equal footing with the original States in all respects whatever," except that slavery was forever forbidden.

The plan worked remarkably well. In its contiguous continental area, the United States has never had *colonies.* As it has from time to time absorbed more land—by war, purchase or otherwise—there has been always an easy and orderly transition from wilderness, through the stage of sparsely populated "territories" governmentally, to that of full and mature statehood. The Northwest Ordinance provided a way for the full incorporation of new lands. The plan was so good, its terms were so simple, so just and so well understood and accepted, that as the nation extended and settlers went into newly acquired lands, they never felt that resentment so often experienced by the settler of colonial status against an overlording central government. Every settler knew that as soon as his territory had been built up to the minimum and easily attained population requirement, and had adopted a constitution in accord with American principles, his "colony-territory" would almost automatically become a state with all the rights enjoyed by even the oldest, such as Virginia or Massachusetts, and that he personally would become legally and politically as much of an American as any other citizen anywhere in the Union.

Our Westerners might be pioneers and colonists but they never were "colonials." Thus the sense of complete equality which was one of the most notable characteristics developed in America received not only no set-back by the development of our growing empire but actually a tremendous impetus from the Northwest Ordinance and all that flowed from that masterstroke of statesmanship. The sense of freedom and unlimited opportunity which were bred by the "wide open spaces" met no counter-check from any sense of political or social inferiority due to a colonial status. From the start the men of the Western Waters had all the old freedom and equality and in addition the new freedom and boundless hopes of the great valley. The Mid-westerner was in time to become the most democratic and the most American of all Americans.

The growth of the Union, from its original thirteen members along the Atlantic coast to forty-eight, covering our entire expanse across the continent to the Pacific, has come about with such ease and so little friction, that we are likely to forget our debt to the men who in their wisdom framed the two Northwest Ordinances as our basic method of state building.

The effect on the American has been profound. The inhabitants of the new lands were not to enjoy—or dislike—colonial or even Dominion status, tending towards independence in some distant future. Instead they were to be free men from the start and to share liberty and equality with the older Americans in no long time, dependent only upon their building up their own sections. We have spoken at different periods of the American becoming cocky. The development of his nation, on the basis of the Northwest Ordinances, from a small part of the continent to the immensely rich band of some 3,000,000 square miles stretching across it, and the increase in the number of the population from about 3,000,000 to the estimated total at this moment of 135,000,000 have served to give him an enormous self-confidence, and the feeling that if he has done what he has, in so expanding and absorbing peoples of all races, yet binding them into one people, free, independent and equal, why cannot others do the same? Of course, there are many reasons why not, but the feeling is that of multitudes of Americans, and it springs in large part from what we have just been describing.

The American has had enormous good luck, as, for example, the sort of country that he settled in, the political alignments in the Old World at critical periods, the coincidence of the age of invention and machinery with that of his own expansion, and so on. These have given rise perhaps to the old saying that "God looks after children, drunks and Americans." Anyway, that idea is pretty well imbued in the American. On the other hand, the American has shown a vast amount of common sense and, in the long run, dependability, on the part of the ordinary man. Also, even though the English considered him as colonial and provincial, he and his leaders showed a political sense that well outran that of the statesmen of the Old World.

We have just been speaking of how the American solved the problem of colonizing vast areas without creating a colonial status for their inhabitants but by forming a single united nation of equal citizens. The America with which he dealt, and which dealt with him, in the earlier centuries, helped him greatly because of its continental instead of scattered global character. He has not yet solved wholly satisfactorily the problem of Alaska, nor the more difficult ones of Porto Rico, Hawaii and other island possessions, though the Northwest Ordinances point the direction in one way, and the immediate acknowledgment of the independence of Cuba after the Spanish war, and the promise of independence to the Philippines, point the way in another. In both cases the basis is the American's love of freedom for himself and others.

Glancing ahead from the time of the Ordinances, we may note one or two interesting points as showing how America molded the American. Obviously a Northwest Ordinance would have been of no use for the British Empire. That needed a Statute of Westminster. In other words, the government of a contiguous continental area is one thing; and that of an Empire made up of bits, and chunks and very big hunks of land in all parts of the world, widely separated, is another. As the American advanced his domain, it was, for most of his history, by adding lands adjoining those he had already possessed and settled and brought from frontier to old settlement. The same people and institutions just kept on moving westward, a bit at a time, allowing always, of course, for the new strains coming as immigrants from Europe. It was not, however, like making a lot of separate pieces of cloth but a continued lengthening of the same strip of material on an almost endless loom.

This was quite unlike the spreading out of the English from their little island to the position of owners or governors of one-quarter of the globe. The American problem was simpler, and it was America itself which both posed it and helped to solve it. One result, among many others, has been that as old colonial boundaries and later, after the Union, state lines, became in many ways, particularly economic, more or less artificial barriers, America has been more and more tending towards centralization, whereas the British Empire has equally tended towards decentralization. Such loose links as exist today between, say, the Dominions and Britain would be unthinkable as between the Federal Government and any one of the forty-eight states. For example, the Dominions now have the right to maintain their separate diplomatic relations with other countries; to decide whether they will or will not join with the rest of the Empire in an imperial war; to make separate peace treaties; even to secede peaceably. We cannot imagine a United States with each of the forty-eight states holding that relation to the Union. It is the vast continental area we settled which has thus bound us together and formed our concept of America as a nation and of all Americans as one.

On the other hand, if American political thinking in the eighteenth century and since was largely influenced by the continental area of America, it was also influenced by the Atlantic Ocean. The wisdom of some of our far-seeing leaders, aided by the pressure of the public opinion of the pioneers over the mountains, in determining that the states carved out of the West should be admitted to the Union on equal terms with the old eastern ones, was considered extremely dangerous radicalism by many conservatives in the East, particularly in Federalist New England. It was the continental mass, plus John Doe and Richard Roe, with their axes and rifles and coonskin caps, which made the nation. As they went, step by step and mile by mile, from their old homes into the wilderness, they saw no reason why they were not as good as or better than the people they had left snugly and comfortably settled back East, and why they should not, in their new but contiguous environment, vote on the same questions and in the same way.

The colonies and the nascent United States, however, had also had another experience. They had seen themselves and their affairs regulated, or attempts made at regulating them, by a wholly different group of citizens with their Parliament across three thousand miles of ocean. The Americans had come to the conclusion that such a distance precluded the possibilities both of unbiased and disinterested governance from England or of any satisfactory system of American representation, which would always be an ineffective small minority, in the Parliament in Whitehall. Ordinary Americans, or propagandists writing as such, sent letters to the *Boston Gazette* asking "Do your honors really believe that North-America was created for the sole emolument of your very respectable dinnerizing corporations? . . . Have they or any other highborn British mechanic, an indefeazible right to the agonies, toils, and bloody sweat of the inhabitants of this land and the profits and produce of all their labors?"

This was the language of the street and tavern but thinkers in provincial America were also giving sound advice, about a hundred and fifty years ahead of British thought. For example, in two quotations which I have used before, a writer in the same *Boston Gazette,* wrote: "The true plan of government which reason and the experience of nations point out for the British Empire is to let the several parliaments in Britain and America be (as they naturally are) free and independent of each other. . . . And as the King is the center of union . . . the various parts of the great body politic will be united in him; He will be the spring and soul of the union, to guide and regulate the grand political machine." Another writer (or perhaps the same!) in the *New Hampshire Gazette* elaborated on the theme. He accepted the idea of separate parliaments with one King head of all, and wrote: "The government thus united in one Sovereign, though divided into distant Parliaments, will be actuated by one Soul. It will have all the advantages of a powerful Republic, and an extensive Monarchy. . . . If the supreme Legislature is considered as only in the Majesty of the King as the common Head of all his Parliaments, and exercising his authority with their [several] consents, while no one of them encroaches upon the rights of the rest, harmony will reign through the whole Empire; every part will enjoy freedom and happiness; it may be extended farther and farther to the utmost ends of the earth, and yet continue firmly compacted until all the kingdoms of the World shall be dissolved." It is quite probable that both the passages quoted were from the pen of Joseph Hawley of Massachusetts, but such plans presaging the future British Commonwealth of Nations were being formulated about 1764 not only by him but also by Benjamin Franklin of Pennsylvania (then in London), and by Richard Bland of Virginia.

In the foregoing paragraphs we get some glimpses of what has made the American, in addition to all which we have noted before. The quotations regarding imperial organization might have been written into the Statute of Westminster passed in 1931 instead of a possible one of 1776. What I here point to is that the American of the eighteenth century was successively faced with two different problems, namely, how to build a nation out of people gradually expanding over an immense contiguous territory, and how to build one out of a people scattering over all parts of the globe. He solved them both. The Northwest Ordinances and their results are proof of the solution of the first problem, and the present organization of the British Commonwealth of Nations is proof of the solution of the other. In a word, the Americans of that day may have been colonials, provincial frontiersmen, "buckskins," and all the rest, but somehow as a whole they had as good political sense as any people in history. Perhaps Lincoln, in his estimate of the common people, was right.

But America has not been made wholly of the common people, though they have helped and guided and balanced to an extent that the ultra-conservatives have not yet recognized. At great crises we need leaders, but we also need a sane commonalty, and the special interest of this chapter is in showing the balance between the two.

Before we go on, however, to the solution of another great political problem we may note one more point as to what we have just been saying. If the Americans of the period we are considering were, as we say, a hundred and fifty years ahead of the British in their views as to how the problems of an ocean empire should be met and solved, it was not necessarily because they were wiser, more learned or even more generous and liberty-loving than the people and leaders in England. Many over there heartily agreed with Pitt when he exclaimed: "I rejoice that the Americans have resisted." What made the difference in imperial thinking was the Atlantic Ocean. The British on their island were at the center of a growing colonial empire. They saw things from one standpoint. The colonials were on the periphery. They saw the same problems from another standpoint. British and Americans develop their "ideas" more from experience than from any logical process of abstract reasoning, and as the experiences had been different in this case so the progress of ideas also was different.

So here was another instance of how the ocean was to play its continuing rôle in making the American. Just to illuminate the point, it is interesting to glance ahead. The expanse of ocean and the expanse of land in the west have been two of the greatest geographical factors in molding the thought as well as the character of the American. After the second war with Britain we turned our eyes away from the Old World and busied ourselves in developing the West. For about a century the ocean was looked upon as a barrier against any attack from Europe, and so tended towards emphasizing that desire for isolation, and belief in its possibility, which has always been false yet powerful. But then the ocean, for far-seeing Americans, began to be better understood and to influence us in another direction. The ocean might be a barrier but it also might be a highway leading to our doors, a highway which would have to be defended by ourselves unless it were guarded by a friendly nation. That nation was the British Empire, which held the two gates through which European attack might come—the English Channel and the Strait of Gibraltar. Jefferson almost alone among early American statesmen realized this, but it was largely lost to sight until the twentieth century with its two World Wars. Thus what had been a factor in developing isolationist sentiment has now become a powerful one leading to the working together again of the English-speaking peoples in a common effort of self-defense against the greatest menace to civilization since the earlier hordes of barbarians broke the defenses of the Roman Empire. Just as the sea itself ebbs and flows, so likewise has its influence on the American.

To return again to our domestic political problems after our independence was acknowledged in 1783, we note that at the very time when the Continental Congress, about to abdicate its power and functions, passed the Ordinance of 1787, it had also arranged for a convention which was to draw up a new Constitution for the government of the Union as a whole.

The need as it had developed is interesting as showing again how, as I have said before, among the English-speaking peoples, great constitutional changes usually come about from trying to meet a practical situation in a practical and limited way instead of from wanting to make the world over on a basis of abstract theory. The American Constitution, now the oldest written one in the world, was not the result of revolutionary or abstract logic on the part of a few, but was an effort to solve practical problems by very practical, if also very able, men who understood their country and their time.

Among the conditions which led after several years to the great Convention of 1787 in Philadelphia we must differentiate between those which seemed to demand calling the Convention in Annapolis in 1786 and those which changed that trade meeting, so to describe it, into the great Constitutional Convention of the following year.

We have had frequent occasion to note the jealousies and inability to unite on common policies shown by all of the original thirteen colonies, now become states. These attitudes continued after independence had been won, and although we are not interested here in all the historical details of what John Fiske called *The Critical Period of American History,* what is pertinent to our main theme is what problems the particular American conditions posed to the American, how he solved them, and what influence his solutions had on his later development.

If the link of the British Crown and the legislative claims of Parliament had been weak as factors uniting the colonies into larger consolidated political units, the Continental Congress had been almost equally so. The difficulties with taxation, the currency, enlistment, pay and commissariat of the army all through the war, had demonstrated the weakness with altogether too much clarity to men in responsible positions, such as Washington. The war won, even the slight cohesion and willingness to work together and sacrifice together, which a common struggle for a common end tends to engender for a time, more or less evaporated.

We have come in the century and more following to know much too well the evils which modern nationalism breeds. The America of the 1780's was suffering from the same evils, as expressed in "statism." Among these were trade tariffs and the problems of how to conduct trade between small and adjoining states which were really dependent on each other for their prosperity. New York, for example, had to do business with her neighbors of New Jersey and Connecticut, but all three states claimed the right to pass tariff and other laws governing trade in the waters of Long Island Sound and New York Harbor. In a similar way Virginia and Maryland had been squabbling over trade relations across their boundaries and in the waters of Chesapeake Bay.

It was this latter dispute, among many, which finally led to the calling of a Convention at Annapolis in 1786 to devise methods of settling such matters. Representatives from only five states attended, and it is unlikely that any more, or as many, might have been present if the stated purpose had been broadened to that of a complete change in the whole form of Union and Government. However, the preliminary step had been taken, and whether in accordance with prevision and plans or not, some of the most prominent men attending, such as Washington, James Madison, Alexander Hamilton and others, suggested that another Convention be held, at the invitation of Congress, the following year, to improve the form of national government. This proposal went through all the necessary stages and the great Constitutional Convention in Philadelphia was the result.

We must now go back a few years to see why the leaders and also many of the John Does and Richard Roes should have agreed that such a step was called for. It was one of the most momentous steps in the history of the modern world.

There were two general causes operating on all sorts of people. One stemmed from the war and the situation of America in conducting the negotiations for peace. The Confederacy and the Continental Congress had proved weak reeds on which a buoyant and ambitious nation could lean. Washington, trying to keep an army together, an army which out of a population of some three millions never numbered more than twenty-five thousand at any one time; trying also to keep it paid, willing to fight and unwilling to mutiny, knew the story. Other leaders, trying to keep national finances afloat and foreign loans negotiated and paid, knew the story. The common soldier to a great extent knew the story.

Then victory, with the help of the French, was won. Next came the usual post-war economic cycle. This always runs in four ups-and-downs, regardless apparently of changing conditions. At the end of the Revolution there was as yet no machine age; there was no modern credit system or instalment buying;

there were no modern inventions; yet the four ups-and-downs, allowing for a small difference in the length of each, formed the same pattern as in the post-war world of 1919–29. This is in large part because the cycle, although it is called economic, is really psychological.

During a war, people have been denied many things they have been accustomed to think of as necessities, even though they may really have been luxuries. With the coming of peace, every one thinks all will be normal again. With the signing of the Treaty of Paris there was no Warren Harding to coin the atrocious word "normalcy," but people were thinking in that term though they did not use it. During the war many people of all sorts had made money. Farmers had got high prices for crops; privateers and others had made or lost fortunes; army contracts had yielded fat returns; many had gone into debt, farmers among them as usual; there were new rich, ready to spend, as well as new poor and a new crop of debtors; the same old story.

So, as always, when peace came, merchants stocked up and people bought, for a while. The "while" lasted about two years after the signing of peace in Paris in 1783, as it did after the signing of another peace there in 1919. But war profits are largely ephemeral, and war always destroys an immense amount of real capital. A readjustment is always called for. There is a primary depression. After that, with every one trying to scramble back, there is a period of speculation, and then the real crash. In our first war, we got it in 1791; in our second, mentioned above, in 1929.

We had had, as I have said, two years of wild spending after 1783. Then came the primary depression, but it was extremely severe in hitting the men who had been particularly notable in fighting the war of the Revolution in the beginning, the farmers and others in New England and especially in Massachusetts. Farms were seized for debt—mortgages or taxes—and could not be sold for enough to satisfy creditors. A very serious uprising, known as Shays's Rebellion, because led by a Daniel Shays who had been a captain in the Revolutionary army, broke out and courts were closed by the populace in arms. The state, which was considered to be one of the most conservative in the new Union, was in turmoil. The state government proved itself utterly incompetent to cope with the situation, and even the former agitator Sam Adams, who had become a hard-shell reactionary, denied that the people had the right even to voice their grievances!

The episode of Shays's Rebellion had two effects which were of great importance in the formation of the American. It brought leaders like Washington to the belief that if America were to survive as a Union and as a strong nation, there would have to be a stronger government than the old and dying Confederation, and so led to the transformation of the trade conference at Annapolis into a Constitutional Convention in Philadelphia, and to the drawing up of the American Constitution under which America has lived ever since. But if it led the leaders to this conclusion, it and other discontents of the poorer classes led also to the inclusion of clauses in that Constitution which might not otherwise have appeared in it. Again we have the leaders among the wealthy and cultivated united with John Doe and Richard Roe in making America and the American.

For our present purpose we need not detail the story of how the Constitution was drawn up and adopted, nor analyze too closely its phrases. There are certain broad aspects, however, which are pertinent to our main theme.

First of all we may speak, perhaps, of why it is "written," for there is a good deal of misunderstanding about that. It is frequently said, for example, that the American Constitution is written, whereas the British is unwritten. This statement is only a half truth. The "Constitutions" of the United States and Britain are different in important respects, but "written" and "unwritten" is only a matter of degree. We need merely note that any constitution made as the foundation of a new government, and especially one which combines formerly independent states, *must* be in writing. A single people governing themselves down the centuries in one territory may have a constitution "broadening down from precedent to precedent" but if others are brought in, there must be some agreement which is clearly understood and beyond question of misunderstanding.

For example, the Act of Union, stating the terms on which the kingdoms of England and Scotland were finally united had to be put in writing and legal form in 1707 and is most certainly part of the British constitution. The only common tie between the original thirteen colonies was the link to the British Crown, and when that was broken, and each colony became independent, if they were to unite to form a nation, a written constitution was inexorably called for. There just was not any "precedent to precedent" to bind them together as a united nation. It is surely obvious that if the nations of Europe may ever unite—should it prove possible or even desirable—in a "United States of Europe," there would have to be some written document to form the basis of union and to which they could all refer in case of dispute about the terms on which they had combined. The League of Nations *had* to have a written "Covenant." The question is not whether a written or unwritten constitution is more desirable but what conditions demand at the time when a constitution is adopted. The thirteen separate states of America uniting in one nation could have had nothing but a written constitution.

We may add that the British constitution is also largely written, because of similar necessities from time to time. We have spoken of the Act of Union, but there are also the Statute of Westminster and others, which, although nominally Acts of Parliament, could hardly be changed without splitting the Empire. England has given her word in writing that they will not be changed. So much for that. We had to start with a written constitution but that does not mean that it was rigid. Later, we shall speak of the various ways in which it might be and has been changed.

What interests us here is how all these varying Americans, jealous of and often heartily disliking each other—the New Englanders, New Yorkers, Virginians and others—got together and formed any constitution at all, and what they put in it, and why.

First, we may note that the process was democratic, and I say that in spite of much which others have said. The Constitution was adopted only after two debates. One was in the secret meetings of the leaders of America in Independence Hall in Philadelphia, and the other was in every newspaper and tavern and home throughout the land. The first debate produced a Constitution but the other changed it materially. In other words, not only the leaders but Doe and Roe also had their say. Here we come to the economic interpretation of it, as put forward by certain authors, more notably about a generation ago when such interpretation of all history had become a fad among certain historians.

We had been familiar with the theory for long in its earlier Marxian form but for some reason it suddenly took hold in America, and its influence is still widespread. For example, a while ago I received in my "fan mail" a letter, which was merely a sample of others, from a student in one of the largest high schools in New York. He asked how I could write as I did about the Constitution when it was well known, as his teacher told him, that it was made only by the rich of that day for their own benefit? A brief consideration of the economic theory of historic determinism as applied to the Constitution may do something to illuminate the problem of the American—then and perhaps now.

The theory itself appears to me not only wholly untenable but extremely pernicious. It is untenable because, after all, history is the story of how human beings have acted, and it would seem impossible for any one who sees life steadily and sees it whole to believe that throughout a long life a man or woman acts only from economic motivations. Did Washington, for example, serve at Valley Forge and through some eight years of war and responsibility, refusing all pay, just from an economic motive? Or was that all which motivated Lincoln when praying and toiling for the preservation of the Union? Or a Father Damien when devoting his life to the lepers on a lonely island? To those who have read a carefully tabulated list of the members of the Constitutional Convention with the sort and amount of property they owned, I suggest that they also glance at a similar though far shorter list made by Roscoe Pound in his *Formative Era of American Law.*

Dean Pound's own comment, published in 1938, would be worth quoting with regard to human nature in general but is particularly so with regard to human nature in America, where the opportunities for variation have been so great. "Each of these men," he writes, speaking of three great judges who helped to lay the foundations of our law, "long dominated the highest court of an important state, from which many newer states took their legal traditions and upon whose decisions these newer states built their course of decision. The differences in their parentage, bringing up, social environment, political affiliations, and economic surroundings should, according to the psychological and economic determinists of today, have determined their judicial action decisively and so have led to three different judicial traditions. Yet they cooperated in making a consistent body of law on the basis of the tradition they had been taught in the offices of lawyers whose training (through office apprenticeship) ran back to barristers trained in the Inns of Court." In the pages following, he continues to demolish the theory of economic determinism for law as well as for history.

All this is important not only for the proper teaching of American history today but for the understanding of the American in the period we are more particularly discussing in this chapter. We have already spoken from time to time of the great variety of motives which induced immigrants to come to the New World and which were fostered in them likewise by the conditions of American life. They ran the entire gamut of human nature—sex, food, money, wages, land—all the economic motives in their widest range—religion, ambition, the desire to rise and shine, love of adventure—in fact every possible motive. We had them all in 1787 as we have had them before and ever since, and each individual has had them in varying proportions.

The population of any nation at a given moment is made up of all sorts of people. There are the young and old, the prosperous and unprosperous, the energetic and the shiftless, the lucky and the unlucky, the radicals and the conservatives, the leaders and the led. All these types cross one another, in spite of justified generalizations. Thus, the old are usually conservative and the young radical; many people similarly classify the rich and the poor, but this by no means holds good. We know of old men, such as the late Justice Holmes who was a liberal at over ninety, and young men who are extreme reactionary Tories; many of the labor class are excessively conservative, and we know of multimillionaires who are "parlor pinks," Socialists and Communists.

Admitting much truth in the generalizations, however, what was the situation when Americans were faced with the task of devising a form of government? It was feared that no plan would be acceptable to all the states and classes, and that anarchy might ensue. As Washington, perhaps the most silent chairman of a great Convention in all history, said in the only speech he made: "It is probable that no plan we propose will be adopted. Perhaps another dreadful conflict is to be sustained. If, to please the people, we offer what we ourselves disapprove, how can we afterward defend our work? Let us raise a standard to which the wise and the honest can repair; the event is in the hand of God."

Who were "we" and "the people"? "We," naturally, were the members of the Convention and other leaders who were in touch with them, and "the people" were those who were being represented and who would have to decide on and accept or reject the work of the Convention. Let us consider the members of the latter first. Naturally each state—except Rhode Island, which declined to send delegates, and Vermont, which had not yet joined the Union—tried to send distinguished men to represent them, which meant in those days, perhaps any day, that they would be men who had achieved a leading position by means of wealth, learning, culture, sound judgment, or by other means. They were distinctly not demagogues, but neither were they old and rich, "crusted port."

Generalizations as to the relation of age to liberalism or radicalism are impossible, but people often think in general terms and are easily misled by words. Regarding these two familiar errors we may point out that the Supreme Court was never composed of "Nine Old Men" and that John Marshall, the particular *bête noir* of radicals today, was barely forty-five when he began his epoch-making career as Chief Justice. We may also note that of the fifty-five delegates who actually attended the meetings of the Constitutional Convention and drew up the Constitution which was submitted to the states, over ten per cent were under thirty-one and only about one-fifth were over fifty-four, including Washington and the aged Franklin. Thirty-three were lawyers; eight were in business; six were planters; three were physicians; and about one-half of the total were college graduates.

They were, almost all of them, men of learning, wisdom and substance. To an amazing extent they were able to take all history for their guide and knew why societies had failed and crumbled in the past. They also knew America and believed in its future, but on the whole they were conservative. There were various reasons why they should be. For one thing, the war had been won. The *destructive* work was considered to be past and the *constructive* had to begin. The mood and tenor of thought of men who are engaged in building are different from those of men bent primarily on destroying. The extreme radicals had largely disappeared from the center of the stage. The fiery Patrick Henry, though asked, declined to participate in building a new ship of state to replace the one which he had so effectively helped to scuttle. Sam Adams had become a dull reactionary instead of the arch agitator. In fact it was no time for the rabble-rouser but rather for the sane conservative-liberal, if we may so designate the men who drew up the Constitution. It is enough to say that of the fifty-five present, eight had risked their necks and all their property by signing the Declaration of Independence; eight had taken part in forming the revolutionary constitutions of their several states; seven had been governors of the states in rebellion; and twenty-one, almost one-half, had fought in the Continental army. Evidently these were no counter-revolutionists.

They were sane men trying to form a stable nation out of thirteen almost warring states, at a time when such a nation would of necessity be weak, when all the lessons of history taught that complete democracies always had failed, and when Americans themselves had been indulging in all sorts of mob violence in the name of liberty. Shays's Rebellion had been the culminating incident of a long train of events which had frightened all sober and honest men. The seamy side of the American Revolution was long concealed by patriotic historians of the Bancroft school but the men who sweltered through that hot summer in Philadelphia in 1787 had first-hand knowledge of what had been going on—the controlled and sometimes uncontrolled mobs who burned and looted homes at the nod of their leaders; the tarrings and featherings and ridings on rails, of those whom they had grudges against; the confiscations of estates on false charges; and all the rest. Altogether too many Americans had acquired property for a song or nothing by bringing charges of disloyalty against neighbors whose bit of land they coveted. This is a chapter of history far too little known, but it was well known to those who found themselves responsible for forming some sort of stable and safe government for the new-born but obstreperous nation.

The men who framed the Constitution knew all this. They believed in freedom; in the future of America; but they also knew the conditions then prevailing. They believed that the rights of property were human rights, not for themselves alone but for all others. It must be recalled that at that time ninety per cent of all Americans were engaged in agriculture, and that property was obtainable by all who were energetic, ambitious and hardworking except the Negro slaves. In protecting property they felt that they were protecting the rights and opportunities of all Americans. Property in America was owned by all classes. There was no attempt in the Constitution to protect the property of one class as against another or to expropriate the property of any one class, as in the French Revolution.

We must draw a distinct line, now often overlooked, between *privilege* and *property*. The rich may have wanted special privilege while the poor abhorred it; but poor as well as rich wanted property; and no class considered that earned property became changed from a thing called a property right to a thing called a human right by the simple thimble game of taking some of it from a man who was a little richer and giving it to a man who was a little poorer. If there is any one idea which every American immigrant, from Jamestown and Plymouth Rock, down to Ellis Island and other ports of entry, entertained, and which was later borne in on him by all his American experiences and opportunities, it is that of the right to make and keep property so long as he does it honestly and does not harm others in the process. He wants equality also. Yes, but equality of opportunity, which is American; not equality of property, which is about as un-American as any idea or motive could be. Had equality, or even virtual equality in that regard, been required from the start, there would simply have been no America or American as we understand them.

The framers of the Constitution had before them, however, the lesson of all history as to the course of events in a pure democracy, and they also recalled, not as long-past events read in their classics but as personal experiences, what had been going on in almost every neighborhood in America in the preceding fifteen or twenty years.

On the other hand, all the conditions of American life for a century and three-quarters had emphasized the tendency towards democracy. This had been brought to a mental and verbal focus by the propaganda of the war and of the pre-war years of agitation. Thus, the Constitution, as drawn up by the Convention, did not wholly measure up to the demands of the people. The leaders had done their best, and then Doe and Roe took a hand in the discussion as to whether or not the document as prepared should be approved. The civil war between the two branches of the English-speaking peoples, and the Revolution, which were two different things, had to a considerable extent upset the balance between conservative and radical, as war upsets the normal ratio between the sexes. The sixty to a hundred thousand Tory émigrés (according to different estimates), who had left America, had all been what we would call conservatives, and it must be remembered that they were of all classes from wealthy down to laborers. It had been another case of cutting across the lines of too easy generalizations. But those who had emigrated formed an appreciable proportion of the total population, and having all been conservatives, they added another burden of responsibility to those conservatives—or what you will—who were left to start the new nation on its way.

The members of the Convention had done a remarkable job. How remarkable is evidenced by the fact that the Constitution which, in the main, they drew up is still, after a hundred and fifty-six years, the basis of government of the greatest democracy the world has ever known, directing the lives of 135,000,000 citizens living and working together in harmony and peace. It could not have had that record had it been motivated solely by the selfish property interests of a few in an economic world as different from ours almost as was the Roman Empire or early Greece. There was evidently wisdom in it somewhere. We shall speak presently of the changes in it, changes which were provided for by the men who drew it up, and of its "rigidity," which is a tradition insisted upon by some as much as the other tradition that it was made by the rich for the rich.

However, Doe and Roe improved it.

First let us speak of the Constitution as it was finally framed in the Convention and submitted to the states for ratification. We need mention only a few points for our present theme which is "the American," and not narrative American history. The Anglo-Saxon ability to compromise rather than to fight to a finish appears all through the work of the Convention. The Constitution framed by its members is full of compromises. To mention only a few, there was the great compromise, as it has been called, to settle the difficulty of big versus small states, by which each state had the same representation in the Senate but representation in accordance with population in the House. There were the compromises between the slave and free states. There was what may be considered the compromise between a monarchy and a democracy in the system of representative government as set up. There was the compromise between a confederation and a consolidation of states in the new idea proposed and accepted that citizens should be such in a dual capacity: citizens first of a state but in other respects citizens of the Union and directly under the control of the Federal government. As a result of long and varied experiences of the dangers to be apprehended from the executive power, the legislatures and the courts, there was what amounted to the compromise of the system of checks and balances.

Suffice it to say that, as far as the American was concerned, with the problem of bringing order out of chaos he proved himself at long last able to rise to full stature and forget his local jealousies, to compromise time after time in order to try to devise a workable union which would make a nation. That is what the leaders did, and we must mention one point more. The Constitution, for the reasons given, had perforce to be a written one, but it was not intended that it should be rigid and unchangeable, so methods of alteration or amendment were also provided for. These, due partly to the terms of the written Constitution itself, and partly to the political genius of the people and *their* ability to compromise, were to make the instrument far more flexible than the framers would perhaps have desired or than many writers today would have us believe. In fact, the two most pernicious errors taught about the Constitution in the past decade or so have been that it was drawn up only for the rich and that it is antiquated and almost impossible to change. Each statement is as false and misleading as the other.

And now we must turn for a moment to the part of the people in forming our basic law. A post-war period always tends to be one of radicalism and innovation, both in ideas and manners. Also, as we have noted, there had been a heavy draining-off of the more conservative elements not only of the richer class but of *all* classes, due to emigration. "Leader" is a somewhat vague and often misused term. We think of leaders as those who are prominent in the public eye, but any man may be a leader. One may have a state or national reputation and another may not have either and yet be a leader in his neighborhood or working group. I have in mind at the moment, for example, a man whose name is probably unknown to many of the rich and prosperous in the wealthy and extensive New England town, still run by the old town-meeting system, in which he lives, but who can always count on five hundred votes on a question which he tells his followers is important. Aside from the more violent Tories who had emigrated, and whose absence helped America to become America, there were lacking, after the war was over, many of just ordinary conservative people in all colonies and of all ranks. In addition, the propaganda employed during the years of contention and actual war had been of such a sort as to emphasize enormously the tendencies towards democracy, individualism, the desire on the part of the ordinary man for freedom from governmental, or indeed any, control and yet for a voice in government, which we have already noted as fostered by all the conditions in America. All the above factors helped to form the background against which any sound and lasting form of government had to be devised and approved.

In September 1787 the members of the Convention set their signatures to the document they had drawn up, with no more than a faint hope that it might prove acceptable. Then the public debate began. The Constitution was not to be approved by direct individual vote of the people, and it must be recalled that at that time the franchise was a limited and not a manhood one. The proposals were to be passed on by conventions in the several states, chosen as representative of the citizens at large. The debate, however, was general. Articles and letters in the news sheets; conversations over fences by neighbors or talks in taverns by cronies; pamphlets, speeches; all the means of expressing public opinion which had been employed in the war propaganda, were brought to the fore. The most important articles printed during the discussion were made into a book, *The Federalist*, one of America's best contributions to the theory of government. It may be noted that the authors, Hamilton, Madison and Jay, were, respectively, thirty-one, thirty-eight and thirty-two years of age. Evidently the Constitution was not the product only of the old, rich and reactionary!

It is probable, however, that under the conditions of the time it might well not have been accepted by a full manhood suffrage vote of all the people. Like the Constitution itself, the endorsement of it was a compromise. Most of the ordinary men of the laboring classes of the old settlements or the pioneers on the frontiers would never have been able to draw up the document itself with the breadth of historical and political knowledge of the leaders who had sat in the Philadelphia Convention, but, on the other hand, if they could not make a Constitution, they could analyze one. From their strongly voiced criticisms came the Bill of Rights in the form of the first ten Amendments, which are generally considered an integral part of the original instrument.

That instrument had been adopted by many of the state conventions by only narrow margins of votes, such as nineteen in Massachusetts and three in New York. Even so, it would not have been accepted unless it had been understood that the amendments proposed by the people would be voted and adopted, as they were in December 1791. They have come to be considered one of the most important parts of the entire Constitution, including as they do the clauses guaranteeing freedom of religion, of the press and of speech; the right of the people to assemble peaceably and to petition the government for a redress of grievances; security of citizens as to their homes, persons, papers and effects against unreasonable searches and seizures; the right to a speedy and impartial trial; and all the rest of these ten Amendments, which should be known by heart by every American. Many improvements could be made in some of the provisions of the main body of the Constitution, such as the method of electing Congressmen as contrasted with the method of electing members of Parliament, but there can be no better Bill of Rights. That was the contribution made by John Doe and Richard Roe.

Allowing for the disturbed conditions of the time and for what we may call the ultra-radical mood of the moment, even if the Constitution might not have been adopted by a nationwide vote of manhood suffrage, it was, happily, accepted peaceably by all the people. The disgruntled and dissatisfied—and there must have been many—did not form revolutionary groups or break into armed revolt. They bowed to the decision of the majority, which had been growing into a fundamental American dogma, never to be forcibly resisted on a large scale save in the Civil War. With that one exception, it has been, ever since the Revolution, one of the most notable characteristics of Americans to fight their political battles fiercely, but to accept the decision and carry on as friends the day after, whether the decision has gone in their favor or against them. This is something for both our own people and foreigners to realize. It had been left for Doe and Roe to write into the

Constitution freedom of speech and of the press, and they have abided by it loyally and in the spirit in which it was intended.

Other points may be suggested, as indicating the nature of the American. One was his insistence on placing a fundamental law above the passing whims or wishes of the electorate. No other democracy in history has done that. In view of rapidly changing conditions, of the varied racial groups in our melting pot, of the rise of the masses, with their mass emotions, it was one of the wisest things any people ever did. Another point is that most of the provisions of the fundamental law were based on experience and were not the result of abstract thinking. It is true that there were some new ideas, such as the representation compromise arrived at to allay the fears of both the big and little states, or the dual citizenship—state and Federal—of all citizens. For the most part, however, the whole Constitution was made up of what the colonists had already become familiar with in the workings of their local colonial governments, their charters, and their relations with the central government in England. The Supreme Court, for example, was no innovation. For generations colonial laws had been passed on by the Privy Council to determine whether they were or were not in accord with the higher law of Britain and the terms of the charters. Incidentally it may be noted that in this the Americans merely led the way, and that in the dominions of the British Commonwealth today there are Supreme Courts with functions similar to our own.

The fact that the framers of the Constitution relied to such a great extent wherever possible on the known and tried forms of government accounts largely for the fact that we have today the Congressional instead of the Parliamentary form. At the time we split off from the Empire the present form of cabinet government in Britain, and as adopted by such dominions as Canada, which drew up their constitutions long after the British system had taken its present shape, had not come into being. Neither the British nor we foresaw its growth, which came about slowly and naturally in England by the usual method of meeting crises with practical solutions in each case. We could hardly have been expected to suddenly invent it in Philadelphia, or rather some similar system in which a more or less non-political president would have had to be substituted for a hereditary monarch, without the glamour and long historical tradition of the latter. Undoubtedly the present British system has many advantages over ours in flexibility, quick responsiveness to the public will, and other ways. Those, however, who demand a sudden and complete change in our own way should remember that a people and a government have to be adjusted to one another. A political system is not like a suit of clothes which we take off or put on at will. It is rather like our skin, which is part of us. When we were forced to adopt a Constitution, after severing ourselves from the old relations with the Empire, we saved as much of the old ways as we could, and in a century and a half we have grown into new ways.

Possibly the Constitution will have to be altered in many points, as it has been in the past, but those who would have us change it all suddenly remind me of the efficiency expert who was being driven to a factory in very cold weather by a countryman in a sleigh. Trying to impress his own importance on the driver the expert said he could find a better way of doing almost anything. "For example," he said, "if you had put this buffalo robe over my knees with the skin outside and the fur inside, it would keep me much warmer." The driver thought for a few moments and then said: "Too bad the buffaloes didn't know that." There are advantages in both the Congressional and Parliamentary forms as used by us and the British, but both have grown naturally, and as Professor Allan Nevins wrote in a review of a book advising a complete change-over to the British way, it may yet be, in spite of the drawbacks of the Congressional way, that "in a country so large, so heterogeneous and so varied, a system made for caution is still better than one made for celerity."

Thus, in spite of the disorder of the post-war period, of the new conditions and characteristics developed by a hundred and fifty years of life in colonial America, the American had shown himself in this great crisis both conservative and far-seeing. He had clung to the known and tried as far as he could, and in dealing with problems which called for new solutions, he had shown himself capable of a statesmanlike view. All the leaders did not agree by any means as to the form of the new government, nor did the ordinary people. It is now utterly impossible to say just what the majority for or against adoption might have been had every nose been counted, but the main point is that enough of all classes of Americans approved of the Constitution, and were of a character to acquiesce peaceably in the decision as to what, in spite of all the dissentient voices, evidently satisfied at least a very large part of the nation. That new nation had been saved from descending into the Balkanic anarchy of a lot of conflicting small states, none of which would have been strong enough to resist conquest by a European power, and had agreed on a union which would not only grow to vast strength, but which in its continental sweep would offer the greatest free-trade area in the world.

The Northwest Ordinances, the Constitution as drawn up and the Amendments constituting the Bill of Rights were documents which distinctly stamped the Americans who produced, accepted, and used them, as having political ability and stability of a most unusual sort. If the American produced them, they in turn were to have a great molding influence on future Americans. The American has been the result of a constant interplay of influences between the geographical environment of America and the mind and nature of the American himself. The geography was there, but the American himself, in the historic documents which we have mentioned in this chapter, built the political structure on a geographic foundation that would permit of a future nation of 135,000,000 today and perhaps of many millions more tomorrow, all of one language and nationality if not of one race, and of a continental free-trade area which would demand free trade, mass production, and "national brands" even at the expense of individual craftsmanship and of interesting diversity. In other words, the American of today stems directly from all we have been speaking of, both physical and mental.

Before going on to other conditioning influences we may mention briefly just one more point. We spoke of the fact that the Americans of that day, both the leaders and ordinary folk, were far-seeing enough to limit even themselves by a fundamental law, but that, although they wanted a structure of government which would not be subject to every gust of popular emotion, they did not believe in an absolutely rigid basic law which could never be altered to meet new conditions. Consequently, provision was made for amendment. We have seen how this method of change was brought into play at the very beginning, how the ten amendments constituting the Bill of Rights, so called, were made by 1791. During the following century there were comparatively few more made, and the tradition grew up that the method was cumbrous and slow. In fact not only were alternative methods of amendment provided for, but amendments have become much more frequent in the past generation, with continued diminishings of the time required for their passage. There are now twenty-one, and there is no reason why an amendment cannot be passed within a few months *if public opinion is beyond question in its favor.* It can certainly be passed, in such circumstance, in less time than it takes for the supposedly omnipotent House of Commons in the so-called "unwritten Constitution" of Britain to pass a Bill over the veto of the House of Lords.

There are also, however, other methods of bringing the Constitution up-to-date. The Supreme Court by its decisions interpreting the original document with its several formal amendments is practically a Constitutional Convention in continuous session, though it may or may not at any given moment be in harmony with the *emotional* rather than the *considered* views of the nation. In addition, there are yet other ways in which the Constitution can be altered without either formal amendment or Court decision. For example, the original Constitution provided, because of the fear of democracy at the time it was drawn up, that neither the President nor members of the Senate should be elected by direct popular vote. Senators are now so elected, as a result of a formal amendment, but the President is so also to all intents and purposes by the growth of custom which has resulted in changing the functions of the members of the Electoral College from that of free agents to that of rubber stamps registering the will of the people. Finally, the Constitution is under constant alteration by means of the delegation of powers by Congress to Boards and Commissions, a form of change which is raising serious problems in all departments of government, notably for the Supreme Court. The point is not the problems which may be raised by one method or another of alteration but the fact that the Constitution is not nearly so rigid as many reformers in a hurry would have us believe when an overwhelming popular approval seems to them slow in catching up with their particular desire for change.

The new form of government, replacing the old Confederation, got quietly under way with the election of George Washington as the first President, and after a short delay, due mainly to difficulties of travel at the time, the new ship of state slipped down the ways to float on the boundless ocean of the future. The period in which all these plans had to be made for establishing a new nation under new conditions had been not only a post-war one but also a post-revolutionary one, yet, amid all the unrest, Americans had shown themselves capable of clear thinking and of conservative action. Washington's acceptance of the office, against his cherished personal desire to live quietly at Mount Vernon after the eight years he had devoted to public service during the war, undoubtedly helped greatly to bind the nation together, as had the grants to it by the several colonies of their western land claims. Both Washington (one of the fathers of the West), and the West itself, were two of the leading factors in the making of that united and expanding

America which was so profoundly to modify the American. Washington had risked his life as a traitor had America not won the war. He was devoted to liberty and self-government, but was not a democrat. America had been making democrats, and the West was to be profoundly democratic in its influence. The American, having adopted, to create the nation, the great measures we have spoken of in this chapter would now turn to making it no less free or staunchly based, but ever more the land of the common man, of the American Dream for all.

CHAPTER XII

AMERICA BIDS FAREWELL TO EUROPE

ALMOST a generation passed between the ratification of the Constitution in 1788 and the confirmation by the Senate early in 1815 of the Treaty ending the second war with Britain. It was an extremely complex period, full of incidents, which included the formation of the new American government, the beginning of political parties, difficult international relations, economic changes at home, and much else. What the period did to the American was to make him more consciously democratic; an almost complete isolationist; more boastfully and fundamentally an American; and to lay the foundation for an unhappy and jealous division between whole sections rather than, as of old, between colonies or states. All these points were to be important, and for the most part lasting, as aspects of the American mind.

The Constitution had charted the course of the governmental system in general terms. It had provided, for example, the method of electing a President and members of the Senate and House. This was duly done, but, when some months later owing to difficulties of travel and communication, these various members of the somewhat sketchy government were finally able to get down to business in the temporary capitol of New York City, almost all else remained to be organized or slowly developed. The Constitution had provided for a system of Courts, but to translate the general phrases into a practical working plan, a Judiciary Act had to be enacted. The government and state debts and finances had to be handled, an especially thorny problem. The paper Constitution made no provision at all for the place of political parties in running government. In fact, Washington and many others had no conception of parties, which they referred to as "factions," and our entire party system, so essential to the operation of our form of government, was to be built up by the people themselves wholly outside the Constitution. That instrument had provided vaguely for a Cabinet in the clause which stated that the President might require the written opinion of the heads of the executive departments when he so desired, but such departments remained to be created. Only four were at first set up—State, Treasury, War and Justice.

Washington appointed their heads, who became the first "Cabinet." Two of these were negligible for our theme but the other two are of supreme importance. Thomas Jefferson became Secretary of State and Alexander Hamilton Secretary of the Treasury. We need not bother at all in this book about their quarrels, or even the measures which each carried through, or tried to, in this first period of our national history. Their strongly contrasting ideas, however, have left such a permanent impress on the American that they must be considered. The environments of the Old World and the New, and the traditions, beliefs, ways of life, and ideas, of both have all played their part in the making of the American of today. We Americans are made up of many strands. Hamilton, the extremely brilliant (and because of divorce laws, or the lack of them), illegitimate son of a Scotch father and a French mother in the island of Nevis, was distinctly European in outlook. This is no slur. It merely means that during his short life he somehow remained largely untouched by those special influences in the American environment which we think of as making the American. We can imagine Hamilton employing his extraordinary abilities as the finance minister of a Louis XIV or George III, as readily as we can picture him as the Secretary of the Treasury in America, appointed by George Washington. He did a magnificent job, and we owe him a great debt for his various services, but his mind always struggled to float against, instead of with, the main current of American thought and life.

That life was fluid, mobile, democratic and individualistic. Very possibly it was too much so, but Hamilton understood none of it, except that he married the rich heiress, Miss Schuyler, and so allied himself with wealth and the then "interests." Sent to America by his aunts—his father had no money—he always took the aristocratic, special privilege point of view, and despised the ordinary man, in whom he had no trust. In fact he had no confidence in humanity in general, and believed that the only strong government was one based on satisfying the selfish interests of those who might support it. His good citizen was that myth, the "economic man." His idea of government was a strongly centralized control, binding together the threads of the economic longings of its supporters. Human nature being what it is, there is much to be said for Hamiltonianism, and to him we owe, not only the rescue of the national finances on a basis of honor, but also the whole system of protective tariffs and log rollings in Congress ever since.

The American Dream was for Hamilton merely a nightmare. In a land where above all others in history the poor and common man was to have his chance to rise, and to demand it, Hamilton could see firm government as established only on the foundation of wealth and pressure groups. In a land where the people hated privilege above all else, Hamilton wanted to establish a government on the basis of privilege, in the form of tariffs, and other appeals to self-interest which government could offer to the faithful.

Government *must* be strong. As Washington wrote at the time of Shays's Rebellion "Government is not *influence*." The point is where should the strength of a government lie? Hamilton was right in believing in the need for strength but ran counter to the main current of American thought when he conceived it as emanating only from the rich and privileged classes. He would have preferred a monarchy and a hereditary aristocracy. He did understand America enough to know that those were impossible, so he fought valiantly for the adoption of the Constitution, and under that did the best he could with a republic and the creation of a plutocracy. What he did was to go far to make America rich and powerful. He is the father of

American manufacturing and the tariff on which it has thrived. The Hamiltonian strain in our thought has been lasting and of enormous influence. Like the climate, geography and other natural factors, his ideas and the classes he helped to foster have had much to do with the making of certain types of Americans and certain phases of the American outlook. He was an extremely lucid and logical thinker, although a hopelessly diffuse writer.

Contrary to the opinion of many, Jefferson's mind was no less lucid and logical than Hamilton's. He was far from the hazy-minded dreamer and radical which the ultra-conservatives of his day believed him to be. Perhaps no thinker in our public life has been more misrepresented both by his enemies and those who have tried to use his name and supposed theories to back their own political fortunes. Like Hamilton his views and words have been continuing factors in the formation of the American.

We may point just for a moment to the differences in the background of the two men, differences which have also continued down the two currents of American life, differences which we may designate briefly as those existing between a boy brought up among the rich in a city and a boy brought up on a farm. New York on Hamilton's arrival was perhaps the most "business-minded" and politically cynical of all the larger centers in the colonies. Turning up there for his education, with a brilliant mind and a consuming ambition, but nothing to back them except a bar sinister and a little pecuniary help from aunts unknown in the city, the young immigrant may well have had an inferiority complex (though I dislike Freudian interpretations of the obvious). When he made his way into the inner citadel of wealth, society and reactionary politics, he would naturally become, like new converts to a religion, "more Catholic than the Pope." The clever but penniless young outsider who married the daughter of General Schuyler may have been compensating for many mortifications when he declared that "the people, Sir, the people is a great Beast."

The background of Jefferson was utterly different. His mother, a Randolph, belonged to one of the highest placed families socially in Virginia. His father, one of whose favorite sayings was "Never ask another to do for you what you can do yourself," had settled in what was to prove one of the finest pioneer counties in all America, Albemarle County in the Blue Ridge. Within a hundred miles of one another, four boys were growing up at the same time—Jefferson, Patrick Henry, James Madison and John Marshall. This was evidently no ordinary frontier. Owing to his father's untimely death, Jefferson was left with heavy family responsibilities but comparative wealth when very young. That was *his* background. Now for his political philosophy.

As contrasted with Hamilton's cynical belief in money and distrust of human nature, Jefferson always maintained a dislike of business and finance and a profound trust in the ordinary man *under certain conditions*. It must, as always, be remembered that America was then ninety per cent agricultural, and although all country boys were not Jeffersons and Madisons and Marshalls, and perhaps Albemarle County was the pick of all frontiers, yet it was more American than the New York in which Hamilton had to create a career for himself. The consequence was that the philosophy which Jefferson developed was more typically and soundly American than that wrought out by Hamilton, though both, like the two faces of Janus, represent aspects of the American.

Jefferson's philosophy, briefly, was this. He believed that power should be decentralized and not centralized, and that the functions of government should be as limited as possible consonant with the maintenance of order, safety and opportunity. This did not mean, however, that he, any more than Hamilton, believed in a *weak* government. The difference between them consisted in their divergent ideas as to where strength lay.

Jefferson believed that the base to count on should not be formed of a few very rich individuals or groups but of the great mass of self-respecting, self-supporting citizens of moderate means. He believed profoundly in the common man, but only the common man who had certain qualities and who was formed by certain conditions. There is no greater error than to think he believed that because a man was a human being he would *ipso facto* be a good citizen and should have all the rights and duties of one. Jefferson was one of the most scientific and progressive farmers of his day. He knew the innate difference in quality and possibilities of his horses, cattle, dogs and slaves. He believed in both heredity and environment. When he wrote that "all men are created equal" he did not for a moment mean that they were all born with equal capacities or virtues. All his writings prove *that* beyond a doubt. What he meant was that they should be equal before the law and be given equal opportunities according to their natures and abilities.

What he considered to be the soundest human being in general was neither the very rich, nor the wage-earning proletarian of the cities, but what we might call the yeoman farmer or the moderately well-to-do planter. In such a man, owning his own land, with a stake in the community, independent and individualistic, Jefferson found what he considered the best sort of citizen to support a stable and honest government. That being his premise, all his philosophy as expressed in his writings and attempts at legislation both in state and nation, was articulated with an entirely logical consistency.

"I think," he wrote to Madison, "our governments will remain virtuous for many centuries; as long as they are chiefly agricultural; and this will be as long as there shall be vacant lands in any part of America. When they [the people] get piled upon one another in large cities, as in Europe, they will become corrupt as in Europe. Above all things I hope the education of the common people will be attended to." Let us see how closely knit all his ideas were.

He made successful fights against the laws of entail and primogeniture in Virginia, which won him much unpopularity in all parts of the country and gave him the reputation of being an enemy of privilege and property, because he believed that the engrossing of huge tracts of land, permanently taken out of the market and the reach of the ordinary man, would substitute for his class of widespread moderately well-to-do farmers, a group of a few rich families who would rule in their own interest. His purchase from France of the Louisiana territory, of which we shall speak again later, almost doubled the size of the United States, which then afforded in his opinion enough free land for almost a thousand years.

His dislike of manufacturing, which he later had to modify to some extent, sprang in large part from the fear of a too rapid growth in population and of the rise of a city proletariat which, as he pointed out from his own European experiences, would not provide the material for a sound citizenry in a democracy. Thus in opposing tariffs and the rise of a manufacturing interest, in cutting off the "dead hand" of entail and primogeniture, and in his deal with Napoleon for the West, he thought he was helping to ensure for centuries a sound agricultural economy of small holders.

However, he was no blind worshipper of the small farmer as such or of the common man as such. He not only disapproved of universal suffrage and was in favor of a small property qualification, but his idea of democracy and the "equality" of men was shown most clearly in his scheme for that public education which he considered so essential.

Briefly, his plan was that every child, girls as well as boys, should have free education for three years in the primary schools, where they should be taught the three "R's," and in which their school readers should give them some idea of Greek, Roman, English and American history. Above the primary were to be the grammar schools but to these were to be sent at *public expense* only such students as were culled out as the "best and most promising." These were to get two years of this higher education free, and after a second culling process, certain of these would get two years more. Finally, the best of these four-year pupils would be selected for a free college education of four years. As the plan of the system was published in 1786 in a French edition of Jefferson's *Notes on Virginia,* Professor Chinard thinks it not unlikely that it formed the original basis for the system which has so long prevailed in France. Jefferson is considered our great "democrat," and one of his main interests all his life was education as preparation for citizenship. The above plan, carefully graded according to ability, is therefore of the greatest value as a gloss on what he really meant when he spoke of all men being equal. He quite evidently believed that talent in any economic grade of society should be developed for the good of society at public expense; but that public money should not be spent in trying to cultivate talent or ablity which did not exist.

His fight for religious liberty was another stone in the edifice, dedicated to personal liberty of thought and opportunity, which he was trying to build. We may also add one more point. From the day of the drawing up of the Mayflower Covenant until the present perhaps the political principle most deeply engraved in the mind of the American is that of "majority rule." It was, of course, not a new idea, but perhaps among no other people of the earth, except possibly the English, has it been accepted so completely or been so instrumental in avoiding violent revolution and bloodshed. There has been plenty of mobbing, violence, and fanaticism in America but on large questions the nation has ever preferred ballots to bullets, with the exception noted of the Civil War. Jefferson referred to this doctrine in his First Inaugural Address in 1801 but interpreted it in a way as to which Americans have for the most part agreed and as to which it is profoundly to be hoped they always will. He called on all citizens to obey the "sacred principle that though the will of the majority is in all cases to prevail, that will, to be rightful, must be reasonable; that the minority possess their equal rights, which equal laws must protect, and to violate which would be oppression . . . Having banished religious intolerance, we have yet gained little if we countenance political intolerance, as despotic, as wicked, and capable of as bitter and bloody persecution."

A whole volume could be written on Jefferson's political philosophy but the above mere skeleton indicates how deeply American it was in many respects as contrasted with the European doctrines of Hamilton. We have taken space to contrast the two because we have now reached the period in which the words and thoughts of American leaders were beginning to be lasting forces in molding the American of today, and rank with the more impersonal forces of nature or society. The work which many men in America did in the seventeenth century was of great importance, but although their work has been wrought into the fabric of American life, they are seldom or never quoted nowadays by Americans or much thought about as individuals. With Jefferson and Hamilton it is different. The number of "Hamilton Clubs" throughout the country, the constant "Jefferson dinners," and references by politicians to the authority of one or the other leader of more than a century ago indicate that they are still alive in personal influence and appeal. This explains the heat engendered when their views are discussed and the seeming difficulty which all biographers encounter in trying to write their biographies without rancor or bias.

At present, although there is a good deal of irony in the claims made, Hamilton is the patron saint of the Republicans and Jefferson of the Democrats and the differences between them had much to do with the origin of parties as essential factors in our governmental machinery. There had, of course, been parties before Independence—the Whigs, who favored America, and the Tories, who favored the Empire. Again, there was wide difference of opinion in the discussions over the adoption of the Constitution. There were, in a sense, two parties, but after its adoption there was an odd hope on the part of many that parties might disappear, since they were dangerous to the peace of the country. Practically no one questioned that Washington should be the first President, and no party machine opposed him. But as his first and second terms went on, the split which had occurred over the adoption of the Constitution became more marked over its interpretation and application, and men divided between the views of Hamilton and those of Jefferson, Hamilton, of course, being a leader of the Federalists and Jefferson slowly building up an opposition organization known then as Republican or Democratic. After the eight years of Washington, who refused a third term, establishing the tradition against it (never broken until Franklin Roosevelt), and the four years of John Adams, the situation had ripened to the point at which there were two strong parties in the field, as there have been in general ever since.

Jefferson, who was a superb political organizer, had built up his organization on the basis of the farmer and the city worker, a rather incongruous and antagonistic combination, as we have noted before. It became, however, the party of the poor and what is now called the "underprivileged," while the Federalists represented business, wealth and privilege of one sort or another. Obviously, Jefferson's party conformed more closely to the trend of the American Dream as determined by conditions of American life, but naturally he was considered a dangerous radical by the Federalists. New York and, even more, New England were particularly bitter in their opposition and in the vituperative epithets applied to the Virginian liberal-aristocrat.

However, in the election of 1800, one of the fiercest and vilest ever fought in this country, in which even leading New England clergymen employed language which would not be tolerated today, Jefferson won.

One effect of the election was to show the common man that, with a leader, he could win against all the entrenched power, especially mercantile and financial, which had been opposed to his view of what America meant in the long run. The "Revolution of 1800," as Jefferson referred to it, was perhaps not as great a revolution as he believed, but it was an immense stride forward towards making a reality out of all the propaganda of the pre-Revolutionary and Revolutionary periods in which the ordinary Americans, John Doe and Richard Roe, had been taught what America might be for them if they would fight for it. The election definitely helped to set the direction of the development of American thought and life. It heavily underscored democracy as against aristocracy or plutocracy. It practically finished the Federalist Party and what it stood for, for the time being. Moreover, it helped very greatly to take defeated Federalist New England out of the main current of American life, and make it a disgruntled and sulking section instead of a leading one.

We are apt to think of sectionalism in the extreme terms of southern secession and the Civil War, but sectionalism has been ever present more or less and, aside from the earlier intercolonial jealousies and dislikes, national sectionalism began in New England, and in this period. There was, first, the election of 1800 in which New England took a good drubbing and had to bow to the national will, leaving her sore and licking her wounds. Then came Jefferson's purchase of Louisiana Territory, which so greatly expanded the West. Always provincial and to a great extent cut off from the interior by the geographic factors we have already noted, New England feared that as the nation expanded, it would find itself more and more an unimportant backwater. Moreover, everything made the West democratic, whereas the leaders of New England were Federalist and aristocratic or plutocratic. The West had been enormously enlarged in 1803 by the Louisiana Purchase, and with a new empire to develop, it appeared that in time the population of the West might far exceed that of the East, and control pass to what was regarded by many of the Federalist leaders as the raw, ignorant, ultra-democratic, radical pioneers.

In addition, the election of 1800, followed by Jefferson's purchase of Louisiana, including New Orleans, and the opening of the Mississippi, bound the West to the South both politically and economically. It seemed that the Northeast and particularly New England would be encircled and cut off.

There were other factors at work in this period to emphasize tremendously the growing sectionalism. Some of these were due to geographic conditions and some to the wit of man. We have already noted why the South became a country of great staple crops, needing only such simple operations in cultivating them as were within the scope of the Negro mind, and therefore why slavery was economically useful there whereas it failed in the cold climate of the North with its varied small crops and intricate and canny ways of making a living. Nevertheless the sections were not so badly balanced until around 1800.

Slaves, which were then moderately priced, were employed in both sections, though, of course, far more numerous in the South. That section led the North in the value of its exports, although it possessed little shipping of its own. It was the period of the Napoleonic wars in Europe, and the era of invention was at hand. The impact of these two forces was to affect America and the American profoundly.

In 1791 the South had exported 200,000 pounds of cotton. The demand from abroad was moderate, and production was limited by the slow and laborious manual labor involved in separating the seeds from the cotton fibre. Suddenly things happened, and the machine began to exert its control over American destiny, as well as over other sections and types of Americans. In 1796, a New Englander, Eli Whitney, invented the cotton-gin, which made the separation process so easy as to open unlimited opportunity for production. At almost the same time, the inventions of Hargreaves, Arkwright and others in England greatly increased the demand by introducing textile machinery. The results of all this were that the South's export of cotton rose from the 200,000 pounds of 1791 to 64,000,000 in 1807; and the price of a slave jumped to $1,000 or $1,500, coinciding with the increased demand and the constitutional ending of the slave trade in 1808. Both socially and economically the type of the ante-bellum South was suddenly beginning to take form.

On the other hand, if the South, from circumstances with which it had nothing to do, became permanently agrarian, with its rapidly mounting wealth almost wholly in the form of land and slaves, and was to demand free trade politically, an equally great change had come over the Northeast. Its shipping interest would naturally share in the profits resulting from the increased export of cotton and other goods, and from 1791 to 1799 the exports of all America rose from about $18,500,000 to well over $33,000,000. There was, however, another factor and another set of figures. The South had almost no shipping of its own. Owing to the Napoleonic wars, America, which in this case meant chiefly New York and New England, took over a vast amount of the ocean carrying trade formerly belonging to the vessels of the French and British, and the re-exports of foreign products in American bottoms rose in those same years from $512,000 to $45,523,000! Manufactures in that section were also getting into their first strong stride, to be much accelerated by the needs and scarcities of the War of 1812.

Obviously Northern wealth was swelling fast, but it was chiefly due to trade and factories, and not to land or slaves or crops. It was a form of wealth, and a social and economic society, at least as far as the leaders were concerned, which fitted into and demanded a Hamiltonian philosophy of government, and was strongly Federalist. I have purposely brought the figures in the second group down to 1799 because their trend shows clearly why the North and particularly New England were so bitterly opposed to, and terrified by, the Jeffersonian revolution of 1800.

In the next dozen years or more, other factors worked for the increasing sectional feeling in New England. First, there was Jefferson's interesting but unsuccessful effort to use economic pressure to stave off war by use of his Embargo policy. On account of the huge profits they had been making, New Englanders were bitterly opposed to having their ships rotting at the docks when money lured them to the waves. It might have been thought that when war with Great Britain finally came, ostensibly because of her impressment of American seamen, New England would have been in favor of it. In fact it was not, and the war had really been brought on largely by the young western "War Hawks" who saw a chance, among other things, to invade and annex Canada. New England feared the West, and certainly any addition to it. It contemplated its own navel chiefly, and looked overseas for profits to line that part of its anatomy behind it. By an odd chain of circumstances, Boston, with its hinterland, which for a hundred and fifty years had been anti-British, became the most pro-British section of the new nation, and was long to remain so. So strong was the feeling in New England against the rest of the country, that not only did it flout Federal laws and refuse during the war to bear its proper proportion of the financial burden, but for some years, culminating in the Hartford Convention, it was seriously considering, or its leaders were, secession from the Union. Although the "embattled farmers" of the section were independent old fashioned Americans, the people of the section were curiously under the domination of the so-called leaders, families and individuals. Among the latter, the most important were the clergy and the rich—what the Federalists called as a party, "the wise, the rich and the good."

These got wholly out of the main current of American life and aspiration. They were at odds politically with the South. They feared, and opposed the expansion of the West, the "manifest destiny" of other Americans. They fought democracy. In the years of turmoil and Revolution, New England had furnished national leaders, but we may merely note that from the formation of the national government in 1791 until 1824 that section which claimed to be the wisest and most intellectual in the nation furnished only one President, the only one in that period not to be re-elected for a second term, and contributed only a sprinkling of the leading figures in national life.

Before we go on to speak of the development of isolationism

in the American during this period, we may touch for just a moment on one point. When the United States won its independence, the states and population were scattered up and down a fairly narrow strip of coast from Maine, then a province of Massachusetts, down to Georgia. Travel over bad roads was extremely slow and wearying. Because of that and of the jealousy existing among the states, the problem of where to locate the capital and the seat of the new national government was a difficult one. The vast westward expansion was not yet visualized, but distances north and south had to be reasonably fair to all. New York was selected for the moment, with agreement to move to Philadelphia later temporarily, but the question of a permanent location was almost bound to result as it did in Australia which, after federation of bitterly jealous states, had to locate and build its Federal capital in the waste, and found Canberra. The site chosen for the United States was the bit of Virginia set off as Federal Territory in the District of Columbia.

The main point for us is that in the city of Washington we never had a genuine capital of the country such as England has in London, France in Paris or Italy in Rome. It is not merely that, owing to our westward march, it is nowhere near the center of the country, but that, although it has become a beautiful city, it never has been, and never will be, a metropolis or a center of the nation's life. It is a huge government bureau, built at first on a few hills and the intervening marshes of a wilderness. It is true that it has some of our finest institutions, such as the Library of Congress and the National Museum of Art. What it may be in the future, no one can foretell. The only point I make is that in London or Paris, for example, the capital is really the capital, and the focus of all the most important currents and aspects of national life—government, politics, art, drama, literature, music, commerce, business, finance, science, publishing, book selling and all the rest, with the resulting assemblage in them of leaders of all sorts, or at least enough of them to afford a variety of experience to those who live there—a really national center which binds all the rest of the nation together.

In the cities mentioned one feels, though far from the scene of English country and provincial life, and of the French peasantry, at the center of the nation where one senses its heart-throbs in all its endeavors. In Washington one feels oddly off-center and outside of all the important national activities except politics and specialized national bureaus. Perhaps we are too big and sprawling, and our distances are too great. However, it is somewhat of a misfortune that those who go to visit the capital from all over the country do not see a metropolis, and those who remain there in government service live more or less apart in a sort of political monastery, cut off largely, except by appointment, from leaders in other departments of the cultural life of the nation.

America, however, was becoming very conscious of its destiny, and the new city to arise had been planned on a grandiose scale, by the French Major L'Enfant, who had been an officer in our Revolutionary army and served through the terrible winter with Washington at Valley Forge. He had already by remodelling turned the present City Hall in New York into what is perhaps the most perfect building architecturally in America, when called on to plan the national capital to be located in what was then merely a piece of wilderness ten miles square bordering on the Potomac. No other modern capital city of equal size and world importance has been so carefully laid out, and before we leave it, there are one or two points connected with it which help to illustrate the American.

One is that there was no historic background as in London or Paris or Rome or Vienna. There was nothing to start with but swamps and scrubby hillsides, but the American, who had been learning more and more to live in the future as almost a present reality in his dreams, saw the city as it was to be and could ignore its muddy streets and shabby boarding-houses and generally unfinished state, so distressing for a while to European diplomats stationed there after 1800. Moreover, although

L'Enfant was a great architect, architecture was the first art in which the American was to excel, and aside from the beauty of the buildings we were to develop, we have become in time builders on the grandest scale witnessed since the Roman Empire. For scale we need mention only our dams, and skyscrapers or to contrast such railway stations as the Pennsylvania or Grand Central in New York with any railway terminal in Europe. Perhaps the American, like the Roman, was subtly influenced by the vast extent of his empire. He came to like to do things in the grand manner, such as a tree belt 1200 miles long, or the road just completed extending 1500 miles from the United States border across Canada to Alaska, built through the wilderness in five months. In the period of this chapter he had already learned to live in the future, but the planning of the city of Washington was the first evidence of this new trait of the big and grandiose which he was developing.

The spirit of the American when the new nation was formed is well expressed in the Great Seal as designed, and any one who on reading this happens to have a current dollar bill in his pocket can study it. On the reverse side he will find reproductions of the front and obverse of the Seal. The latter shows a pyramid, unfinished at the top, with thirteen courses of stone representing the thirteen states, and two Latin mottoes which may be translated as "Favor my undertaking" and "A new Order begins in the Ages." These represented the sentiment of the time, and have a bearing on our next topic, the growth of isolationism. The American was indeed becoming more cocky than ever. He felt not only that he had beaten in battle the greatest power on earth—the British Empire—but that he was top-dog in every way. Indeed, the House of Representatives in 1796, even before we had acquired the great Louisiana Territory, suggested that we announce to mankind that we were "the freest and most enlightened [nation] in the world!" As Henry Adams pointed out in his history of the period we had nothing to match the work of a Goethe, Schiller,

Mozart, Haydn, Kant, Scott, Shelley, Wordsworth, Beethoven, Hegel, Cuvier, or other contemporary European musicians, poets, artists, scientists or philosophers. That, however, was the way the American was coming to feel as a result of his environment and his relations to the Old World.

Those relations were about to give another turn to the screw, and to leave an impress on the American which was to be marked for considerably more than a century to come.

The Napoleonic wars naturally dislocated all international relations including those of the young new nation in America. We have already noted the great growth of American shipping due to the difficulty of transport in either French or British bottoms. As the tremendous struggle between the British and the French Empires grew in intensity, with Napoleon trying to conquer all of the Continent, and Britain using the embargo and control of the seas as one of her most effective weapons, the neutral rights of America were more and more infringed. Between the insatiable ambition of the Emperor and the desperate resistance demanded of Britain, sometimes with allies and sometimes alone, to preserve herself and freedom, an innocent bystander in the form of a neutral but young and untried nation like the United States, was bound to be mauled without much consideration.

Decrees by Napoleon and Orders in Council by the English followed each other with supreme disregard of American commercial rights on the high seas, and we have noted how important those rights, in terms of money as well as of national honor, were becoming to America. There were, however, other factors at work which were tending to foster an isolationist attitude on the part of Americans. The Orient had as yet hardly risen above the horizon of our interest. Africa did not count except as a source of slaves or of irritation on its north coast due to the Barbary pirates. The European states refusing to join us in our decision to end the shameful demands for tribute by the Barbary States in return for the right of passing through the Mediterranean, we fought a successful little war of our own against them, 1801–05, and another little naval campaign in 1815, both of which gave us additional self-confidence, but certainly added nothing to our respect for, or confidence in, the powers of the Old World.

That world, during the two score years or so of the Napoleonic wars, was for us almost divided between the warring powers of France and Britain. Their interests conflicted with each other at every point and appeared no less to conflict with ours. For us there seemed little to choose as between the injuries inflicted on us by either. Spain, however, as a European though decaying power, had done its best to close the Mississippi to us, and the growing West felt that this old European Empire was still trying to throttle the growth of the new Republic and the maritime commerce on which depended some of its dreams of future wealth. There was talk of the West's seceding from the East if that section did nothing to help its growth.

Recently, ourselves, emerged successful from a war and revolution for freedom and liberty, we had to a large extent been sympathetic, especially south of New England, with the early phase of the French Revolution, but that sympathy was steadily alienated by the excesses of its later stages and the rise of Napoleon to dictatorship. In addition, the French representative, Genêt, had behaved in an insulting manner to the American government, and greatly irritated not only Washington and Hamilton but Jefferson and almost all Americans likewise. Then came the X.Y.Z. affair, when Talleyrand tried to hold up the American representatives in France for money, giving rise to the famous cry at home of "Millions for defense but not a cent for tribute." War was narrowly avoided in 1789 and staved off only by the personal moves of President John Adams. Later, under Jefferson, came the revelation that France had acquired the Louisiana Territory from Spain. Spain was a decadent and failing power, and in spite of the irritation felt by the westerners we had thought we could bide our time so long as she remained our neighbor on the west bank of the Mississippi. But the rising star of Napoleon was a different matter. Jefferson remarked that if such a power as France should control our future in the west we should have to "marry ourselves to the British fleet and nation." Napoleon, fortunately, however, needed money, and Jefferson was able to buy the territory from him for cold cash, without war with his nation or an alliance with England.

We had ample grievances and cause for dislike in connection with that nation also. Briefly, neither Great Britain nor the United States had lived up wholly to the terms of the peace treaty of 1783, and each failure on the part of one became an excuse for a further failure on the part of the other. Britain had not turned over the posts in the Northwest Indian and fur country, claiming that we were not facilitating the payment of debts due British merchants, as had been agreed. In a long letter, Jefferson, then Secretary of State, took the ground, interesting in view of the post-war debts due us after 1919, that if a creditor himself placed obstacles, which had not existed at the time that the debts were incurred, in the way of the debtor, the latter could not be held to the original terms. After 1919 the obstacle took the form of the big rise in the tariff. After 1783 the obstacle claimed was the hampering by Britain of our old accustomed trade with the British West Indies. We could hardly secede from the Empire and still claim all the accustomed rights of a member of it, although it probably would have been wisdom on the part of the British to have allowed the old trade to continue.

Then came the Jay Treaty, which settled many points but was immensely unpopular in America, even with Washington backing it. Later came the problem of impressment of American seamen by British naval officers. The number is unknown and very variously stated but certainly ran to several thousand. We naturally objected to having our ships stopped and having American citizens taken off them, but the laws of citizenship and naturalization were different then, though they are still mixed enough, and it must be allowed that there was much illicit traffic in citizenship papers, and it was hard to distinguish a British Englishman or Irishman from a *bona fide* American citizen.

This particular grievance did not extend to the French, who would have had no more objection than the English to taking their claimed citizens off our vessels, but the difference in appearance and speech, combined with the small number of French in the United States, could give rise to only a negligible number of mistakes, real or pretended.

In general, however, between the causes mentioned above and others, it was hard to say whether Britain or France was injuring our interests and our honor the more. We narrowly averted war with France in 1798, and Jefferson, during his Presidency, tried to avoid it with both nations by his policy of Embargo, which immensely irritated and almost ruined the shipping sections of the country, and added to the sectionalism we have already briefly discussed. Subsequently, under President Madison, who was fooled by Napoleon, and due to a combination of other unfortunate circumstances, we finally entered the war on the side of France and against England.

All the conditions we have described naturally led a young, not too strong, but very touchy and rather conceited new nation, to desire to wash its hands of the Old World altogether. We wanted peace. We wanted to develop our trade. We wanted to exploit the riches of our own land to the west. The eternal quarrels of Europe seemed to be hindering and endangering us in all our efforts and wishes. Meanwhile, Washington, towards the close of his second term, having noted our then weakness, the different interests at that time of the Old and New Worlds, the danger to our national unity in taking either the French or British side in the wars, had advocated in his so-called Farewell Address an attitude of complete isolation as far as was possible, which he said "Our detached and distant situation invites and enables us to pursue."

Here we meet again the supposed protection of the three thousand miles of ocean under the then conditions of time and space as related to travel and communication. We have reached the period in our history in which the words of great leaders, as we have noted in the cases of Hamilton and Jefferson, begin to have a continuing formative influence on the American, as important as the physical environment, the inventions of the machine age, or others. There is no way of telling with any accuracy what Washington, with his stalwartness, forthrightness and common sense, would have thought about isolation in 1898, 1914 or 1941, but it is unquestionable that what he did say, applicable to the circumstances of 1797, in his Farewell Address, has been one of the strong forces making for isolationist sentiment in America ever since. The geographically "detached and distant situation" which he envisaged has been completely altered, but his words remain, and it is an odd trait in the American that although in his daily and practical life he lives in the future rather than the present or the past, he nevertheless has an almost Chinese reverence for certain aspects of that past, preserved in the words of great Americans of earlier generations and in his abnormal preoccupation with genealogy and the mere names of his ancestors, whether they signify anything important or not.

Before turning our back on the Old World for a considerable time, there is one more strain in the American which stems from this period to which we must allude in order to understand him. That is his anti-British attitude.

Colonial America can hardly be said to have been anti-British. There were influences at work which were making the colonial American a somewhat different sort of person from the stay-at-home Englishman, but as we have mentioned, so strong a patriot as John Adams estimated that at the time the Declaration of Independence was drawn up only one-third of the people were in favor of separation whereas one-third were opposed and the remainder were indifferent. There had been, of course, the usual conflicts in points of view between a colony and a home country, accentuated by the factors we have emphasized in the American situation in the seventeenth and eighteenth centuries.

New elements came in, however, which changed the relationship. First, there was ill-feeling aroused on the part of many by the events of the dozen years or so before 1776, and especially by the propaganda promoted by Sam Adams and others. Then came the long-drawn-out war with its intensified propaganda, emphasizing every possible fact or falsehood which would play on the emotion of hatred. "War," as General Sherman said almost a century later, "is Hell," and naturally leaves bitter memories. Moreover, some sixty to a hundred thousand of those Americans particularly attached to England had been forced to emigrate. Then came the twenty years or more of controversy and semi-declared war with both France and England. As it turned out we finally, by a series of accidents, joined Napoleon instead of England, although the latter was the one who was fighting for freedom for the world against the ambition of the French dictator.

The result was that, with renewed war propaganda, France, especially in view of the aid which she had given us, for purely selfish reasons, in the first war against England, was played up as our eternal friend, whereas Britain was made to seem the eternal enemy. Once more, we were a young, self-conscious and cocky nation which had won its independence and place among the nations of the world by fighting England. We were not a people who had slowly evolved down the ages but one which had sprung from battle. For a long, long period, it seemed essential to orators and historians that all Americans should be described as angels of light and the British as devils of darkness. It was natural, in that age and under the conditions prevailing, even if unfortunate and untrue. War and imperial secession had to be justified. The easiest and most emotional way of doing so was to continue the hate for the Empire. The second war between England and America held little glory for either. We had some brilliant naval encounters on both sides, mostly between individual ships, but the land operations bogged down, and both we and England were glad to conclude the strife with almost nothing said about what each had been fighting for. Much bitterness had been engendered, due to our burning of British towns and the British burning of Washington, but nothing had been gained, and if ever there has been a "peace without victory" it was that consummated between the two nations at Ghent the day before Christmas 1814.

However, the pattern had been set. The United States had fought Britain again, and if we had not won, we at least had not been licked. There was a new store of dislike laid up for the future which in the decades ahead could be exploited by the politicians who herded in the big Irish vote that came to our shores in the 1840's and after, and could be played upon in the difficult times of our Civil War when the British upper, but not lower, classes were largely against the Union and in favor of the South. The wars between Britain and Napoleon were world wars. The intervention of the United States had little or no effect on the result, except for Anglo-American relations. We were then much like a little pup which tries to take part in a fight to the death between a lion and a rhinoceros. The only effect was to make the lion sore and the pup walk off with his tail in the air.

When the war was over, with a sort of posthumous victory of the Americans over the British at New Orleans, in a battle which was fought after the treaty of peace had been signed and which could not have taken place had we then had an Atlantic cable, the American turned to what he had been wanting to tackle all along, the development of the West, so vastly enlarged by Jefferson's taking advantage of Napoleon's need for cash. In a way we owe it to England, because if that country had not been pressing the Emperor so hard in his plans for conquest, he would never have sold it but would have kept it to build up the new French Empire in America of which he dreamed. Had he refused to sell, we would probably have been forced to "marry the British fleet and nation" as Jefferson said, and to enter the war on the side of England, with immense differences during the next century in our attitudes towards that nation and towards France.

We now have to turn from Europe, as did the American of that day, and see what, with a free mind, he would do to the land of the Western Waters and what that land would do to him. For democracy the Jeffersonian revolution of 1800 had been important, but the Jacksonian lay ahead, and was wholly due to the West.

CHAPTER XIII

WESTERN DEMOCRACY

BEFORE we concentrate too completely on the American domestic scene we may mention one more step taken in the direction which was helping to make the American an isolationist internationally. In 1823 James Monroe was President and John Quincy Adams his Secretary of State. Two pieces of disquieting news had reached the young government in Washington, still scarce a generation old, as to possible designs of foreign nations on the territory of the Americas. Russia had set up pretensions that none but vessels flying her flag should be allowed to touch on the Pacific coast of North America north of latitude fifty-one; and in South America there were intimations from the British government that some of the European powers were considering the reconquest of the possessions of Spain which had recently acquired their independence. In fact the British Foreign Secretary, George Canning, suggested that Britain and the United States should issue a joint declaration in order to prevent this eventuality. Our own government preferred to go it alone, an indication of how America had come to consider itself. Adams drew up a proclamation which the President signed almost without change of wording, and which has since been known as the Monroe Doctrine. This was, briefly, to the effect that all non-American nations must thenceforth keep their hands off the New World, and that any attempt by them to oppress, or to control the destiny of, any American nation would be viewed as manifesting an unfriendly disposition towards the United States.

For a while the world paid little attention to it. In fact to the present day Germany has never accepted it, and we ourselves overlooked some very minor infringements for a few years. Nevertheless as time went on we did refer to it and invoke its validity, on one occasion after another, until in spite of varying interpretations of just what it did mean, it became a sort of sacred cow and, to change the metaphor, a corner-stone of our foreign policy.

In so far as the American has been molded by documents it is fair to say that the two which have had the greatest influence in orienting him as to world affairs and his own place in them have been Washington's Farewell Address and the text of the Monroe Doctrine. Probably John Doe never read either of them, and certainly could not quote them, but from long reiteration he has become deeply imbued with the idea that somehow disaster would overtake him if he mixed up with the Old World or allowed it to get any foothold in the New. There are other factors which have made for isolationism, such as the oceans, the seeming remoteness from danger, between their two rampart chains of mountains, of the dwellers in the Mississippi Valley, provinciality, self-satisfaction, dislike of the foreigner on the part of many, and others, but the words of Washington and Monroe (or rather Adams) still reverberate in the American mind. The Monroe Doctrine is not part of international law. When we were engaged in our Civil War France attempted to flout it and build an empire in Mexico, but it has been recognized now for nearly eighty years by many other nations as being so deeply imbedded in our own national emotions as to prevent them from infringing on it unless certain that we could be conquered. This has increased not only our isolationist sentiment but added to our national pride and sense of power and superiority. The promulgation of the Doctrine was received at the time in America with immense satisfaction. Perhaps nothing gives a man more of a sense of "being somebody" than the chance to put up a sign "Keep Out." The young nation had done that and felt pretty pleased with itself. Meanwhile after the peace of 1814 it had been developing south and west with amazing rapidity.

It had also been becoming more distinctly American. Some

years later a friendly foreign traveller commented, even in the heart of New York State, that "A stranger cannot help meditating on the vast materials of human happiness which are placed at the disposal of the real administrators of this great country. How great is the apparatus to be yet put to use! Here, where life is swarming all around, how few are the habitations of men!" It was again the story of unlimited resources lying open to exploitation by unlimited ambition. During the twenty years or more of the Napoleonic wars, immigration had practically ceased. The Americans already here had, so to say, a breathing spell in which to consolidate their Americanism, for better or worse.

We have spoken several times of the influence of the environment and life here, and of how the American, even of English descent, had become different from the Englishman at home. By this period the difference had become pronounced. To mention only a few instances we may note that what Mencken has called "the American language" and what Samuel Johnson in 1756 called "the American dialect," had been veering off markedly from contemporary English. Just as we had borrowed architectural ideas from our varied immigrants, such as the log cabins from the Swedes, the step type of roof from the Dutch, and others, so we borrowed a large vocabulary. For example, such words as skunk, hickory, squash, succotash, caribou, porgy, raccoon, squaw, wigwam, canoe, catalpa, moccasin, tomahawk, and toboggan came from the native Indian. The French gave us prairie, bogus, chowder, gopher, portage and others. The Dutch, such words as cruller, stoop (for front steps), scow, boss, cookey, pit (of a peach), span (of horses), and waffle.

These were all strange to ears in Old England, but so also were those nouns the Americans had coined for themselves, such as bull-frog, egg-plant, snow-plow, cold-snap, trail, popcorn, back-log, sophomore, schooner, cat-boat, shingle and many others, or such adjectives as handy, kinky or chunky. In addition, many of what English people often consider "Americanisms" were merely old English words which we had retained from the England of our first period of settlement and which had continued in use here while being discarded or forgotten in England itself. That settlement occurred in the period in which the English language was perhaps at the height of its glory, serving the King James version of the Bible, Shakespeare and the other Elizabethan and Jacobean dramatists. It is the irony of illiteracy that the English should consider as Americanisms words which we had brought from England itself at the period of greatest verbal richness. Of course, we developed regional dialects here, just as they had done in England, and regional modes of pronunciation. But we may note that the flat *a* was brought from England, where the broad pronunciation was not used until the third quarter of the eighteenth century, when the "Oxford accent" began, to be copied later by the Anglophiles of Boston and Harvard.

Somewhere in this period, although it cannot be dated accurately, American humor, which observers from Europe mention as one of the peculiarly American traits, seems to have diverged completely from the English type and become one of grossly exaggerated over-statement instead of the under-statement which is often the soul of an English joke. England was a small island which could be tucked complete into more than one of our states, whereas America was huge, sprawling and with illimitable opportunities. Apparently, geographical conditions had something to do with the change, and with the development of the so-called "tall stories" which were to grow in the West, but it is straining the point to decide how much. In any case, the change occurred, and the two varieties of humor are at opposite poles today. We obviously cannot make a joke book, but can give two samples to show the difference. There is the tale of two Englishmen looking at Niagara Falls. One remarks, "Not bad, eh?" (precisely the remark I heard an English girl make about the Bargello in Florence, Italy). The other answers, "Oh, don't gush." Compare this with the tale of the plainsman who said he saw two prairie dogs carried twenty feet into the air by the wind and "digging like Hell to get back to the ground," or Davy Crockett who claimed to be able to kill a coon with his own hideous grin and once found he had mistaken a knot in a tree for a coon but had grinned all the bark off the tree. We could add the answer of the Mississippi steamboat captain in the days when steamers were set on fire and boilers blew up because of the piling of wood in the fire boxes when racing. He was asked whether his boat had a good draft. "Draft? Hell yes," he said, "every time a nigger puts a log on the fire he is sucked right up the stack."

Better examples might be chosen, but the fact seems to remain that, as one English traveller commented, "The immensity of the continent produces a sort of intoxication; there is a moral dram-drinking in contemplation of the map," and, we may add, the chances to turn the map into a fortune, with all a fortune might mean. In the Old World ordinary John Doe had no chance. The very exceptional man, as general, statesman, merchant or courtier, might rise and found a family. But in America a lucky turn of the wheel of fortune might do the trick for any one.

America had become American and not colonial English, and many other things followed the same course as language or humor, or the folk-lore we shall mention later, and for the same reason. Conditions had become wholly different. Visiting New York City in 1834 Harriet Martineau, a very able and friendly Englishwoman, noted, looking from the window of her room in that then small city, where the katydids still made a disagreeable noise on Broadway, "I cannot conceive what travellers mean by saying that there is nothing foreign in the aspect of New York. I beheld nothing at this moment that I could have seen at home, except the sky and the grass of the courtyard." Contrast this with life in England. I recall during my years there spending several afternoons in the village of Ewelme in Oxfordshire and commenting on the fact that standing in the churchyard of the old church built about 1450 one could not see in the landscape anything built by man which did not go back to the fifteenth century, with the sole exception of a telegraph wire running down into the valley and up over the opposite hill. In the church, among other monuments, was the tomb of a Duchess of Suffolk who had come from some other county and who had died in 1475. The doddering old sexton who showed me around told me that his ancestor had come as a servant to the Duchess and that his family had been in the village ever since.

That sort of thing does something to you, just as the constant movement of American life does also, in its different way. To have lived for centuries a more or less unchanging life in the same locality whether as "master" or "man" (terms now unused in America except in the advertisements of snobbish "realtors" who advertise so many "master" bedrooms in the houses they offer), places you, and unconsciously colors your view of life. America has always been on the move, and Dixon Wector in his *The Hero in America* writes that "The father of Abraham Lincoln—a relative by marriage of Daniel Boone—liked to tell about a family who had moved so often that their chickens knew the signs of a new journey; the fowls would then walk up to the wagon, lie flat on the ground, and put their feet up to be tied for another trip." The story, whether true or not, is certainly, as the Italians say, *ben trovato* and points to the eternal restlessness of the American, which gave rise to many American traits.

When the War of 1812 ended, all America seemed on the march. After the acquisition in 1803 of the Louisiana Territory Jefferson had planned a scientific expedition to discover what there was in the great unknown western half of the continent. That expedition, led by Jefferson's private secretary, Meriwether Lewis, and young William Clark, is our national epic of exploration. In two years, 1804–06, the party had revealed the vastness of the Northwest, ascending the Missouri River to the mountains, crossing them to the Snake and Columbia Rivers, and following the latter down to the Pacific Ocean. Nearly four thousand miles had been traversed and had disclosed the fertile lands of the lower Missouri, the hugeness of the buffalo plains, and the infinite timber resources of the Pacific coast. Almost limitless new possibilities of trade and agriculture were opened to the vision of Americans in this possible new western empire. Moreover, it was only the first, though greatest, of the expeditions which were made following the Louisiana Purchase. In 1806–07, for example, Zebulon Pike, an army officer, after having explored the upper Mississippi, made the famous trip which revealed to us the extent and character of our newly acquired Southwest.

The American was indeed becoming intoxicated by the map. The magnitude of his possessions, and the possibilities of following the star of Manifest Destiny still farther, had not only their social, economic and political effects but psychological ones. As the immensity of his nation and its potentialities burst on his dazzled vision no wonder that the ordinary man, in the light of the gigantic task he saw ahead for himself in America, began to look down on the little crowded countries of the British Isles and of the continent of Europe. It is true that he then saw no value in the plains, and that the Southwest was to appear on maps as "the Great American Desert." Nevertheless there were evidently untold riches, though some, like the gold and silver and oil of a later period, had not yet been glimpsed, and the mere size of it all was bewildering. The American realized as never before the magnitude of the fortune which he had inherited, and it was natural that it should take him, like all who come into a huge fortune suddenly, a long time to resolve the confusion between material and spiritual values. It was, in fact a confused period for a couple of generations or so, and we shall now touch on that aspect of our picture.

First we may note the confusion in the movements of population. There were three main streams which may be mentioned as having profound effects on the American and all departments of American life. These were the vast numbers who were passing from the East, including the North and

Upper South, to the West; those from these same sections who were pouring into the rapidly growing "deep South"; and the renewed immigration from Europe, which began again after the defeat of Napoleon and became a torrent by the 1840's.

After the peace of Ghent was ratified in 1815 hordes of settlers almost choked every gateway to the West: the poor on the seaboard who glimpsed a new chance; former rich who had been ruined by the war which, like all wars, had made its new rich and its new poor; adventurers and ne'er-do-wells; farmers and peasants from Britain and Europe who were escaping from the war-ruined Old World in hope of finding a better. How vast this movement was can be traced in all the statistics and writings of the time. For example, one author stated that "Nothing so strongly indicates the superiority of the western country as the vast emigration to it from the eastern and southern states. . . . I was informed by an inhabitant of Cayuga, in April 1816, that more than fifteen thousand wagons had passed over the bridge at that place within the last eighteen months, containing emigrants to the western country." Counting only five to a wagon, and there were probably more, that would be over seventy-five thousand passing that one village. Two years later another writer and traveller wrote that "Old America seems to be breaking up and moving westward. We are seldom out of sight, as we travel on this grand track, towards the Ohio, of family groups, behind and before us." He adds that about twelve thousand wagons passed from Philadelphia and Baltimore to Pittsburgh that year. To these, with their four to six horses each, had to be added the stages, the light wagons, the travellers on horseback or even on foot, all making for the Ohio and the West, "a scene of bustle and business" truly wonderful, he concluded. It was the same on the rivers, whole families with their cattle, chickens and furniture crowding the waters on rafts and flat boats.

We can get an idea of the magnitude of the changes going on from another angle. Taking the figures of the first five Censuses, from 1790 to 1840, for New England alone, we find that on the basis of formerly customary natural increase the population showed a decrease of over 1,300,000 from what it should have been, representing loss by emigration less the number added by foreign immigration. Between 1820 and 1845 the latter amounted to about 100,000, and was rapidly rising. This immigration was mostly composed of the Catholic Irish, forced from home by famine, and these people congregated almost wholly in the seaboard cities and towns, and did not go West.

How amazing was the growth in every way of that section may be illustrated by a quotation from Miss Martineau, who toured it in 1834 and was particularly charmed with Cincinnati, where she was entertained by a Dr. Drake, who, she says, "entered Ohio just forty-seven years before this time, when there were not above a hundred white persons in the state, and they all French, and when the shores were one expanse of canebrake, infested by buffalo." When she was there the city had 35,000 inhabitants, churches, schools, factories, and two banks (the last, as well as a new church and "a hundred and fifty handsome private dwellings" all built in the preceding year). There were also published a magazine and four daily and six weekly newspapers. We may glimpse here some of the causes of the devastating financial panic, due in large part to overexpansion, which was to come in 1837, but for a century the country was to meet and take such things in its stride, and meanwhile the rapid growth of everything—cities, business, rural communities, and all else—was to burn into the American an irresistible belief in himself, his country, and the future of any personal or national undertaking. Many towns indeed did not grow but if hopes failed, well, move and graft yourself on another spot. On the other hand, the story of Cincinnati was to be repeated on a moderate, or often far larger, scale so often that the failures did not count and were forgotten.

It was not only the West which was growing. The early South was immensely changed in the first third of the century we are now discussing. Four important factors were the invention of the cotton gin and the rise of "King Cotton"; the Louisiana Purchase; the acquisition of Florida from Spain by the Adams-Onis Treaty of 1819; and a few years later the final transfer of the remnants of the Cherokee Indian nation, which had owned the larger part of Georgia, Alabama and other rich sections. The story is one of the most shameful in the long one of our relations with the red men, but we allude here only to the fact that in the period we are now discussing the "South" had been given its present boundaries, and was all open to exploitation. From 1812 to 1819 Louisiana, Mississippi and Alabama were admitted to the Union as states.

Cotton is raised throughout all the Old South but the richest section is that known as the "Black Belt," on account of the color of the soil in Alabama and Mississippi, most of which was opened to settlement by a Cherokee cession in 1816 although the real rush did not begin for about a decade. When it did set in it was comparable on a smaller scale to the rush to the West that we have described. The extraordinary fertility of the section, the rise of cotton, the wearing out of the soil in the northern tier of tobacco states of the South, the desire for quick money, and the general speculation of the period, all tended to develop the deep South quickly, and to make of it a section quite different in many ways from the old South. Northern merchants, capitalists and speculators took up land and started plantations. Many Yankees of a low type went down as managers and slave overseers. There were younger sons from impoverished families of the Carolinas and Virginia, and ambitious farmers who were slipping down in the social and economic scale in other parts of the South. Negroes, especially fitted for cotton culture, were poured in from other Southern states, especially Virginia, where their numbers augmented by natural increase, created an almost insoluble economic problem for their masters as the yield from the worn-out tobacco plantations declined. The Gulf states became a new frontier, of a type different from any other we have had. In Alabama at one time the slave population numbered about 87 per cent of the total, giving a new and sinister significance to the term "Black Belt." Again there was confusion in the movement of American population. It was as though some power were using a great spoon to stir up all the people together.

Of the influx of foreigners, beginning again at a fast growing rate, we have spoken briefly, and need only add that in the ten years from 1830 to 1840 their number, for the whole country, quadrupled that of the preceding ten.

We may now turn to consider the effects of these changes on the American, and may speak first of their sectional aspects, after mentioning one general characteristic of the American in *all* sections. This was that he felt assured of a reasonable chance to rise by his own exertions, and insisted that they be his own.

A distinguished foreign observer noted that "Mr. Webster owes his rise to the institutions under which he lives; institutions which open the race to the swift and the battle to the strong." Until the present century it was indeed the swift and the strong who gloried in the opportunities of America, though it was the environment and general atmosphere rather than the institutions, which may be considered responsible. The Constitution did not make America, though it helped. It was America that wrote the Constitution. American life from the very beginning had, as we have seen, always called for work and self-reliance on the part of all—men, women and children. Life in America was harder and more dangerous than in Europe, but people were willing to work harder and take more risks provided that they were sure of retaining their reward, or a big prize if they gained one, and that they should be free to do it in their own way, and receive reasonable social recognition of their worth as individuals.

Of course, for some, wealth had accumulated by inheritance, marriage, favors or lucky strikes, but for the most part only plutocratic and not aristocratic families could be founded on it. Many of the older families had built up substantial fortunes.

though they were often, like so many in America, ephemeral. Speculation in land and rapidly growing cities, and in new avenues of overseas commerce almost as speculative, were creating new fortunes for new men, such as John Jacob Astor, who arrived in New York as a German immigrant by way of the steerage in 1784, with $25 and a tiny stock of musical instruments. On his death in 1848 he left the first really huge American fortune, $20,000,000. It was, however, to be some generations before, in the snobbish days of the 1890's and of the social "four hundred" in New York, a wag could translate *Sic itur ad astra* as "This way to the Astors."

The ordinary or garden variety of American, who for the most part is the real American we are trying to discover, and who was so important, because as Lincoln said "God must love the common people, he made so many of them," did not rival Astor's ability, success or meanness, but he had other qualities and satisfactions. He did not object to people making money. He hoped to make it himself, but he *did* object to pretensions of superiority, to patronage and to money made through privilege. He did not object to work—but he wanted that work to have at least its fair chance of reward and himself to be respected in his community.

We have written in an earlier chapter of the unfortunate effects, socially and economically, of the competition of Negro slave labor with that of the free white workman and small farmer in the eighteenth-century South. A somewhat similar situation was now about to develop in New England, which we shall mention in discussing the next period. In this we may take a few soundings to see what the ordinary American was like. Between an Astor in New York, with his sometimes questionable means of making money, and, say, the boatmen on the Mississippi, "half-horse, half-alligator, with a cross of the wild-cat," the "most riotous and lawless set of people in America," as was said, there was the vast mass of just plain Americans, who were building up themselves and the country. We shall glance at them before we go on, though in a country so vast and varied, to give a full cross-section of the people, their ideas and ways of life, would take a volume in itself.

First, let us quote a few comments from good observers. We have spoken of the feeling of independence and dislike of assumed rank or superiority. A visitor to West Point, in the 1830's, speaking of its value as a training school for officers in war and as a meeting ground for youths from all parts of the country, noted that although its management must "be watched with the greatest jealousy," nevertheless there is "an indignant and honest cry raised against those who would abolish it on account of its aristocratical tendencies." Again, we get a comment on the decline and "aristocratic character" of Harvard, as well as the increasing cost of attending that university, and, almost impossible to believe, we learn that a "diligent professor, with a large family" was frowned upon for attempting to increase his income by "a literary venture!" The main point for us here, in the long criticism of the college from which we quote, is that although it had been suggested that more young men with less income than then sufficed could be brought into the classes by financial grants, the difficulty was that they would rather go elsewhere and pay their own way than accept such help. We may also note, as a straw in the wind, the case of the young artist in Cincinnati whom some wealthy citizens wished to send to Rome to study. "His reply to every mention of the subject is, that he means to go to Italy, but that he shall work his own way there."

America had its early Ruggleses of Red Gap. There is an amusing account of Washington, the capital, in 1834. "The foreign ambassadors," it says, "are terribly plagued about servants. No American will wear livery, and there is no reason why any American should. But the British ambassador must have livery servants. He makes what compromise he can, allowing his people to appear without livery out of doors, except on state occasions; but yet he is obliged to pick up his domestics from among foreigners who are in want of a subsistence for a short time, and are sure to go away as soon as they can find any employment in which the wearing of a livery is not requisite." Another incident of the period is that of the American who attended a Passion Week service in St. Peter's in Rome, and who was almost mobbed because he would not kneel as the Pope passed by. The people all knelt, he said, and "tugged at me to do the same; but, said I, 'Excuse me, I can't.' So, when the old pope came as near to me as I am to you, he stopped and looked me full in my face, while I stood bent, and my hat raised as before, and thinking within myself, 'Now, sir, I am paying you the same respect I would show to the President of the United States, and I can't show any more to anyone': so, after a good look at me, the old gentleman went on." What he thought will unfortunately never be known.

As to "servants," who in the less sophisticated parts of the old America are still called "hired help," we get a picture in the reminiscences of Samuel Goodrich of Connecticut, the sixth of ten children of a clergyman who brought them up well on a salary of $400 a year. "In families," he writes, "where all were laborers, all sat at table, servants as well as masters, the food being served before sitting down. In families where the masters and mistresses did not share the labors of the household or the farm, the meals of the domestics were separate. . . . Our servants, during all my early life, were of the neighborhood, generally the daughters of respectable farmers and mechanics, and, respecting others, were themselves respected and cherished. They were devoted to the interests of the family and were always relied upon and treated as friends." They were not, he adds, "Irish; they had not as yet imbibed the plebeian envy of those above them which has since so generally embittered and embarrassed American domestic life."

Until about 1840 the same was true of the employees in the rising mills and factories. Until the new wave of immigration, with its temptation to the owners to drive the American out by use of cheap foreign labor, such mills, for example, as those in the textile industry in Lowell, Waltham and Lynn, in Massachusetts, were for a while models of what could be done even with the industrial revolution. Most of the workers were young women, daughters of farmers not far away, who worked in the mills and lived in its dormitories, for a few months or years, in order to earn money to pay off a mortgage on the home, send a brother through college, make up a trousseau or help to build a home for themselves when married. They, and the men working in the shoe industry, largely in their own homes, were as far from forming a "proletariat" as is possible. They all worked hard, even up to seventy hours a week, unaware of the lurid dangers now conjured up regarding the health or efficiency of any one who even in wartime should work more than forty-eight hours.

Perhaps the English traveller, Miss Martineau, was too favorably impressed by the American workers as she saw them, though she made plenty of unfavorable criticisms of many things, but her comment is worth quoting as indicating some conditions and molding factors in this period which more or less marks a turning-point in American history.

> There seems to be no doubt [she wrote], among those who know both England and America that the mechanics of the New World work harder than those of the Old. [This is still true but, speaking of domestic service, all three maids I had in London earned together only what one does here.] They have much to do besides their daily handicraft business. They are up early about this, and when it is done, they read late, or attend lectures, or perhaps they have their houses to build or repair, or other care to take of their property.

If we want to know why they were contented with hard work and long hours, we need only read further:

> They live in a state and period of society where every man is answerable for his own fortunes and where there is therefore stimulus to the exercise of every power.
>
> What a state of society it is when a dozen artisans of one town —Salem—are seen rearing each a comfortable one-story (or, as the Americans would say, two-story) house in the place with which they have grown up! when a man who began with laying bricks criticizes, and sometimes corrects, his lawyer's composition; when

a poor errand boy becomes the proprietor of a flourishing store before he is thirty, pays off the capital advanced by friends at the rate of two thousand dollars per month, and bids fair to be one of the most substantial citizens of the place! Such are the outward fortunes of the mechanics of America.

The old American of the real type was not afraid of work; not afraid of danger; not afraid of risk of any sort to his money, labor or life, so long as he was assured of a chance to win.

Let us now call at the homes of a few John Does and Richard Roes, who were, economically, above the bottom but very far from the top. We shall begin with that of a man near Ridgefield, Connecticut, who had been a tailor but had saved money and become a farmer, for, as our narrator states, a "thrifty mechanic . . . usually ended as the proprietor of an ample house, fifty to a hundred acres of land, and an ample barn, stocked with half a dozen cows, one or two horses, a flock of sheep and a general assortment of poultry, including turkeys." There were, of course, an orchard and wood lot. The house was roomy but the kitchen was the largest room, cool in summer and warm in winter with its huge fireplace blazing with logs of hickory.

The furniture was simple but ample, and there were homemade goose-feather beds and homespun linen sheets. The cellar by autumn would contain three barrels each of pork and beef, twenty of cider, and bins filled with potatoes, turnips, beets, carrots and cabbages. In the attic would be quantities of dried pumpkins, peaches and apples, various herbs, and piles of wool, flax and tow. Men, women and children of the household worked hard at the proper seasons, but they had independence and security. Now the family might be taken up as hoarders; then they were merely hard-working, forward-looking, and thrifty. There was no rent to be met every week or month; no bills from butcher or grocer; no gadgets to pay for, saving work in some ways but making more work and worry in others. Hard work, yes, but self-respect, a rightful place in the community life, and no fear of the loss of a "job."

We pass to the deep South, skipping the great places in Maryland such as the Donreaghan Manor of the Carrolls or the declining plantations in Virginia, to see what was then happening to a moderately well-to-do family in the new South, where the service was slave. One might think that where there were a fair number of slaves, household or field, the servant problem would be solved, and that, like her successor in a modern apartment, the mistress of the household might have little or nothing to do. Let us cull a few extracts from the note-book of a visitor.

> The waking in the morning is accomplished by two or three black women staring at you from the bed posts. Then it is five minutes' work to get them out of the room. (Breakfast, then.) Your hostess, meantime, has given her orders, and is now engaged in a back room, or out on the piazza behind the house, cutting out clothes for her slaves; very laborious work in warm weather. There may be a pretence of lessons among the young people, and something more than pretence if they happen to have a tutor or governess; but the probability is that their occupations are as varied as their tempers. . . . Your hostess comes in at length, and you sit down to work with her; she gratifies your curiosity about her "people," telling you how they burn out their shoes at the toes, and wear out their winter woollens, and tear up their summer cottons; and how impossible it is to get black women to learn to cut clothes without waste; and how she never inquires when and where the whipping is done, as it is the overseer's business and not hers. She has not been seated many minutes when she is called away, and returns saying how babyish these people are, that they will not take medicine unless she gives it to them; and how careless of each other, so that she has been obliged to stand by and see Diana put clean linen on her infant, and to compel Bet to get her sick husband some breakfast.

Allowing for a certain amount of exaggeration, the above picture is a fairly true one of the work which a woman as head of a slave household had to do, and the more slaves the more responsibility and work. The woman mistress of a slave plantation had a never-ending round of work, just as did the mistress of a northern household or farm in a different way.

She had clothes to look after, was doctor, nurse and many things else. One important point was that work was not done which competed with or was similar to that done by the slaves. In the northern self-sufficing household, the children would work at trades, domestic service, or in the fields, but on a moderately prosperous southern slave plantation the children could not. A consequence was that they grew up with a sense of superiority but not with the training of hard work in a family group.

We shall now turn west, to another sort of home, a sort which I myself have known in the yet remaining frontier of the Carolina and Tennessee mountains. This is the description by a circuit rider in western Virginia. "The cabin is twelve by fourteen feet, and one story high. The spaces between the logs are chinked, and then daubed with mud for plaster. The interior consists of one room, one end of which is occupied by a fireplace. In this one room are to sleep the man, his wife, the fifteen or twenty children bestowed upon them by Providence —for Providence is bountiful in this matter, upon the border— and as the woods are full of 'varmints,' hens and chickens must be brought in for safekeeping, and as the dogs constitute an important portion of every hunter's family, they also take potluck with the rest. Fastened to a tree near the door is a clapboard upon which is traced in characters of charcoal a sentence to the following effect—which you may read if you are keen at deciphering hieroglyphics: 'Akomidation fur man and Beast.' In this one room the family are to perform their manifold household offices. Here their sleeping, cooking, eating, washing, preaching, and hearing are to be performed."

People were always moving farther west, and we may go ahead a very few years to listen to "Grandmother Brown" tell of her experiences. She and her husband after a western remove had been comfortably settled in Ohio but Brown heard of better and cheaper lands west, and went. Well, the Browns went to Iowa, where Brown had bought 220 acres for $17.50 an acre. It was so wild and lonely that Mrs. Brown wanted to go back without unpacking, but, as she wrote, "We had bought the farm and there we were." Their house had four rooms, cellar and attic but "No shutters, no porch, no closets. Not even a nail to hang a dishrag on! Just house!" In this they lived with their children and "hired hands, when we had any." The Brussels carpet, the one article of luxury they had brought with them, could not be used. It was difficult enough to keep bare wood floors clean of the mud tramped in. Grandmother Brown had plenty of work to do, "cooking, cleaning, washing, ironing, and baby tending," looking after the chickens, eggs and butter, even, on one occasion, making a casket for a dead baby. "Such a way of living is hard, *hard,* HARD," she wrote, "the only thing that makes it endurable for a woman is love and plenty of it." Yet, speaking of the many tasks she had to do in her earlier life in Ohio, she remarked that "We had all the things really necessary for our comfort in those days, and we had quite as much leisure as people have now."

The coastal Northeast, from Pennsylvania northward, was turning more and more to business and manufactures. The changes, however, were most acutely felt in New England. That section was continuing to drift out of the main current of national life. The production of a President of the United States is not perhaps the best gauge of importance, but nevertheless it has its inferences. No New Englander was ever re-elected President. But, more, no New Englander ever became President after J. Q. Adams, except by the back-door of the Vice-Presidency, with the exception of the pale figure of Franklin Pierce. After Pierce, the only two Presidents in our history who came from New England were Chester Arthur, who succeeded to the office on the assassination of Garfield, and Calvin Coolidge, and it is questionable whether the former can be considered a New Englander, as it is uncertain whether he was born in Vermont or Canada, while from boyhood he was a New Yorker. Coolidge, a genuine Vermonter, was elected only after he had been President for part of a term, succeeding to office on the death of Harding.

New England exerted an immense influence on the nation for a generation or so through its authors, publishers, lecturers, reformers, and innumerable "isms" but it had certainly lost touch with the aims and aspirations of ordinary Americans. This had been largely due to the fear on the part of its leaders, political, economic and social, of the rise of the West.

The ordinary folk of New England contributed immensely to the development of the northern band of expansion from Portland, Maine, to Portland, Oregon, but the higher class, which remained, so to say, within sight of the sacred golden cod in the State House in Boston, as a cockney has to be born within sound of "Bow Bells" in London, did not emigrate, and they felt their national influence waning in relation to that of the growing South and West. They had already glimpsed the future, with the acquisition of the Louisiana Purchase by Jefferson, but they felt it more or less sealed to them by the building of the Erie Canal, which carried the commercial advantages of western expansion to New York City rather than to Boston. The railroad era lay yet in the future—in the entire United States in 1830 there were only 23 miles—but this canal, opened in 1825, was one of the great factors in the development of America and the American. Freight rates between New York and Buffalo, the gateway to the Northwest, at once dropped from $100 a ton to less than $8. Western produce moved east and eastern manufactured goods moved west in such sudden and vast quantities that the canal tolls alone amounted to a million dollars in its first year. The destiny of New York as the greatest city and port in the nation was settled then and there. Later, there was to be a rail line from Boston to Albany, but this obviously could not change the tremendous advantage of New York's all-water route. The effect on the West also was magical. Population increased by leaps and bounds, although the great highway of the Mississippi River still determined the main markets for western products, with effects, which we shall note a little later, in linking it to the South.

We have already pointed to some of the human results of raising only, or chiefly, great staple crops, whether in our South, the West Indies, or elsewhere. For the laborer, such an economy calls for only a very limited mentality, and results also in a low standard of living. For the owner of a large plantation, with slave or low-paid free labor, or even for the small proprietor of a few acres, such an economy has marked effects. The fact that the crops cannot be utilized as food or in other ways but must be sold for cash, and that this occurs only once a year, tends to make him dependent on his factor or other money lender for all the rest of the time. A succession of years of bad crops or low prices lands him hopelessly in debt, while a sudden bonanza year induces extravagance. Yet he needs money for the purchase of food and all sorts of manufactured goods.

This situation existed in connection with the staple crop of tobacco, but the sudden expansion of cotton-growing greatly intensified it. Wealth was thought of only as land, slaves and cotton. In the cotton belt diversified farming and food-raising were reduced to a minimum. Food came down the Mississippi from the West. Although there were ample natural resources for manufacturing, as the post-Civil War development of Birmingham and other centers showed, the pre-war South had neither the capital nor the labor for manufacturing, so its tools, clothing and other goods were largely imported from the Middle States of New York and Pennsylvania, from New and Old England, and it was chiefly dependent on the latter two for the marketing of its cotton.

Although this was only vaguely realized, all these factors made the section extremely vulnerable economically. What the South, particularly the far South, did believe was that Cotton was King, that it would create enormous wealth, that the world was becoming dependent on the southern states for an essential staple in world economy, that to raise cotton slaves were essential, that there was an increasingly wide gulf between free North and slave South, between the tariff-demanding manufacturing North and staple-crop South, whereas there was a tie which could not be broken between its need for the food of the West and the need of the West for agricultural markets.

In 1820 the Missouri Compromise, which had come as Jefferson wrote "like a firebell in the night," had brought home to all the nation the definite sectionalism and danger which were developing. The admission of Maine as a free state to balance Missouri as a slave state, and the declaration that slavery must be confined below latitude 36° 30′ in the remainder of the Louisiana Purchase territory, was clearly to many only a stop-gap to fend off an ultimately pending struggle. In 1832 came the Nullification attempt by South Carolina in connection with the higher tariff demanded by the North on goods which the agricultural South wanted to buy cheap. Later, in the same decade, came the discussion over Texas and the refusal of the North to allow its annexation because it would enlarge slave territory.

In spite of great expansion and such growth as we have noted the period was one of general national financial anxiety, culminating in the terrific crash of 1837 when it is said one-half of the property in the United States changed hands, recovery not coming until after 1841. What we have called the confusion of these decades was felt especially in the North and South. Of the cross-currents of thought and feeling in New England we shall speak more at length in the next chapter. We need note here only the nervousness of that section over its loss of power in the nation at large; the emigration of large numbers of its most energetic and ambitious people, young and old, to the West; their replacement in part by Irish; and the increasing clash between those dependent on southern cotton and trade with those zealous reformers who were the beginners of the radical Abolitionist movement; the struggle between New England business sense and love of profit, and that hardy plant, the New England conscience. There was neither contentment nor happiness, but a vast uneasiness.

The same was true of the South. As Miss Martineau wrote:

Nothing could be gayer than the external aspect of these entertainments [in South Carolina]; but it is impossible for a stranger to avoid being struck with the anxiety which shows itself through it all. I think I never was in society in any of the Southern cities without being asked what I would do if I had a legacy of slaves, or told, in vindictiveness or sorrow, that the prosperity of the North was obtained at the expense of the South. I was never in Southern society without perceiving that its characteristic is a want of repose. It is restlessly gay or restlessly sorrowful. It is never content; never in such a state of calm satisfaction as to forget itself. . . . You reproach yourself because you are anxious and cannot be deceived; and feel as if it were ingratitude to your entertainers not to think them the secure and happy people which, in alternation with their complaints of all the external world, they assure you they are.

The American, who like the native Indian before him, had become a nervous, high-strung animal, was getting the jitters. The freeing by Britain, in 1833, of all the slaves in the British West Indies, did not conduce to the American's self-satisfaction, nor did the general trend of world opinion. North and South, men and women were trying to compromise with each other and themselves, on fundamentals, such as slavery and national unity. The Missouri Compromise was one example. President Jackson's refusal to allow nullification by South Carolina, to be followed by a lower tariff Bill and the nullification of his Force Bill, was another. The American was squirming. He was trying to dodge. Both Northerner and Southerner had an uneasy feeling that somehow there were, so to say, worms at work in the core of the fruit which they pointed to with pride as the biggest and finest and most beautiful in the world. What the American of the future would be would depend on whether he would always squirm or whether he would finally face the issues. We may now turn to the West, which in this period was perhaps the only satisfied and hopeful section, especially in its northern half.

That portion of the country had been set apart for freedom by the Northwest Ordinance. All the West, however, was growing rapidly and had the buoyancy which goes with such a condition, in spite of the temporary setback of the financial panic and its aftermath. Moreover, the West was the most democratic portion of the whole country. At the very end of the eighteenth century, Kentucky and Tennessee had set the rule for "over the mountains" when they were admitted as states with full white manhood suffrage, and this example had been followed by every other western state as it entered the Union. The West was crude and much of it still frontier, with all that this means in lack of standards of comparison. To be President of the United States did not call, in the minds of most, for more ability than to be a leader in some frontier community. That outlook is true of all small and restricted communities or societies. It still holds good in many small places. I recall a local history I once read, of Easthampton, New York, by a college graduate, who said that when he was young there were enough men of ability living on the main street (farmers and small shopkeepers) "to form a Roman Senate." Whatever we may think of the Roman Senate at its various stages, we must also recall that public affairs were far simpler in our own earlier days than they are now. President Cleveland had only one telephone in the White House, and after nine in the evening he would answer it himself!

At any rate, the "men of the western waters" had reached the point where they could decide a national election. Of the total population of the United States in 1828 over 4,000,000, or nearly one-third, lived west of the Appalachians. Obviously, the balance of power between the eastern North and South could be exerted by the West, and what New England had feared when Louisiana had been purchased in 1803 had come to pass. The Jeffersonian Revolution of 1800 had done much to overturn the old order and to emphasize the essential democratic trend caused by American conditions, but Jefferson had been fundamentally an aristocrat who was a democrat intellectually only and, as we have seen, with many mental reservations.

What the people had come to want—whether a majority or not, an election would show—was a man as nearly in their own image as they could find. They were tired of the aristocrats and intellectuals—Washington, John Adams, Jefferson, Madison, Monroe and John Quincy Adams. There was also the problem of "the interests"—particularly the banking interest, with the ever-present antagonism of frontier to old settlement, and debtor to creditor. The Western democracy found its man in General Andrew Jackson of Tennessee, the hero of New Orleans and always a picturesque and colorful figure. Joined by the South, which voted against its enemy the North, the West placed him in the White House.

Much has been made of the tumultuous and almost riotous proceedings in that dignified mansion when Jackson's followers attended the levee after his inauguration, but the main point was not that the voters were crude but that they had chosen wisely. Jackson himself was neither uncouth nor illiterate, as some of his enemies pretended, and the Jacksonian Revolution had much more far-spreading results than the earlier one of Jefferson. It is true that he introduced the "spoils system" into our politics on a scale hitherto undreamed of, but self-government, on which a democracy has to function, must be a party government. There must be two strong parties, one for administration and one for opposition, and France and other countries unskilled in the working of such a system have shown how government by groups instead of parties results finally in the downfall of freedom.

Even if Jackson made mistakes, his election and his political manipulation first established a genuine party system, and thus ensured, for a long time at least, the more fundamentally important fact of self-government. He also demonstrated that the only way in which a people can carry out its wishes is to have a strong leader backed by a strong party. A strong opposition is equally essential, but up to the time of Jackson's election the necessary function of parties in a democracy had not been understood. From Washington, who considered party as "faction," down to J. Q. Adams, who was too high-minded to soil his hands with patronage, no President, except to a certain extent Jefferson, had understood the essential nature of government by parties. There had been no provision for them in the Constitution. The general form of government had been laid on the table, so to say, and its operation was largely left to the people to work out. The campaign of 1824 had demonstrated what could happen. Five candidates ran for President—Jackson, Adams, Crawford, Clay and Calhoun. Calhoun withdrew and became a candidate for Vice-President on two of the remaining tickets, but none of the candidates received a majority of the votes in the Electoral College. The American had been left in the beginning to work out his own salvation in organizing machinery to operate the Constitution, and it was not the statesmen or the intellectual leaders of the first forty years who worked it out, but the John Does and Richard Roes of the extremely dirty campaign of 1828. The system, which is certainly neither dignified nor perfect, with its almost unbelievable nominating conventions, its wild campaigns, and its spoils system, still somehow works, or has so far, and it was developed, as all democratic institutions must be, in the heart and brain of the ordinary man.

We must not be too shocked by the scenes in the White House on Inauguration Day, the muddy boots on damask chairs, the pails of rapidly consumed punch, or the undignified rescue of the President himself from his over-ardent admirers through a side window. What was important was that the American, the very ordinary American, had been learning how to run his government for himself. He had conducted town meetings, parish affairs, revolutionary committees, and established law and order on frontiers where writs did not run from any near central authority. Now he was learning how to run a nation. In the generations to come he would take many a tumble and fall in the dark, but his guiding star was his belief in himself, in America, and in the American Dream.

When discouraged or made fearful by popular movements it may be well to recall the wise words of Edward Everett Hale a generation or so later. "The great mistakes in our government," he said, "have all been the mistakes of theorists. The great successes have been wrought when the people took their own affair in hand, and pushed it through." Or, again, "The whole history of government in America from 1620 [of course a Bostonian *would* forget Virginia and 1607!] to this time, is one illustration of the people's success in doing what no statesman or theorist, though he were John Locke or John Adams, could do single-handed. You start with the charter of a trading company. You come out at the end of a hundred and thirty years with organized constitutional government. In that hundred and thirty years you have not one Numa, or Solon, or Lycurgus; but you have the people." That is another slant on the American.

CHAPTER XIV

FROM OLD AMERICA TO NEW

THE quarter century from 1840 to 1861 was the most confused and tumultuous in our annals, but we, in this book, are concerned solely with what the American *was*, what he was *becoming* and, only in relation to this, with what he was *doing*. Many of the factors at work were, of course, not of the American's own choosing. There were, for example, things done to him by others, by social forces which played on him without his understanding them, or by sheer accidents, such as the discovery of gold in California.

In the first category we may mention briefly international relations. We have spoken of the various influences tending to make the American an isolationist. In the period now being considered there were frequent incidents which tended to set us against both France and Britain. The so-called Spoliation claims, of which there were two different sets, both arising from infringements on our neutrality and damage to our vessels during the Revolutionary and early Napoleonic wars, made constant friction with France until 1836. We had assumed responsibility for one set ourselves in part payment for Louisiana, but France had finally agreed by treaty in 1831 to pay 25,000,000 francs on account of the other lot. She then refused to make the payment until President Jackson threatened war, and five years later diplomatic relations were severed. France then paid, but only after intense feeling had been kindled against her for her lack of good faith.

There were also many incidents with England which made hard feeling. Troubles over the Maine boundary led to the undeclared and happily bloodless "Aroostook War" in 1839, when Congress voted $10,000,000 and a force of 50,000 men for the possible struggle. Fortunately, Britain agreed to a settlement which was incorporated in the Webster-Ashburton Treaty. In 1840 there was the McCleod incident in connection with the Canadian revolt of three years before. The details do not concern us but only the fact that Palmerston, the peppery British Prime Minister, threatened immediate war. That too was happily settled but only after American opinion had been deeply aroused. There were also clashes in the Oregon country and constant disputes until in 1846 the boundary between Canada and the United States was agreed upon as practically the 48th parallel of latitude, though our own cry had been "54° 40′ or fight." Moreover it was believed that England had designs on Texas, which had revolted from Mexico. So great was the fear created that it had much to do with our annexation of that slave-holding province in spite of the strong opposition of the North. Many Americans were bitterly opposed to the annexation, because it would enlarge the slave area, but it appeared an even worse evil to allow Britain to attain a dominant position in such a great region jutting up between our East and the Pacific.

Most Americans have been expansionists but not imperialists. That is, they have had an instinctive feeling for westward expansion on our own continent, but have shrunk from conquering alien peoples and from going southward or overseas. "Manifest Destiny" was an instinct, but as meaning ownership of the broad band from sea to sea which is now the United States, and in which there were no alien races, save the comparatively few Indians, to be governed, assimilated or wiped out. Texas was in the belt of Manifest Destiny, and was largely inhabited by Americans who had crossed the border.

To the southwest of us, there had been the Spaniards to deal with, and after their revolution, the newly independent Mexicans, there and in Texas. The governors, customs house officers and others had not endeared themselves, to say the least, to the extraordinary assortment of American settlers, traders and adventurers who came into contact with them.

There was not, perhaps, much to be said for either party to innumerable transactions, but the Americans said it, and emphatically.

Between the recovery from the deep depression of 1837 and the panic of 1857, there was a period of great material prosperity in America, and of misery and disaster in the Old World. Partly due to America and partly to conditions over which Americans had little or no control, these two factors were to be of enormous influence on the future American.

The factors were closely intertwined but we shall take the European ones first. In Ireland the successive potato famines and other economic distresses had brought about the direst misery. The choice was starvation or emigration. For emigration the United States was the country of choice above all others. Irish had already settled here, and the new emigrants hated England but did not want to settle in a wholly foreign land. In the United States the people spoke English but had won their independence from, and fought two wars against, Britain. The climate was favorable. Rapid physical development offered an insatiable market for men who had no capital but their muscles. America was the magnet which drew the human filings to it with irresistible force.

The other great stream of immigration during this period was from Germany. In that country, or rather the then group of countries which we think of under that generic name, there had also been economic distress as well as political oppression and upheaval. Efforts on the part of some to make government more democratic and popular had been ruthlessly suppressed. Those who came to us from thence were workers, farmers and a considerable number of intellectuals and leaders of liberal thought. They were the "Forty-eighters" who, fleeing from the balked revolt of that year in their home lands, just preceded our own "Forty-niners."

These two sets of immigrants who came to our shores by the tens of thousands to help build and influence America were forced from home, it is true, but that is only part of the story. Americans employed every possible method to induce them to come here. Thus these movements of peoples, so important in many ways, were in part forced on us and in part fostered by us. Westward expansion was creating a boom. Manufacturers in the East wanted more and cheaper operatives; railways wanted a reservoir of laborers to build the fast expanding lines; they and the West in general wanted more settlers to develop the land and to give them business. Not only was literature, much of it highly deceptive, circulated in the countries which might possibly supply immigrants, but agents went over to collect them. Needless to say the new steamship lines took part in trying to drum up immigrant traffic.

In considering the influence of these new Americans, we may note first what induced them to come. They all wanted freedom from oppression. They all wanted a chance to get ahead. Great numbers of them were accustomed at home to a low scale of living and freedom. What was much below the accustomed scale for Americans here, to them seemed fabulously high. To put it in its most materialistic form, the "Paddy" who had fled from famine at home was delighted with bad living conditions and fifty-cents-a-day wages here. This was to be of extreme importance in the future drift of America, which was growing with incredible speed but had a scarcity of both capital and labor, for the scarcity of the latter had largely impeded the accumulation of the former. The South thought it had solved the problem by slavery. It had not, nor had the North solved it.

Much misinformation was handed out to the immigrants before leaving the Old World, and there was much cheating of them on arrival in the New. In addition these poor people suffered intense misery on the voyage over, sometimes lasting two and a half months. Even with the new steamships, conditions had not improved much, if at all, as compared with a century earlier. Lack of food and water, overcrowding, bad ventilation and disease took a heavy toll of life and served as strainers which sifted the weak from the strong on the "floating coffins," as the emigrant ships were called. Only the daring and adventurous undertook the American gamble willingly, and only the strong survived. Whether the predominant motive might be desire for political or religious freedom, or for social or economic betterment, for the most part the newcomers brought over fresh injections of vigor and hope, of will and determination. After the long lapse in immigration this new tide, which lasted until the Civil War, was to be important in many ways in making America and the American. It has been said that one reason why the American often comes to feel a profound disillusionment is that he is so compact of mere will and action that when these fail of success or when the success achieved fails to afford the satisfaction expected, he has nothing left. This was not yet true, however, of this period of hurry, bustle and optimism, except perhaps in the South, and the shadow which it cast over the future of other sections.

Whatever sufferings the immigrants had had to bear, and however they had been misled as to particulars, they *did* find here, for the most part, conditions so much better than those they had left, that the Land of Opportunity largely fulfilled their dreams and stimulated their energies.

All America, as we have said, was hungry for increased population and manpower. The Germans after landing went mostly to the Middle West, which has been their stronghold ever since. Everybody, except perhaps the sage who had long since been laid to rest in his grave at Monticello, wanted the land to fill up as quickly as possible. Settlers wanted neighbors, which meant doctors, schools, churches, company. "Bigger" *was* "better" in those days. Owners of land wanted to see it rise in value. Villages wanted to become towns or cities. Manufacturers wanted markets. Canals and railways wanted freight and passengers.

The West opened its doors wide. In 1850 Michigan gave the franchise to all who had lived in it two and a half years and who merely declared their intention of becoming naturalized. Wisconsin had done the same for those who had lived there only one year.

The Germans, and the lesser Scandinavian immigration of this period, brought to the raw West and frontier some notable qualities, such as thrift, orderliness and love of music and singing, to offset some of those which conditions had bred in the older Americans. What America in turn did for them is clearly evident. We have spoken of the quick rise to the franchise in two states, and the same was true of others. This not only gave the newly arrived almost at once the feeling of being free citizens of a free country, but opened careers to them which would have been impossible in Europe. The opportunities, real and seeming, were so great that almost every man was led instinctively to make the most of them as fast as he could.

Among the Germans we may take Carl Schurz, if not as a typical at least as a sample case. A refugee from the German revolution of 1848, within five years of his coming to America, and while not yet a citizen, he was running for the office of Lieutenant-Governor of Wisconsin; soon became a national political figure; and four years later was appointed by Lincoln United States Minister to Spain. No wonder America was a land of dreams. But if all immigrants who passed to the West were not to become great figures, there is ample evidence that dreams came true for the little men also. "There are no large estates here," wrote one Swede from the Northwest, "whose owners can take the last sheaf from their dependents and turn them out to beg." "My cap is not worn out," wrote another, "from lifting it in the presence of gentlemen." Another sent word home that "It is no disgrace to work here. Both the gentlemen and the day-laborer work." There are letters which paint the opportunities in far more sombre color, and others which are much more extravagant in praise, but the three just quoted give a fair picture of conditions which were making Americans.

The West, especially the Northwest, was growing with amazing speed, and the effects were felt in the East. The West developed largely from expansion from the East, but not wholly. If the great modern transformation of the West was due largely to the seaboard it is as much a mistake for the Easterner to think of the West, at any time this century past, as only a less developed East as it is for an Englishman to think in similar comparative terms of Britain and America.

We must now turn to see what was happening to the American of the northern Atlantic coast through the influx of the other great stream of immigrants, at the time—the Irish. By 1850 they accounted for two-fifths of all the immigration then in progress, although in another decade they were to lose the lead to the Germans and Scandinavians. However, while the Irish influx lasted, it was to leave a deep impress on America. It was not merely that in time the heart of Puritan New England, Massachusetts, was to become a Catholic state and Boston a great Irish city. The effects were far more varied.

New England had been losing population rapidly to the West. On the other hand, it was also rapidly increasing in wealth due largely to shipping, and to the production of manufactures for other sections. With rising wealth, the demand for household servants had notably risen, and also the complexity of social life. In America, especially in the slave South, the fact that alien races were looked down upon as inferior led the older-time American to regard the work they did as beneath his own dignity. It has been one of the blots on American life. The cheap Irish male laborer and the women of his family drove the native Yankee of both sexes out of work which they had done with complete self-respect up to this time. Labor of any sort had always been scarce in America. It had become scarcer than ever, but with the influx of the Irish, who would work for almost any wages, New Englanders thought they saw their chance, just as the Southerners had seen theirs in the use of slaves, and with somewhat the same result. The independently minded southern white workman or small farmer moved away if he could, or was ambitious enough to do so, so as not to compete with the Negro. In New England when the Irish women took up household work, not on the old basis of Yankee semi-equality and friendliness but as "servants" in a new sense, the old relationship was broken up. The "mistress" of the household adopted a new attitude, and the former friendly "hired girl" refused to put herself on a level with the then looked-down-upon Irish peasant, and to become a "servant" instead of a "helper." Although for long after, in innumerable households, the old familiar and, if you will, feudal relation, of mutual respect, affection, rights and duties, was to continue, the American "servant problem" had begun, and America was to that extent the less "America."

The same revolution occurred in other lines. In old-time America the real American had taken his turn in working on the roads, in the factories, at all sorts of manual labor, in building canals or railways. With the ambitious men of this class leaving the Northeast for the West, and with the Irish coming in, the situation altered radically. The Irish immigrant, as contrasted with the German, was usually illiterate. He had been used to a low standard of living and to much misery. The Americans felt that these Irish were undermining American standards and the American way. America owes much to them for its rapid development, but there is no use denying that at this time and under the circumstances they were considered an inferior race. For those who had been through all that these had—eviction from their lands, the starvation of their families and all the rest of the doleful tale of Ireland in the 1830's and 1840's—work at even fifty cents a day and a home in the slums, but with freedom, food and at least the dream of a chance to get ahead, were enough to lure them.

But just as Irish servants largely drove the old help out of the homes, so Irish competition largely drove old American labor out of the mills and other lines of work, and as old American labor became even scarcer than ever, and the new proved so cheap, capitalists adopted a new attitude towards their employees, just as the "mistress" of the home felt differently towards those who as "servants" did the work formerly done by friendly "help." In the mills, for example, which had often been models of right relationships, the farmers' daughters and others from nearby disappeared, and "black slavers," as the wagons were called, began cruising through remote villages of New Hampshire and Vermont, their drivers enticing girls to go to work in the mill towns, and the farther off the better as they would then have less chance to quit and go home. The growth of the country and the demand for manufactured goods were sending profits rocketing, but labor was needed and the cheaper the labor the greater the profits.

In business the corporation instead of the individual owner or partnership, was coming into more general use, and this, like the change in the character and race of many of the workers, again tended to widen the gulf between the employer and the laborer. In the manufacturing sections of the country the industrial revolution which had begun so benignly as compared with that in England, and which at first had not seemed destined to change the American, began rapidly to take on the aspects of the class struggle in the Old World. The outrages of excessive child labor, long hours for all, low wages and high profits, the speeding up of labor by new methods and machines, the growth of slums in cities, all tended to change a very considerable proportion of New Englanders into quite a different "American" from the canny, hard-working, self-reliant, self-respecting, self-sufficient Yankee farmer who owned his farm, felt himself as good as anybody else, and took his often cantankerous and parsimonious but independent part in public affairs in town meeting or in state government. There were plenty of them yet, scattered over the countryside like the rocks in their stony fields, but it was becoming difficult to recognize in many of the urban population living in slums, or in those now working as laborers on the great public and private projects, such as canals and railroads, the traditional "Uncle Sam."

The East, or at least the Northeast, was changing. There was the enormous area as well as the riches of the West to be exploited. There were the new inventions. To use a somewhat crude simile, changes were passing over the land like a herd of jumping kangaroos, and with every leap there seemed almost to coincide a new invention which hit the kangaroo in the back, and made him take a longer jump. We had the raw materials, the markets, the increasing variety of machines, while conditions abroad were at last almost forcing on us cheap labor to run the factories, build the transportation plant, and send settlers to people the West, feed the East, and expand the markets still more.

We have spoken of how quickly the new arrival in the West could become a voter. The effect both on him and on us was not bad; indeed, perhaps the contrary. The Germans, English, Scandinavians and others mostly became free-holding farmers with a stake in the community. The situation was wholly different with respect to the Irish, and it was by no means their own fault. Owing to the conditions at home which were forcing them overseas, the great bulk of those who came were uneducated and desperately poor. Considering their long and unhappy experience of misgovernment and their own earlier racial institutions, it is no wonder that they thought of their public duties or opportunities far more as those of clan members following a leader than those of independent citizens bearing the responsibilities of self-government.

Just about the time that the heavy floods of Irish were reaching our shores our political life was rapidly degenerating. Influence had always been important in America, as anywhere, for the rapid gaining of wealth or privilege, and even godly Puritan leaders had wangled large land grants out of godly Puritan legislatures. But in early days the economic, social and political structure had been comparatively simple. With the Revolution had come the rise of the new class of lawyers and of notable politicians, such as Sam Adams, who learned the value of "the mob." Last had come the Jacksonian Revolution, with its slogan of "to the victors belong the spoils," and the modern politician had become full-blown.

Moreover, with the rapid development of the country, and of invention, machinery, business and commerce, the "business man" not only emerged into a new and important rôle different from that of the earlier landed magnate or colonial merchant, but his chances to make money were multiplying so fast that he ceased to care about public life. He could be as nationally notable, as powerful, or as active an empire builder, by being a John Jacob Astor as by being a United States senator or a state governor. Also the transfiguration of business was sweeping everyone (outside the agricultural sections) so completely off their feet that even an Emerson could lecture on the divine uses of railroads and insurance companies.

Business was coming to be regarded as not only transcontinental but as transcendental. The Puritan had believed that getting ahead in the world was a sign of God's approval of the individual life. Prosperity became a religious virtue. Then, in building up the young, new, independent nation, the wealth and power of each was supposed to contribute to the wealth and power of all, and business success became a patriotic virtue. Now under the lead of Emerson it was becoming a sort of mystical one. All these influences, added to the very understandable liking for becoming rich and influential, were irresistibly driving the American to thinking that business and wealth were good in themselves. When Emerson talked of the "divine uses" to which corporations could be put, it was sugar-coating for many a bitter pill.

The business man wanted much from politics but he was too busy to engage in them himself. He found it easier to hire people, who liked politics, to get what he wanted rather than give up his own precious time. Even so great a figure as Daniel Webster obeyed the behests of his larger business constituents. But if the politician was to be efficient in his own new rôle he must be able to "deliver the goods." He had to build up a "machine" and he had to control votes. If, in the Northeast, the manufacturer wanted cheap labor, the professional politician wanted cheap votes, and both suddenly found what they wanted in the new immigration.

They both seized on the Irish, and, I repeat, it was not the fault of that people. It was rather the fault of the American himself, driven relentlessly by forces and temptations too great for him to resist. But what happened was to have a continuing influence on future Americans. The Irish were admirably adapted to being exploited by the machine boss. They congregated in cities. They were poor and mostly illiterate, and, as I have said, they regarded themselves less as citizens than as followers of a leader, and in clan fashion they expected that the leader whom they helped would, in turn, look after them. Our system of ward politics and leaders is really very much like that of any Gaelic clan of the old days in Scotland or Ireland. With this welcome material to hand for his use, the ward boss got busy. He was friendly and helpful. The warm-hearted Irish, exploited by nearly every one else, rallied round him. He could herd them to the polls on election day to vote, not on seriously debated issues, but for what he wanted. The politician not only bought the votes, but in a sense he largely made his voters, and it was estimated in an election as early as 1836 in New England that one-sixth of all the naturalized voters had obtained their papers by fraud, many of them doubtless without even knowing what offense they were committing.

In connection with the Irish as compared with other immigration for the most part, there was a religious problem. The bulk of the Irish were Catholics, whereas only a small proportion of the others were so. The change effected in New England as the old stock was drained west and replaced, and even more, by the influx of new immigration, naturally had profound repercussions. Quite properly the Catholic Church increased its activities to look after its greatly enlarged membership, opened large numbers of churches and established several Catholic magazines. The Protestants became alarmed, and even so prominent a man as Lyman Beecher, among others, fanned the flames by preaching against the Catholic Church as opposed to liberty and incompatible with a free society.

As a result, in the 1840's there were three highly emotional causes of dislike of all immigrants. The "old Americans" feared the effects of the newcomers on politics and American institutions. The American workers who found themselves not only displaced by "cheap foreign labor" but pushed down in the scale of social consideration were filled with resentment. On top of this there was the religious issue, and the three together made for constant mob violence. For some years there was rioting everywhere, in the Northeast. We need not detail even the more important of these burnings of churches and convents; clashes of workmen in streets; and rows on election days. All this gave a great fillip to anti-foreign feeling and so to isolationism. It embittered the relations between sections and classes; increased the gulf between "old" and "new" Americans; established a new technique of violence which was felt North and South in the agitation over Abolition; and greatly intensified in every way the nervous tension of a period in which nerves were to be on edge with two wars and enormous changes.

There were other things which were making the American nervous, agitated, hurried. If New England was reaping from its manufactures for West and South a harvest which it never could have gleaned from its farms, it was also beginning to create fortunes in one of the most exciting fields of enterprise America has ever entered. With the clipper-ship trade to the Pacific, New England ran New York a far closer race than she could in the struggle for western business. In fact she beat old England in one of the mother country's most cherished trades, the building of ships for the high seas.

The short-lived clipper era was full of romance and excitement. The ships themselves were perhaps the most beautiful vessels that ever sailed the seas, and the fastest. The two main trades were with China, and for a short time, after the discovery of gold, California. Even the cargoes of the China clippers brought romance to the wharves of New York and Boston. There was tea in curious and fascinating Chinese boxes. Lacquer, fine china, sandalwood, wonderful silks, all the perfume and mystery of the Far East, were heaved out on dingy docks when a ship came home.

There was the excitement of great gambles as well. The profits might be enormous. One of the smaller of these ships, the *Oriental*, owned by A. A. Low & Brother of New York, cost $70,000 to build and on her second voyage made a profit on freight of $48,000. In the terrific competition between both the British and Americans, and between firms and ships here at home, speed became not only an exciting game but of the essence. For example, the *Oriental* having made a trip to China during which she reached the equator 25 days after leaving New York; the meridian of the Cape of Good Hope in 45 days; Java Head in 71 days; and Hong Kong at the end of 81 days, was at once chartered there to carry a cargo of tea to London at £6 per ton as against approximately £3 which was what the English clippers were getting.

What did these ships and this trade, created by the American, do to him? For one thing, they added to his immense pride in American accomplishment. To have beaten the British at shipbuilding, seamanship and money-making had no small effect in inflating, and justly, the American's confidence in himself. Also everything connected with what we might almost call the clipper-ship sport helped to weave a halo of romance and patriotism around ordinary business, which was beginning in this era, and which infected even the calm mind of the "Sage of Concord."

Lastly, it enormously emphasized the growing feeling that business was a gamble and that the fellow who got there first would catch the chicken. The vessels—*Flying Cloud*, *Witch of the Wave*, and many others—and their captains, were names as familiar to the public as the most popular heroes of fiction. When the *Flying Cloud* made the trip from New York around the Horn to San Francisco in 89 days, a record never before or since beaten by a sailing vessel, it was a world event. Incidentally, freight rates on this route were $6 a ton, and a fortune might hang on which ship got there first. In the China trade English and American vessels raced from Foo-chow to London, and in one case, on a voyage of 89 days, arrived within ten minutes of each other at Gravesend. So great was the rivalry that in 1852 Sampson & Tappan of Boston offered to match their ship, the *Nightingale*, in a race to China and back, with any other British or American one, for stakes of $50,000.

In the plantation South, life moved at a leisurely pace. Slaves were no longer imported. They could be bought from some other planter, or bred, but the latter process was slow. The great staple crops were planted and harvested once a year. Nature could not be hurried, and the chances taken of seasons, markets and prices, had nothing of the nerve-quickening excitement of Northern business. In the North and West, business was coming to be a great game, and the businessman, always in a hurry, was coming to enjoy the game and his power and prestige almost more than the mere gains.

One thing that made the China trade glamorous was that it was between two different civilizations, and that was true, although to a lesser extent, of that which developed along the Santa Fé Trail between Missouri and New Mexico. The slow-paced Spanish life of the Old Southwest was about as different from that of our roaring, growing, raw West or our business Northeast as well could be, and the Spaniards for long had refused to allow the entry of Americans. The trade had been opened almost by chance in 1822, and from then on the Trail was to see caravans of mules, horses, and later of wagons, taking their goods from the starting points in Missouri —first Franklin, then Independence, and then Westport, to Taos, Santa Fé and even far into Mexico, at enormous profits. One party of traders, carried down about $30,000 worth of goods and returned with $10,000 in furs and $180,000 in gold and silver. What profits might be had for all business as it became interwoven in the new pattern of expanding America can be glimpsed in the statistics. In its heyday, the boom town of Franklin offered Philadelphia twenty to thirty per cent more for goods than they could be sold for in the eastern city, and in turn they were sold at Santa Fé anywhere from forty to one hundred per cent above the prices at Franklin. There seemed no limit to profits in return for work, danger and the gambler's chance.

The Trail was a hard journey always, with Indians, thirst, mirages, deserts, death, and Spanish officials to be reckoned with. It called for young and hardy men. Like the clipper trade it formed a brief saga of a few decades but an important one for the making of the American. It was the tale, now coming to be repeated in so many different parts and ways, of risk, courage, hurry. The story of the starting-points was symbolic. The first expedition had started from Franklin, a hamlet where Kit Carson got his earliest information of the Far West. With the opening of the Santa Fé trade, the place boomed. Mississippi steamboats stopped there, and the caravans to Spanish America came and went. Then the Missouri in one of its vagaries swallowed the whole place. Independence took over and became the entrepôt not only for the Santa Fé trade but also for the Rocky Mountain hunter business. It was a wild place, with its traders, trappers, hunters, saloons, French voyageurs, river-men, cattle, mules, buffalo skins, other furs, gold and free-flowing whiskey. Then it went, the Missouri again having overwhelmed the shore and swept away the docks. Business moved to Westport (now the Fourth Ward of Kansas City). It was the old gamble of the West. Would a center become a city, with real estate values and business opportunities jumping like mad, or would it in a few years disappear?

There were fortunes to be made or a few years of struggle and effort to be lost, but every man was on his own and there came to be a wild exhilaration about it all. And always the sense of hurry. The clippers raced to China and back with fortunes at stake. The steamboats plying up and down the

Mississippi piled the wood on their fires and not seldom burst their boilers and killed their passengers in racing one another. The caravans carrying their goods to Santa Fé and beyond had to try to get there first to get the cream of the market. After a night's camp, when time came to prepare to start, teamsters and traders were awakened with the familiar "Catch up! Catch up!"

But perhaps the greatest scramble of all was to California after the discovery of gold, which was to have incalculable effect on the American. In spite of the protests of Mexico and of the anti-slavery men in our North, Texas had been annexed and admitted as a state almost the last day of 1845. Then followed the Mexican War, which many still consider a vast land steal. By February 1848, for a small payment, $15,000,000, we had got title not only to Texas but to practically all of New Mexico, Arizona, Utah, Nevada and California. We had already, on the eve of the war, wisely settled the Oregon question with England, and so had title to the present state of that name and of Washington. "Manifest Destiny" had done its job, but with complications of which we shall speak presently.

Eight days before we signed the treaty with Mexico, and unknown to the American government, gold was discovered in a stream on the ranch of an early settler in California, John Sutter. Sutter himself oddly ties up many strands of the American story of this period. Born in Germany, he had a somewhat vague career until he came to America and settled in St. Louis. He joined a trading party to Santa Fé, and later went over the Oregon Trail, and on to California then still Mexican. He became a Mexican citizen, got a grant of thirty-three square leagues of land and built up a vast baronial estate on the Sacramento River, a square league by Spanish law being about 4500 acres. When the United States acquired California he thought his property was safe, but oddly enough the discovery of gold on his estate was his ruin. His workmen left, his vast flocks and herds disappeared, hordes of gold hunters came in, and squatters seized his lands. He died many years later, practically penniless, even a small pension from the Federal Government having been stopped. His whole story is an illuminating one as regards this hectic period in the formation of the American business man and empire.

When word of the new El Dorado spread through the world in 1849, and it did so with marvellous speed for that day, there was one of the most amazing rushes in history. From East, West, South, from England and Europe, from China, from almost everywhere, men of all sorts, clergy, nobility, ships' crews, businessmen, day laborers, farmers, every sort possible, and of dozens of races, caught the "gold fever" and tried to get to California to take their chances. They went overland across the as yet only partly known continent, by horse, wagon, and even on foot; by vessel to Panama, across the fever jungle of the isthmus and by vessel again up the coast; or all the way by sea around Cape Horn. Within a year, 1850, there were 92,000 persons in California, mostly men, and by 1860 there were 380,000. Conditions were fantastic. In less than four years after the Pacific Mail Company was formed it sent on its boats from San Francisco to New York approximately $122,000,000 in gold. In California itself prices meant almost nothing. Playing cards sold for $5 a pack; cowhide boots for $45; flour for $60 a barrel; newspapers cost $1 each; even cats, to catch mice in the new stores, brought $50 to $100 a-piece! Laborers were getting $20 to $30 a day; lucky miners were picking up $100–$1,000 a day washing dirt.

Nobody knew how long this sort of easy money gone mad would last. Many who went to the Coast and encountered all the risks and hardships found little or no gold, but the "chance" kept drawing them, and again it was hurry, *hurry*. They might be too late. Speed for the clipper ships too and others! Passengers wanted to get there first; cargoes to be sold at hundreds of per cent profit might bring more if they arrived at the right time and before somebody else's. Speed, every one gambling for millions with the God of Fortune, excitement, tremendous energy, and the zest of empire-building.

Although the cow country and the cowboy lay yet in the future the picturesque West of colorful romance had begun, including the stagecoach, the excitement of which lingers with all who were fortunate enough to have attended the Wild West Shows of Buffalo Bill. The stagecoach meant risk, attacks by Indians, possible death, but—speed. What most fired the imagination of the boys of the period, however, was the Pony Express. It was the most famous mail route in our history, using at its height 420 horses and 125 riders, to carry mail between St. Jo, Missouri, and Sacramento. Each rider covered from 75 to 125 miles, changing horses every ten or fifteen miles at stations provided for the purpose. Arriving at terrific speed, the rider would leap with his pouch from his foam-flecked pony, mount another and be off. Changing not only horses but riders, the letters, carried at a cost of five dollars each, flew across the plains and mountains at a speed of 250 miles in twenty-four hours. Every superfluous ounce of weight was stripped from the trappings of both man and horse, even from the letters themselves, which, like modern air mail, were written on the thinnest of paper. As Mark Twain wrote, giving his impression of seeing a Pony Express go by, it was "so like a flash of unreal fancy . . . that we might have doubted whether we had seen any actual horse and man at all." The wonderful ponies who stood up to the work, and the dash and daring of the young fellows who rode them, fired the imagination of youngsters during the short period when the Express operated, and the effect was no slight one in making the American.

This was America—danger, excitement, to be on your own, to win through in the quickest possible time. This was the air the American breathed. This was the sort of thing that spurred him to work to the limit. He was not thinking of an abstraction called the "national income," or worrying about how it might be divided. He was thinking about his own, and the great game he was playing. If he had thought about the national income he probably would have had the quaint idea that such a thing was only the sum total of all the incomes of all citizens, and that having unlimited opportunity, he would if he seized it before somebody else, increase the national income by increasing his own. It was a simple age. Of course the slaves were clothed and fed and cared for at the expense of somebody else, for whom they had to work as they were told, but who wanted that? Other visions stirred the free American—a rider on the Pony Express, a captain of a whaler at twenty-seven, master of a vessel racing the British from Foo-chow to London, moving west from poor land to rich land, to democracy and elbow-room, dashing to California on the chance of hitting it rich and getting a million. No "social security" but taut nerves and LIFE.

We may now consider a few other factors that exerted a powerful influence on the making of the American. By 1850 there were roughly four quite differentiated sections in the country. There was the Far West lying between the Pacific and the great mountain ranges. It was raw frontier but different from all our others. It was not essentially either farming or hunting. It was mining and business. It had not been settled, for the most part, in the usual way of population gradually pushing westward from old settlement to new but by people from every state in the Union, most of them going around by Panama or the Horn and coming in, in a sudden flood, through a back-door, so to say. It was to be a part, and a most loyal and important part, of the new nation but the "Coast," as it is called, is an empire in itself and has always had its own peculiar individuality. Moreover it faces the Pacific and not the Atlantic, and the immense remoteness of the Coast Region from everything in Europe tended to be another strong element in our isolationism from European affairs.

The other three sections were the Northeast, notably New England, New York and Pennsylvania; the slave South, stretching across the lower Middle West; and the free northern part of the latter. This last section had been subject to special influences, besides that ever-recurrent factor in making the

American, the frontier. The Ordinance of 1787 had declared that the states to be carved out of the old "Northwest" should be forever free. Also there were location and climate. Owing to all these, the section had received almost all the emigration from the free Northeast. It had also received practically all the immigrants from Europe and England who wished to be farmers. Such newcomers arrived from the Old World chiefly through the ports of Boston, New York and Philadelphia and went west by canals and the newly developing railway lines.

The West was becoming increasingly interested in and dependent on these means of transport. Every slave state bordered on either the ocean, the Gulf or the Mississippi River, and had otherwise many transport facilities by water. Almost wholly non-commercial and non-industrial, the South did not experience the need of railways to the extent which the North and Northwest did. As so often has happened in American life, new needs and the means to supply them almost miraculously synchronized. The immigration of the decades from 1830 to 1860 was supplying the upper Mississippi Valley with settlers of the soundest sort, and the manufacturing and commercial East with a glut of cheap white labor, which refused to go either West or South. In these critical years, railway building on a colossal scale seemed an inevitable necessity and a profitable investment. Like all new countries we had had to lean heavily on the old for capital for development, but the tremendous crash of the 1830's had involved very heavy losses to English investors and created, to say the least, intense resentment on both sides. However, in America itself money was now being made fast in the various ways we have mentioned, and in others as well. Also there was the sudden flood of gold from California, which was comparable only to that which flowed to Spain from its American Empire in the sixteenth century and made it for a while the leader of the world. These sources gave us most of the capital needed to build all the railroads we could think of as serving the needs of East and West. We did it. We overdid it. The panic of 1857 was in part a result, but nevertheless the two sections became bound together by most important links of steel as well as of thought.

The steel links were rather more noticeable than the others, though they too existed, under the surface of different mental attitudes, and here we come back to the frontier and its influence in the making of the American.

We must always recall that frontiers changed fairly quickly, and as one frontier pushed ahead of another it was followed by "old settlements," often in an incredibly short time. Going west, culturally, was much like going down stairs, but, as Dixon Fox has pointed out, the stairs did not remain stationary for the lower ones were always rising to the level of the upper. It takes a certain amount of accumulated capital and, if not of leisure, at least of surcease from the incessant fight to keep alive and make a living, to provide a civilization that is something more than a subsistence. A man toiling with all his strength to make a clearing, build a shelter and get some food crops started, had not much time to putter over flower gardens. If he did he would have been considered by the community as an incapable fool, and in fact at that stage he would have been. America could never have become America if it had not had the uncultured ruggedness of the pioneer, nor if it had not slowly developed the culture of the old settlements as time went on. It needed both but in developing the country on frontier after frontier, and in the processes of building up capital, both frontier and old settlement came to consider that the only real American, the one and only red-blooded "he-man," was the one who succeeded in the practical concerns of building, as fast as possible, homes, communities, fortunes, an empire. The man who "wasted time" over literature, art or music—as extensions of the flower garden—was a sissie, not a man, and not worth thinking about. Women, well they were different. If "Mother" wanted a few flowers, or some curtains at the window, a book or pretty dress, it was a whim to be humored. Women were inexplicable anyway, but it was all outside a man's life and interests.

And here we come to a very deep element in American life and the formation of the American—the position of woman, the separation of the sexes, and loneliness in its many aspects.

As to the first, it must be recalled that in settlement after settlement and on frontier after frontier, at different times all the way from Jamestown to California, there were often and for long times extremely few women compared to the number of men. The men may often have been rough and wild, but they were civilized. They did not practise marriage "by capture." That not being allowed, to gain the affection of a woman or wife, a man had to study to please her. The position of the American woman may be said to have begun at Jamestown where, after a couple of years of hardship and only male company, the first women appeared from England. It took little time for them to be married and the competition was great, as it was in the clipper-ship and other trades we have mentioned in this chapter. During all our earlier and frontier periods there was an enormous premium on just being a woman, and as a consequence, the price of women went up. The price was to pamper and please the lady.

In general it may well be asserted that the first placing of the American woman on a pedestal by the American man was due to the simple law of supply and demand. That he kept her there and raised her even higher was due to many causes, of which the most important was that she stood beside him in his toils, adventures, dangers and struggles, and deserved what he could give her. The tradition began at once, and in the Indian troubles in the Jamestown period, a number of women, such as Mrs. John Baldwin, successfully and single-handed defended their homes against the savages until help could arrive. From then on the roll of women—known and unknown—who have displayed conspicuous courage is a long and noble one. But there were other forms of courage called for by women than fighting Indians, being captured by them, or facing the hardships and dangers of pioneering journeys with such tragedies as those of Donner Lake or Death Valley.

For many or most, there was the grinding toil of heavy household tasks; of child-bearing and rearing under the most difficult conditions; the breaking up of old homes and moving to new where the woods had to be felled and the fresh ground broken before even a start could be made; and there was the *loneliness.*

Morris Birkbeck in his travel book speaks of the woman on the frontier who was "quite overcome with 'lone'," and it is an ever-recurring note. "Grandma Brown," in her reminiscences, speaks of how "at night it used to make me so lonesome, sitting at the front door in the dusk . . . to hear the prairie chickens calling over the meadow, 'Boo-hoo! Boo-hoo!' " In the frequent moves, old friends and neighbors had to be left behind. A woman with her family arrived where she did not know any one perhaps, or possibly where there *was* nobody, yet. The first frontier of the prairies was bad enough when it was mostly empty, but the vastness of the plains later made for unutterable loneliness, of which we get a graphic picture in Rolvaag's *Giants of the Earth.* One contemporary commentator on the West says that whatever temperament the emigrants may have had before, "they soon become meditative, abstracted, taciturn."

The story of American loneliness and its many-sided influence on the American has never yet been told. For one thing, it made for a pleasure in welcoming newcomers and strangers which is incomprehensible to people in the established communities of the Old World. The coming of a stranger was not an unwelcome intrusion into a closed circle, to be resented or at best tolerated with such grace as could be mustered. It was an event which broke perhaps the unbroken silence of weeks and was to be welcomed with joy. Loneliness was the fountainhead of that American hospitality which foreigners find so warm-hearted and even almost too overwhelming. I have spoken of the relationship of hospitality to the loneliness of the great Southern plantations but it was true of the poor on the frontier as well.

America is not only a *Land of Contrasts,* as my old friend the late James F. Muirhead of London called it in his book, but it is a land of extremes in climate and wealth as well, and in social relations. The lack of social intercourse for long periods demanded an excess whenever possible. Not only did Americans in general become possibly the most hospitable, "open house" people in the world, but they took revenge on marked social and emotional starvation much of the time, by an excess of emotion and social relations at other times. The wild emotional religious camp-meetings of the simpler people both of South and West, lasting sometimes a week or more, can be understood only against the background of the lonely weeks or months intervening. The American, like the first Americans, the Indians before him, learned to alternate between a starvation diet and an orgy.

Also, just as we have noted that the lack of an historic past and of deep roots reacted on us in the cult of genealogy, so the lack of opportunity to gratify three other needs, that of social companionship, of being singled out for honors, and of costume, resulted in Americans becoming the world's most noted "joiners," and in the multiplication of organizations, of weird titles and dress, of the Elks, Masons, Shriners, Red Men, Daughters of the Eastern Star, the Grange, and innumerable others, with their meetings, rituals, titles and insignia. Just as there was physically at Jamestown the "starving time" so there was in America at large an emotional, social and psychological starving time. To that we can trace many of the traits which strike foreigners as so odd. If we have no gorgeous Lord Mayor's procession, with costumes sanctified in their queerness by centuries of historic association, and have instead a long line of "citizens in carriages," as we used to, made up of uninspiring local politicians in silk hats and frock coats, we are forced to take it out in other ways. We can go back to old Bradford's wise remark as to conditions in Plymouth to the effect that human nature, deprived of its natural outlet in one direction, will find another.

There also came into American life a new sort of loneliness, that in the relationship of husband and wife. Woman was to be put on a pedestal and to enjoy in some respects a position with regard to men unknown to the women of other lands, but, as with everything else, there was a price to pay. In America, woman was in the home and man was in the world. In old and settled societies, both moved along more or less together, but in the swirling tide of America, the home, which was the woman's world, was still holding to its old moorings, whereas the outside world, in which the man was venturing, was moving at top speed over new and uncharted seas.

Emigration brought the first cleavage, but as the business game became more and more absorbing, it spread to even the old Americans. The whole situation was set forth for both sorts of Americans in a comment made in 1834 by a kindly doctor in Cincinnati. He had Welsh, Irish, English, German and Yankee patients, and was a great believer in the immigrant, but, as Miss Martineau wrote, "He told me that, unless the head of the emigrant family be timely and judiciously warned, the peace of the household is broken up by the pining of the wife. The husband soon finds interests in his new abode; he becomes a citizen, a man of business, a man of consequence, with brightening prospects; while the poor wife, surrounded by difficulties or vexed with hardships at home, provided with no compensation for what she has left behind, pines away, and wonders that her husband can be so happy when she is so miserable. When there is an end of congeniality, all is over; and a couple who would in their own land have gone through life cheerily, hand in hand, become uneasy yoke-fellows in the midst of a much-improved outward condition or prospect."

The American woman in innumerable cases had to busy herself about something, and in a world where all around her was humming with activity, get away from the loneliness and monotony of the house. Except for the very unusual woman, or one who was willing in those days to be known more or less as a "crank," business, the professions and politics were barred fields. So countless ordinary but lonely and social and active-minded women began to make a world of their own. It is noteworthy that the West, where perhaps loneliness was most intense, was the section in which, in the 1850's, the movement was started organizing Women's Clubs of the modern type. Woman, starved in so many ways emotionally and intellectually, discovered "culture" and beauty. "The lones" gave birth to Browning Clubs and the House Beautiful. It may all have been somewhat crude but woman had found new interests and new incentives, and a new self-importance which was reassuring. Men might be laying the material foundations of personal or national life with amazing speed, but woman had found a job in building the intellectual and aesthetic life. Mr. John Doe might be acquiring a rising importance as president of the local grocery company or lumber concern or running for Congress, but Mrs. Doe might now become president of the Ladies Literary Society and begin to feel herself a leader in the social and cultural life of the same community.

The gulf between the man's world and the woman's widened still further. If the wife could not follow the husband into business and politics, neither could the husband follow the wife into "culture." He was thoroughly imbued in the new sections of the country, and even for the most part in the older, with the idea of the frontier woman who when offered geranium slips to pot remarked that "She never know'd nobody make nothin' by raisin' sich things." In his absorption in the game of getting ahead he may have had twinges of conscience about not doing enough for his wife, and felt that he was drifting away from the "little woman." When, however, she became active in a woman's mental and social world from which he was himself excluded, the score was evened. He felt he could devote all the time he wanted to business, whiskey and talking business with his men friends so long as his wife was not alone but enjoying herself in "society," having her tea and listening to some neighboring woman read a paper on *Sordello.* That curious separation of the sexes socially and intellectually which was so long to be characteristic of the American had begun.

Another effect of all this for the American was the feminizing of American culture and so of the mental food which had to serve American minds. There was the long period during which no book could be published which might offend the supposed complete innocence of a virgin of sixteen. We had the "ordeal of Mark Twain" with his wife blue-pencilling all his work and cutting out any phrase which might offend a lady. We had all the prurient mental involutions which made Americans speak of a bull as a "male cow," and which even today force many kennels to advertise "lady dogs." To the inhibitions of Puritanism, old and new, was added the limitation of art in accordance with the social proprieties as envisaged by the innumerable female arbiters of Main Street.

If all these effects stemmed more or less directly from the forces of speed, competition, loneliness and others we may mention lastly one of a different sort but which also developed from these causes. If culture was beginning to be pursued even on the prairies and was fiercely driven into a corner in Boston, it was still pretty thin. Lowell tells with ingenuous delight of a party he attended where the number of puns made were counted by "an ingenious friend" and found to be seventy-five in twenty minutes "or a little more than three a minute." For Lowell, as for others, William Page was *the* great American painter, and of all American women authors Lydia Maria Child had "the most of what can be truly called genius." Another glimpse of the arts appears in the circumstances which sent William Wetmore Story to Italy, beginning—except for the Tories after the Revolution—a long and illustrious line of expatriates. Story was an able and versatile young man but he had not made any serious effort at sculpture. However, the citizens of Boston wanted a monument of its celebrated citizen, Mr. Justice Story of the Supreme Court. Who more appropriate to employ for the job than his bright young son? The only trouble was that the son was not a sculptor but that difficulty was got over in the simplicity and good-natured kindliness of the day by sending the young man to Italy to learn to become one, with the commission in his pocket to produce the statue when he had learned. Nothing perhaps could better illustrate the extreme thinness of the cultural atmosphere, so heavy in Europe with its centuries of accumulation and tradition.

For any man who wanted seriously to be an artist of any sort, there was nothing to do but go abroad, as so many were soon to do, and cut himself off from his native scene. It was not merely that there was almost no chance to see an example of great art in the then America. It was worse than that. In almost all of the country the artist could find no understanding or congenial society. It was even worse again than that. In the roaring business development we have had glimpses of, one had to be doing something useful and highly profitable to rank as a man. There was a growing literary group in Boston but Lowell was not only a writer, he was a professor and Minister to Great Britain; Motley was Minister to the Netherlands; Longfellow was a professor; Parkman was the inheritor of wealth. But the man who wanted to be merely a sculptor or painter or poet or musician, was made to feel that he did not belong in America, and the sense of being despised was added to the lack of inspiration or encouragement or even understanding appreciation. Like the earlier women—and he was more or less looked upon as one—he got "the lones." He could not sustain himself on the new women's clubs nor even by spending an evening in the company of a Lowell, inviting his soul with puns at the rate of over three a minute. And so the tumultuous currents of New World life forced out first a trickle and then a steady stream of men whose capacities and tastes were different from those of the empire builders, to absorb the culture of the Old. American life was in time to be enormously enriched by the process, and the successors of the empire builders were to become the greatest collectors of art since the eighteenth-century English Mi-lords or the nobles of the Italian Renaissance. Later, the raw America we have been describing was to become the asylum of the past and possibly the hope of the future.

The American life of the 1840's and 50's was as varied and hectic in other ways as in those already touched upon, due to many different causes and in turn influencing in many ways the growth of the American. It was a period of unbounded optimism, darkened by one heavy cloud to which we shall soon have to refer. We still drew largely on Europe for our ideas, and over there, the gradual recovery from the Napoleonic wars, and the broadening and mellowing effects of the French Revolution as they were making themselves felt, were stirring the waters of great new hopes for mankind. The tide which was moving the hearts and aspirations of men of the Old World washed our shores from thence in many ways, besides the philosophies which started us on such experiments as Brook Farm, New Harmony, and others, which seem unimportant now but had their influence on some of our best minds when almost any new experiment in the way of a better ordering of society seemed possible or at least worth trying.

We have already spoken of the Woman's Movement and the broad causes which underlay it, and which at long last led, during the present century, to the Suffrage Amendment to the Constitution and the opening of almost all lines of work and activity to women. We had also what we may call the Humanitarian Movement. There was at the same time a somewhat similar one in England, proceeding from the great Methodist revivals, and from other causes operating during the early years of Queen Victoria and from the complete change in court life since the days of her more or less worthless predecessors. But in America there had long been special influences at work. We most assuredly had our brutalities and what we think of now as shocking inhumanities, in our prisons for debtors and criminals, and so on, but in America, for some reason, there was from the first a better soil than in the Old World, for humanitarian movements to flourish on, and I say that without forgetting the crimes, particularly since the Prohibition era, and the still occasional lynchings.

The first settlers had come from England and had naturally brought the English mentality and outlook with them, but odd things began to happen. In Elizabethan and early Jacobean England, which gave us our earliest immigrants, the cruel sport of bear-baiting by dogs was a favorite one. It was forbidden by law in the colonies, and the Americans enjoyed it no more than they have been able to enjoy the bull fights of old Spain or of our Spanish neighbors to the south. Moreover, for the most part, certainly outside of Massachusetts, severe punishments, especially capital punishment, were less frequent than in the England of that time. We abolished, before England did, imprisonment for debt except perhaps for failure to pay alimony!

Possibly the special causes working over here were, for one, the democracy of the frontier, not perfect but certainly more real than prevailed in any of the Old World countries with their strong persisting ideas of feudal property and position. If the small frontier settlement bred narrowness of mind—and it assuredly did—it also gave a better understanding of who the other fellow was and what he was like. He was a man, with the same tasks and perhaps temptations as yours. Life was hard for all, so it should not be made still harder, except for the incorrigible. Property was much more evenly distributed, and there was far less crime against it, in the early days, than in the old country. As compared with England, where a man could be hanged for stealing a loaf of bread, he was much more likely in America, if he was out of luck, to be given one. Though England had romantic outlaws who infested Hounslow Heath and other approaches even into London itself, I have never found a case of highway robbery in all the American colonies in the eighteenth century, though roads went for many lonely miles through woods. Other crimes against property, such as house-breaking or burglary, were extremely rare. I think this was due to the more even distribution of property, the chance that each man had to acquire it honestly, and, above all, to the fact that a very great number of the population owned their own land and were self-supporting. Also, in the later humanitarian movements of the period we find the philosophy of the worth of the individual human being, partly derived from the strong religious element in the community and in part from the political propaganda of the revolutionary and constitution-making periods.

The rigors of the old Calvinism were passing and in Concord, while Thoreau, from the vantage-point of his political philosophy, was defying the government to collect taxes from him, Emerson in 1840 was also writing, with the cheerful optimism of the Unitarian and Transcendentalist: "In the morning I awake, and find the old world, wife, babes, and mother, Concord and Boston, the dear old spiritual world, and even the dear old devil not far off." With such an outlook on life, amelioration of the lot of man might seem within early reach, and Emerson was a typical American who for a century had perhaps the greatest influence on American youth of any writer.

There was much that called for improvement, and New England became a seed-bed for every sort of reform and organization. To be in the van of the new thought of the age became a fad. There were labor movements; movements for the improvement of schools, which even in New England and rich New York, were deplorable; for abolishing imprisonment for debt; for improving prisons, some of which in Connecticut were almost unbelievably bad; for improving the care of the insane, and educating the deaf and dumb; organizations to promote world peace; the temperance and prohibition movements; and, above all, that for the abolition of slavery.

We are not here concerned with the record of that movement or of all the events finally culminating in the war between the sections. That war was to have an immense influence on the American. It has been claimed that the struggle was neither an "irrepressible conflict" nor inevitable. In my opinion it was both.

North and South were caught and borne along by forces

which they were powerless to control and which neither had consciously set in motion. For forty years there was a confusion of issues and even after war had been declared, honest and intelligent men on both sides were asking themselves and others what *was* the *real* issue? The Union? An interpretation of the Constitution? Slavery? Tariffs and other economic differences? What? Neither side was completely unified on any of the issues. Lee, one of the most high-minded of Americans, was not fighting to defend slavery as an institution but his state of Virginia. Grant had owned slaves, but was fighting to preserve the Union. And so it went, with an infinite variety of opinions and emotions both North and South. Lincoln, in spite of his "House Divided" speech, did much to lose the sympathy of England because he would not declare that the war was for freedom. He claimed it was for unity, and the English could not understand how an enforced unity could be compatible with freedom. As we try, however, to trace the influences which have made the American, I think we must conclude that slavery if not the sole issue was the fundamental *cause* of the war, and consequently of its effects. Curiously enough, it was a great Virginian, a slave-holder, who disbelieved in slavery and who believed in a loose union, who did much to set the train of events in motion—Thomas Jefferson in his Northwest Ordinance.

Let us contrast the two sections. In the earlier part of the eighteenth century there had been slavery in the North as well as in the South. The institution in the North, however, due to climate and economic factors, had not proved profitable as in the South, and in the North abolition did not involve serious problems. Between 1774 and 1804, either by immediate emancipation or a graduated system, slavery was abolished in the states of Rhode Island, Vermont, Massachusetts, New Hampshire, Pennsylvania, Connecticut, New York and New Jersey, in the order named. The states carved out of the old Northwest Territory had from the beginning been dedicated to freedom by the great Ordinance just mentioned.

As a result practically the whole of the northern part of the continent was free, and, as we have seen, attracted practically all the intelligent, liberty-loving and adventurous immigrants from the Old World. These not only rapidly built up Northern population, provided free white labor, helped to develop our West and the manufactures and commerce of our East, but also in innumerable cases brought with them new ideas germinating in England and Europe and, so to say, kept the mental atmosphere stirred by fresh breezes. Moreover the North, although many of its people were illiterate, had a far larger literate population than the South, with not only its smaller total number of whites but its larger percentage of slaves. The northern market for books and magazines and the general dissemination of ideas was far wider than in the South, and the publishing business came to be almost wholly centered in the North, particularly in Boston and, to a lesser extent, in New York. Again, the North had no sacred cow to defend nor any taboo on a particular institution—unless it was the tariff, in the manufacturing quarters of the Northeast—and so the play of ideas could be freer. The discordant voices may have made a Babel of confusion but at least any one could shout and be heard. If mobbed by some, the speaker or agitator was hailed by many others. Moreover, the North, with its variety of factories, mines, railroads, shipping, business and commerce of all sorts, as well as the agriculture of the old America, was coming not only to feel itself in the main current of American life but was realizing also its growing strength.

On the other hand, exactly contrary conditions had, to a great extent, increasingly come to prevail in the South. Immigration passed the section by. The Irish laborer did not want to lose himself in a mass of Negroes. The sturdy German and Scandinavian farmers did not want to compete with slaves or slave-owners. The South had almost no industry or business or shipping. It offered no career to the ambitious beyond the bounds of a slave economy. Its politicians and statesmen were forced to defend slavery. But although many intelligent, forward-looking and loyal Southerners realized how slavery was retarding the possible development of the section, the South was caught in its toils as Laocoön and his sons were bound by the coils of the great serpents. If the North was gradually finding slavery unprofitable and abandoning it in practice even before it did so legally, the causes were largely economic and climatic and not ethical. In the same way, if the South began to find itself more and more bound by the slave system its situation had also been due to the same causes, but in reverse.

The section's special adaptability to the raising of staple crops, the invention of the cotton gin and the exactly contemporaneous inventions in England, had made cotton "King," and "jumped" the price of slaves and the apparent need for them, while the staple crop economy and the slave's lack of adaptability to factory work had prevented the rise of industry, through the absence of liquid capital and of suitable labor; and the very presence of the slave hindered the introduction of such labor. Moreover—and it was an important factor in the whole case—the tide of world opinion was turning against slavery and condemning it on moral grounds. The freeing of its slaves by the British Empire indicated like a beacon buoy the direction of the new ethical and humanitarian current. The North, which had got abreast of it chiefly from economic motives, could claim virtue, and its reformers, at least, could adopt a "Holier than thou" attitude. The South, which was caught in a social and labor system from which it saw no way of escape, had to try to build up an intellectual and moral Maginot Line against the tide of world thought. The South had some banks, insurance companies and railway mileage, but on the whole the capital of the South, on which its social and economic civilization was based, was in land and slaves, with the latter alone valued at, roughly, $1,350,000,000.

In the repeal of the Missouri Compromise in 1850; in the struggle in the border states, notably Kansas; in Court decisions; in the fiery attacks on their institution by northern Abolitionists; in the incitements to slave revolt; the publication of *Uncle Tom's Cabin*; the admission of California as a free state; and in many other incidents, the South saw portents of the fact that not merely slavery but all that the South had built up was threatened and at stake.

Various consequences ensued. One was that the section in general, including many who disapproved of slavery but did not know how to get rid of it without a complete destruction of all values, had to build up an intellectual and moral defense in favor of it. This brought about a certain weakening of force in its political leaders. Up to the very day almost when the war came, the South was largely dominant in Washington but the men who represented her were far below the caliber of the earlier "Virginia Dynasty" of Washington, Jefferson, Madison and Monroe.

Moreover the South—if it is not stretching a point—was beginning to feel another aspect of the loneliness of which we have spoken. The artists of the North who could not stand against the public opinion of their society took refuge in flight but the South could not, yet it could not but help being affected, even unconsciously, by the fact that not only the other sections of its own nation but large sections of other nations as well were condemning the "peculiar institution" which nevertheless it had to defend. So, to avoid the effects of an inferiority complex, it had to build up a superiority one. It had to idealize and romanticize its own way of life and the Southern landed gentleman in contrast to the crudity and vulgarity of the businessman of the North and West. It went back to the "Cavaliers" as contrasted with the "Roundheads," and the works of Walter Scott were imported by the car-load, literally.

Of course, the wild denunciations and misrepresentations of such Northern Abolitionists as Garrison or Harriet Beecher Stowe were countered by abuse in the Southern journals and in Southern speeches. On a higher plane was the controversy over the interpretation of the Constitution, the nature of the Union and the right of secession. These problems had been discussed, off and on, from the beginning, as for example at the time of the Kentucky and Virginia Resolves in 1798 or of the threatened secession of South Carolina, on account of the tariff, which had been countered by Jackson. The point is that the old discussion was opened anew as a result of the threat to the slave economy.

Given changing world opinion, given the different conditions in the free North and the slave South, given the rapidly advancing superiority of the military strength and resources of the North over those of the South, the magnitude of the issues at stake, and the apparent impossibility of changing the Southern system without a complete disruption of its social order, it was evident that a mighty conflict must ensue. The signal was the election of Abraham Lincoln. The new President was inaugurated on March 4, 1861. On April 12, the Confederates fired on the Federal troops in Fort Sumter in the Harbor of Charleston, South Carolina. The American, Northerner or Southerner, had found a problem he could not settle by talk or work or compromise. He would be a different American if the nation were to be split in two—and if two why not ten?—neighboring but antagonistic small countries as compared with the vast expanse which he had won for perhaps the greatest united people and democratic experiment the world has known. From the early failures, and then success, in settling Virginia, down through the building of other colonies and the expansion across the entire continent, American men and women had confronted every danger and hardship. Now they were to face ordeal by battle, not with savages or foreigners but between themselves, divided families, a divided people. A sudden realization of what Union meant, what America meant, a vast surge of emotion, a passionate resolve to defend the American Dream, swept over the North and West when the stars and stripes were fired on that April morning in Charleston Harbor.

CHAPTER XV

FROM UNION TO EMPIRE

THE half century from the time of the threat to the Union in 1860 witnessed notable changes in the American—his occupations and ways of life, his ideas, even his racial composition if we consider him as a legal rather than as a psychological concept.

We have endeavored to show in part what were the causes which influenced the peace-loving Americans, devoted to getting ahead and with no desire for war or military glory, to fight among themselves the greatest and bloodiest civil war of modern times.

One of the suggestive threads to follow in tracing the growth of the American is his reaction to demands made on him for service at times of national crisis. In the early colonial days, because of the extreme individualism of colonies and colonists, no unified policy or unified force could be built up to fight either the French or the Indians. Everything was local, individual, haphazard. Throughout the Revolution, Washington and the Congress had the same difficulty. Both the men and the officers would come and go as suited them, or leave at the end of a three months' enlistment no matter what the military situation might be. Although, in the Civil War, there was trouble on both sides, with heavy desertions, the average American had evidently become less individualist in the bad sense and more socially minded.

Conscription was first dared in the Civil War, and was successful, in both North and South, in spite of the serious "draft riots" in New York and elsewhere. On both sides the war had begun with a rush of volunteers from among the best men, young and old, in both sections. As always, the war was expected to be short, and the flower of the youth rushed to get into it. With conscription, there was a drop in quality but the situation was somewhat different on each of the two sides of the Mason and Dixon Line. At that stage of our development it was considered right that a man who was conscripted could hire a substitute, and the atrocious system of "bounties" was introduced. In the North the entire population, from top to bottom, could be thus hired as substitutes. This was not so in the South, where 3,500,000 of the lowest laboring class were slaves, and until about a month before the end of the war, the Confederacy did not dare allow the use of slaves as soldiers.

It is useless to try to estimate the comparative qualities of the ordinary soldier in the two contending armies, but we may note a few points. There are bums and roughs in every army, and war is war, or more accurately, as General Sherman said, "Hell." Moreover, war propaganda and atrocity stories do not vary much from one war to another, or as regards one side or the other. Both sides try to slander each other and stir up hatred. But, looking forward to the future American in sectional terms, it was certain that the South would suffer most from the fundamental issue of the conflict. That section claimed the right to secede. The North claimed the right to preserve the Union. Consequently it was the South which would have to suffer invasion and the Hell of war on its own soil and among its own homes.

Some points about the Americans in the struggle stand out clearly. When it started, neither side had any regular army which amounted to anything compared with the numbers eventually engaged. Practically all who fought the nearly five years' war were peaceable Americans drawn from civilian life. Yet they fought bravely, magnificently and with bulldog tenacity, on both sides. Moreover, in spite of all the ordinary crimes of war, such as looting, burning and others, which are bound to occur, the American showed that if he could fight hard when he had to, he also fought clean. There were no massacres, no wholesale brutality.

Those behind the lines—the agitators, reformers and anti-reformers, newspaper editors, women who suffered but could not fight—did their best to fan the hatred between the sections, which was long to persist, for this and other reasons. Fortunately, at the time and later, the men and boys who faced each other in their blue or gray learned to appraise the manhood of North and South at its true value. For example, in a lull in the terrific fighting between Lee and Burnside on the Rappahannock, soldiers on both sides of the river built fleets of toy boats which they sailed across to one another, the Yanks filling theirs with tiny cargoes of sugar and coffee, and the "Johnny Rebs" putting tobacco on theirs. Officers on both sides winked at the infraction of discipline until General Lee decided the soldiers were getting *too* friendly and that the practice should be stopped. He sent General Gordon along the river bank to warn the troops, and at one spot Gordon found evidence of excitement. On investigation, he discovered a very scantily clad Yank in the bushes on the Confederate side. Sternly questioned, the lad admitted he was a Yankee but had thought there was no harm in coming over to "see the boys just a little while." When asked "What boys?" he answered "These Johnnies." "Don't you know, sir," said the General, "that there is a war in this country?" The Yankee soldier admitted he did, but added, "We were not fighting just now, sir." Gordon said he was enormously amused but when he had to threaten the intruding Yankee with prison his Confederate soldier hosts pleaded for him, and said it would ruin their honor if they got him into trouble. The General thought, gave the word, and the almost naked Yank, as the General said, "leaped like a bullfrog into the river" and swam to the other side.

Those who had fanned the flames of war on both sides had tried to make the Southerner believe that all Northerners were merely coarse, cowardly money-makers who would not fight; whereas the Northern war-mongers had pictured all Southerners as bullies and braggarts who would give up the moment their bluff was called. These boys, who sailed their boats and visited one another, where 13,000 had just lost their lives in battle, had learned better. It has often been said that the worst rows are those in village, church or family, and the most bitter of wars are those called Civil. These two little stories are worth noting, as showing how the American soldier could both fight and forgive, though the politicians, editors, and people back home in general might do neither.

An American may be of any race or color, and although the Negro had not as yet legally become an American, he deserves mention in connection with the war. His record was of the best. From the North free Negroes fought well in the ranks, but it was in the South that they showed so remarkably. It must be recalled that Abolition literature, magazines, such books as *Uncle Tom's Cabin* and others, had dwelt upon the cruelties visited upon slaves by their masters. Undoubtedly there were many such cases, and the system was antiquated and bad, but against the Abolition outpourings we have to set the amazing conduct of the Southern slaves. As we have noted, there were 3,500,000 of them, and almost all of these were left at home to run the plantations, get in crops, and guard the master's property and family, though one was occasionally taken along in the army as a personal body servant. The South in the early days had often been fearful of slave insurrections. Now, if ever, was the time for the slaves to rise. The white men were almost all of them at the front. Back of the lines were the three and a half million blacks, and women and children and property. Yet there is practically not a single instance in which a slave was unfaithful to the trust that was placed in him. Women, silver, jewels, all were faithfully guarded. It is one of the amazing facts in history, which Americans should not forget.

Sometimes the curious relation in which a slave stood towards his master took an amusing turn. An officer who had taken his black body servant into the army with him and was about to go into battle, told the slave to stand by the tent and guard the master's property. On returning, he found the slave had taken to the woods when the firing began, and when, after finding him, the master threatened to punish him, he said: "Massa, you done tole me to take care of your property, and *dis* property," touching his own breast, "is wurf fifteen hundred dollars, and I done took good care of it."

Although we cannot go into more detail, we may mention one last point. We have spoken of the slaves protecting the white women and children at home when the white men were away, but beyond that fact we may add that among whites or blacks, on both sides, there was practically no authenticated case of sexual crime committed. With the millions of men involved, it is an almost unbelievable record but even if there were *some,* the record would still be an unparallelled one in time of a great war, and is another sidelight on the American.

Before looking at the home scene we may glance briefly at the international aspects of the struggle, and their influence on the outlook of the American, particularly as an isolationist. Modern Germany had not yet been welded by Bismarck into a great state. Italy, which had been only a "geographical expression" was new as a national unity and not yet a great power. Spain was decadent. The real powers were Britain, France and Russia, and each, as a result of their attitudes during our fight for existence as a democratic Union, played a rôle in forming the mind of the American.

The *ersatz* Emperor of the French, Louis Napoleon, not only desired the success of our South and tried to draw Britain into joining him in unneutral acts towards the North, but flouted the Monroe Doctrine by endeavoring to establish a French Empire in Mexico. With our hands full at the time, we could do nothing, but did force the Emperor to retire from the New World when the war was over, though the attitude and acts of France were not soon forgotten.

During the war, feeling against Britain also became bitter. Various incidents such as those of Mason and Slidell, the *Alabama,* Laird rams, and others, and the unconcealed desire of many of the British upper classes—so-called—to have the great experiment in democracy fail and the South break the Union, inflamed the North. The British Government itself maintained a correct, and even friendly attitude, but the United States was struggling for its life, and felt keenly the cold lack of sympathy of the rich and Tory elements in England, in spite of the hearty good will of some among them and the amazing friendliness of the working classes, who were suffering on account of our struggle. *Punch* sneered and even published a full-page cartoon of Lincoln with horns and hooves. Gladstone made anti-Union speeches. Even such a noted historian as Edward A. Freeman published in 1863 the first fat volume of what was to be a monumental work, with the title: *History of Federal Government from the Foundation of the Achæan League to the Disruption of the United States.* The first volume dealt only with Greece. There never was another. There was no *Finis.* There was only Appomattox.

It must be said on behalf of many freedom-loving Britishers that the case for the North was by no means clear to them, any more than it was to many Americans. For many reasons, which were good, Lincoln had to base the war on preserving the Union rather than on abolishing slavery, but this alienated much sound British opinion which, in the early stages of the struggle, came to view it not as one to free 3,500,000 slaves but to force 5,500,000 free whites into a Union which they had rejected. Many British who would have been on our side if the issue had been freeing the slave, could not see how a Union enforced by bayonets could bring freedom to any one.

However, the result of this, and of much inflammatory writing in the North even by such authors as James Russell Lowell, who should have known better, was to leave post-war Americans extremely sore at both France and England. The nation was to grow with enormous speed in the next generation or more; the sense that the Union had been preserved and was—as a whole—becoming enormously rich, added to the American's self-esteem; and his experiences during the war, added to those earlier experiences, already mentioned, with Europe, led him to dislike more than ever any contact with the Old

World. The isolationism of the American was never just parochialism. It had deep roots.

An odd exception also developed out of the war. More than once in the international history of the American, a belief has proved more potent than a fact. Russia, the old Czarist Russia of the 1860's, was for its own good and sufficient reasons friendly to the North. Stories of the aid it had given, diplomatically and otherwise, were exaggerated, but when in 1867 Russia offered to sell Alaska to us for $10,000,000, and we bought it for $7,200,000 we did it to oblige Russia, and out of gratitude for her supposed offer to use her fleet on our side should either France or England intervene on the other. Nobody wanted Alaska, and it was unknown country. No one realized what a stupendous bargain we were getting, and it came to us out of a misapprehension as to how much obligation we were under.

It is amazing how much of the American empire, if you choose to call it such, the American has acquired by the method of bargain and sale. No other people has ever done anything like it. Let us, for a moment, look both backward and forward. We bought a large part of the Middle West, from the Mississippi to the Rockies (the old Louisiana Territory), from the first Napoleon for $15,000,000. We paid $5,000,000 to Spain to clear our title to "the Floridas." We fought Mexico, but we paid her $15,000,000 and assumed $3,250,000 of claims against her, for a large part of our far West, including California. We rounded out our southern boundary by giving her $10,000,000 more for the "Gadsden Purchase," to give us the best route from Texas to California. We fought Spain in 1898 but gave Cuba her freedom and paid Spain $20,000,000 for Porto Rico, Guam and the Philippines. We bought the Virgin Islands from Denmark for $25,000,000. We finally gave Colombia $25,000,000 for the Canal Zone. Was ever an empire so acquired before? It is another slant on the American, and an illuminating one.

Coming back to the domestic scene after the Civil War we

may note that the winning—and losing—of the war left its deep impress on all sections. Some of the effects were permanent, if slow in being felt. For example, the fact that the Union had been maintained was to be of profound influence. However hair-splitting the logic of interpreting the original Constitution might be, secession as a practical possibility had been ruled out. The United States had become a nation, indivisible. From the day of Lincoln the term "United States" became a singular and not a plural noun. That in time was to give a new sense of greatness and power to all Americans. Moreover, in spite of all that was to come, and the problem of the Negro which is still acute for him and for the whites, the abolition of slavery in America did align the nation with the ideas of the modern world, and was like opening all the windows of a musty house to the fresh breezes and the sunshine. The effects of the war, however, were felt very differently in the various sections, then and for a long time afterward.

We may glance first at the West on which the war had the healthiest influence.

At the beginning of the struggle both West and North lost very heavily financially on account of the default of the South on most of the $300,000,000 which its planters and business men, as well as municipalities and state governments, owed to banks, merchants and investors of the other sections. That these losses were quickly overcome and replaced by enormous prosperity was due to an unusual combination of circumstances and events in both the Old and New Worlds. The American himself, although he was to be molded by them, was only in part the author of them.

For one thing, due to many causes, there was once more an enormous outflow of emigrants from Northern Europe and the United Kingdom. There had been wars, oppressions, crop failures, dislocation of the poorer classes by the industrial revolution, and, above all, that still not wholly explained phenomenon, the huge increase in population, with its resultant "rise of the masses."

Before the war the dream of the Westerner had been of free land, but national legislation had been blocked in Congress by the legislators from the South who feared a too rapid growth of population in the free states, much as New England had earlier feared the growth of the West. The war removed the opposition and in 1862 the Homestead Act was passed by which a settler merely by settling and remaining on a 160-acre tract could acquire title to it without making any payment at all. Under this law, the Morrill Act which we shall mention later, and the huge grants to assist the building of railroads, the government within a generation or so disposed of an empire amounting to some 160,000,000 acres.

The land was there. That was America. Its presence and how it was disposed of was American. But it needed people to use it and markets for their crops. It was Europe which began to pour in the people and to supply, in part, the markets. Although immigration was light until 1862, during the five war years over 800,000 immigrants arrived, of whom 80,000 were carried straight to farms in the West by one railway alone. Within two and a half years after the passage of the Homestead Act over 20,000 farms had been settled under it. In 1864 it was estimated, and apparently with truth, that a young man could get a farm, fence it, build his house, raise his crops, and pay for it all with $500 left over, in the first year. It is no wonder that houses and barns and orchards sprang up like magic, as was said.

America gave us the land. The war permitted the Homestead Act. Europe sent the settlers, but it did more. By 1862, after a couple of bad years, there was a complete crop failure in all Europe. The West began its new career by shipping that year to the Old World 60,000,000 bushels of wheat. Practically no cotton moved. The Wheat Kingdom of the West had supplanted the Cotton Kingdom of the South. One more fortuitous circumstance entered into the pattern which the Great God Luck was weaving. Just on the eve of the war there had begun the great development of agricultural machinery. The McCormick reaper could do the work of ten hired men, and, after 1860, all kinds of machines were invented and improved. The West was wallowing in prosperity, out of debt and full of buoyant hope, living a democratic and sane life on farms and in villages, small towns and only moderately sized cities. Uncle Sam had moved to the prairies.

A combination of circumstances had also brought an abounding, if more hectic and less sound, prosperity to the North. War, in an unregulated economy, makes enormous profits for manufacturers and others. Demand leaps, prices jump, and things must be had at almost any cost, without delay. Delay becomes the heaviest cost of all. At least that was always the situation before nations had learned to try to "take the profit out of war." The North was the manufacturing heart of the nation. How much it had been doing even before 1860 was indicated by the fact that when war broke, New York City merchants alone lost $160,000,000 in bad debts in the South. Even with this, it was clear that the North was bound to make money if the war should prove long and be won at last.

But in addition, other things happened. We have just seen how the West boomed. That section was now closely bound to the North. Before the war, one-half of even the far smaller amount of wheat exported to Europe had gone down the Mississippi and by sea. Now all the new exports went over the Northern railways, through Northern ports and business houses, or remained to feed the rapidly increasing Northern factory population. Further, the needs of the West for manufactured and other goods helped Northern firms. There were to be the usual causes of friction between old settlement and frontier, which we have traced back to Hooker and Winthrop, and of which we shall speak briefly later, but the West had more than replaced the South both as a market and as a source of supply for the North.

Northern manufactures would have been booming in any case; Northern capital busy in Western development; Northern railways carrying heavy business; but just as the inventions of farm machinery played such a sudden and important rôle in Western agriculture, so did the general development of invention and machinery in the economy of the North.

For example, to mention only one or two, in 1862, that *annus mirabilis,* a machine was put on the market which would make a hundred pairs of shoes a day as compared with the former hand process. In another two years, we were exporting 50,000 sewing machines a year, that invention which made possible the whole of the modern ready-made clothing business. Without going into further detail concerning the hundreds of inventions which were speeding up production, cheapening goods and broadening markets, we may just note that if the machines created a dislocation in labor and, in some directions, what we now call technological unemployment, they also created all sorts of new work. The machines themselves had to be made and other machines had to be built to do it. Iron, steel, building materials for factories; shops; salesmen; transportation; new containers for the new goods sold and shipped in new ways—all these opened innumerable sources of profit and employment.

Two other things happened. Although a large proportion of the increased immigration found its way directly to the farms of the West, a large part also remained in the East to supply the factories with the increase in labor needed despite labor-saving inventions. This new supply, in turn, released a considerable part of the labor supply of older American stock to go West and start farms. Finally, as one of those strokes of luck that have so often helped to weave the patterns which have deeply affected the American but for which he himself has only in part been responsible, came the discovery of oil. This was to create even greater fortunes, and more suddenly, than all the precious metals in the West. In Venango County, Pennsylvania, six weeks after war was declared, there was discovered on land which had been worth only $3 an acre, the first flowing well of petroleum, which flowed to the tune of $10,000 a day! In the three years, 1862–65, from various wells over 300,000,000 gallons were produced, creating hundreds of millions of sudden wealth. It was an even greater thing than the finding of gold in California just as we signed the treaty with Mexico. If we believe in chance and luck, and if we too often think that God looks after children, drunks and Americans, the belief has been borne in upon us as individuals and as a nation over and over again. It has been one of the chief molding influences on the American. Of the amazing fortunes of the next couple of decades, and of *their* influence, we shall speak a little later in this chapter, and must now turn briefly to the post-war South.

There the picture is a different and far less happy one. Luck had *not* been with the South. That section had adopted a labor economy based on slavery. That had to go, but no one was wise enough to plan *how* it could go and yet not tear down the whole fabric of society. When the South decided to move alone against the rest of the nation and the world, it had perforce to adopt that view of the Constitution which would allow of secession. It cast the die for that, and war; and lost. Slavery had been of profound importance for the American. It had fashioned the whole way of life and thought of a large section. It had brought on the great conflict. It had left the section desolate and broken. But it is interesting to trace to what an extent the American of all sections had been made by outside forces.

When the end came, the South was prostrate. It had lost practically everything except its remaining buildings and its land, which had to be worked to produce. Bank deposits, currency, securities of all sorts, insurance—all had become worthless, and in addition the billion and a half or so invested in slaves had been cancelled by strokes of the pen and the sword. There was practically no manufacturing or foreign commerce. No gold or silver or oil had been discovered to bring a flood of new wealth. No hordes of immigrants poured in to work in mills or to build up farms on free lands. For nearly a generation before the war, in creating an intellectual self-defense against attacks upon its "peculiar institution," the South had been forced more and more to retreat into romantic dreams about itself, into isolation from the world and the rushing present. During the struggle a large proportion of the flower of the young men of the section had either been killed or had lost the chance of the education they might otherwise have had.

The close of the war found its educational institutions, like all else, bankrupt, and there was no money to start afresh. The best university in the South, that of Virginia, which in 1861 had had 600 students, two years later had 40, and so it went, including actual destruction of plants as well as of endowments and incomes. We have spoken of the contrast with the North and West economically but it held true of education also. The founding of a number of the most important institutions of higher learning in the North, such as the Massachusetts Institute of Technology, Vassar and Cornell, date from the war years, the new fortunes being poured into them. Such men as Vassar and Cornell alone gave over $5,000,000 to found the colleges named for them during the war. In the West, the war had permitted the passage not only of the Homestead Act but of the Morrill Act by which the Union government donated 30,000 acres of free land to the states for each representative they had in Congress, such land to be sold and used for the establishment of the state universities which have since played so large a part in the intellectual development of that section. The South had been caught by a malign Fate. The shackles of the slave had at last bound the hands and minds of the whites, and no one knew how to loose them. Even Lincoln said that if he had all power he would not know. Neither compromise nor reason but blind force finally ended the slave system.

The surrender at Appomattox would have spelled the ruin of the South and enormous difficulties even if reconstruction had not taken the form it did. Slavery again played a malignant part not only in what we have come to call more specifically "Reconstruction" but in its effect on American life and on the American himself ever since.

We have spoken of certain factors at work in the North, some of long standing, such as the intense zeal and bigotry of the Abolitionists, stemming back to the early days of similar phenomena in the Puritan period, and of the tremendous impetus given to the desires of the manufacturing interests as a result of the war and of the development of machinery. Lincoln alone, if even he could have done so, might have held these groups in check, but his assassination released the extreme radical and evil forces of all sorts. From one direction or another came demands for the military occupation of the South; for treating it not as a part of the Union restored but as a conquered country; demands for vengeance; and much else which the passions of other post-war periods have shown crop up almost invariably.

But there was another point. The new Republican party had fought the war. It had freed the slave. It had also stood for a protective tariff. It was anathema to the whites of the South. The radical Abolitionists wanted to humiliate those whites. The North wanted a protective tariff. The Party wanted to keep its hold on power. If whites in the South could be held down a while, and the Negro be given the vote, the latter would vote Republican, and all the radicals, manufacturers, politicians and party leaders would entrench themselves in a whole section of the nation otherwise hostile to them. So came all the various measures for governing the Southern states, the amendments to the Constitution, the carpet baggers, and all the evils and horrors of the Reconstruction period. And thus resulted a bitter sectionalism in the national life; a socially, economically and intellectually retarded South for a couple of generations; a speculative, manufacturing, financial and commercial North; and a new West, agrarian, democratic in the broader sense, radical, opposed to the East, as frontier to old settlement, and tending to hold the balance of political power. These were in general some of the influences which were to make the Americans in the three sections so different until the end of the century, and even later.

We may pause a moment to suggest one influence of the

frontier, and consequently of the West on the East, which is not usually mentioned. The American has been pre-eminently a man who likes "gadgets" and new things. Two brief stories may illustrate what I have in mind. Once in London I asked for an egg fried on *both* sides. The answer of the waiter was "It can't be done, sir. It can't be done because it never *has* been done, sir." As a boy in the early '90's of the last century I was much teased by an uncle of mine who came back to New York from the new little city of Cheyenne and taunted me with the fact that New York had only gas lights and horse cars whereas Cheyenne, where he lived, had electric lights and trolleys. The answer to such little tales is, of course, that in an old community with settled ways of doing things, a *new* way has not only to encounter the inertia-drag of perhaps centuries of habit but also a heavy additional cost. A city which starts fresh can install the latest in everything, but an old city which wants to do so has to sacrifice a very large amount of capital invested in the plant which has become out of date.

I think it a point of very great importance that in America, for three centuries, there have always been brand-new communities and homes growing up which can afford the most-up-to-the-minute equipment of all sorts without having to consider scrapping the cost of the old. The consequence is that there have always been, particularly since the age of invention, models of the best, or most efficient, convenient and novel, for people to look at and envy. Little Cheyenne around 1892 could laugh at big New York, but was bound in time to make New York follow, at any cost. One of the most fundamental facts about America and its molding of the American has been that we did not have *one* frontier and settle it, but that there have been innumerable frontiers ever advancing and influencing the equally advancing "old settlements," in refluent waves. This is different from what has happened, at least on the same scale, anywhere else in all history. It accounts for Babbitt with his love of new gadgets for his car, but also for Mrs. Babbitt with her vacuum cleaner and other releases from housework, with all the resultant effects on woman and the home, and also for America's vast industrial development. No American "planned it that way." It was the result of a whole combination of circumstances, but all helped to make the American in his new phase, and, roughly, we may date it from the Civil War.

Before we go on to the decades following, we may mention one more point with regard to "Mrs. Babbitt" and the American woman in general. As part of the intellectual and humanitarian ferment the position of woman was to be immensely improved, but wars had a good deal to do with it. In the Crimean War in Europe, a few years before our own, Florence Nightingale had immortalized herself, changed the male attitude, and opened new careers for women in hospital nursing and other social work. In our great struggle, women came out of the home as never before, to do all sorts of public service.

Both war and war-time inventions helped the movement. For women who had to earn their own living, outside of domestic service one of the chief occupations had been that of seamstress, the low wages, poverty and despair of which were sung for all time by Thomas Hood in England in his *Song of the Shirt*. The invention of the sewing machine threw great numbers of these poor women out of their accustomed employment, but also made possible the ready-made garment industry. The effect of the new machine would have been felt in any case, but the sudden demand for uniforms and other clothing for the armed forces, in enormous quantities and at almost any price, made the new industry "big business" almost overnight. Women, as we have seen, had already, some decades earlier, worked in mills, but as a rule for a limited time and for specific objectives. What happened during and after the war was different. Women who were looking forward to a lifetime of work, were drawn out of homes, not only by the sewing machine but by others (above all, the typewriter, about 1874), into the work-a-day world of business.

Our Civil War in many ways marked the change from old-fashioned warfare by professional armies and old methods to modern war in which the entire civilian population began to take part. Such an overwhelming number of men had to be drawn from civilian life, that women simply had to replace them, and we need mention only one more aspect of this problem, one which was to have lasting influence on both the American woman and "the American." There had of course, for some time, been women teachers in the schools, but because of the enormous demand for men at the front—in Ohio alone 5000 men teachers left in the first two years—the situation became permanently changed. By 1865, for example, there were about 10,500 women teaching in the Illinois schools, and another step had been taken, which was to be permanent, in the emancipation of woman, the equalizing of opportunity between the sexes, or the feminization of American youth and culture, as it is variously interpreted.

The position of woman in America is peculiar to us among all the great modern civilized nations, and a topic of constant comment. We have mentioned the pedestal on which she has almost always been placed here. A friend writes to me that "When I was a boy in Vermont I used to see the middle-aged and old men going to church, not with their wives, not in front of their wives, but about fifteen or twenty feet behind them. I remember commenting on it to my mother and her saying with a laugh that it was supposed to be the New England way. It was never the way in any other country." We get another slant in the following anecdote. George William Curtis, writing in *Harper's Monthly,* in speaking of the reputation of Emerson when Curtis used to hear him lecture, said that grave parents were "quoted as saying, 'I don't go to hear Mr. Emerson; I don't understand him. But my daughters do.'"

The American after the Civil War was about to become subject to new strains, in a double sense—mental and racial. Men of all types were to make handsome or colossal fortunes, not by war, like the old robber barons, or by the favors of a sovereign but by their own shrewdness, hard work, the help of the Great God Luck, the manipulation of a democratic form of government, and by other means.

There are three chief points to consider with respect to this: the woman; the plutocrat, large or small; and the ordinary citizen.

In general, we may say that every post-war period is one of breaking down of ordinary morals. The years after Appomattox formed no exception, and we need not concern ourselves, as we would have to in a narrative history of the period, with all the scandals in politics and business, such as those of the Tweed Ring in New York City, of the bad smells of the Grant administration in Washington, or the doings of such grabbers for millions as the Vanderbilts, Goulds, Daniel Drews and others of the day. Methods were unscrupulous; the possible loot or prizes were fabulously great; and the race was to the swift and the strong. To get there you had to have the guile of the serpent, the speed of a race horse, and the hide of a rhinoceros. Some had all three, and piled up mountainous wealth, but they worked and worried as men seldom have done. The getting was good, and what they got was *theirs*.

As an aunt of mine used to say on her visits here from Paris at the turn of the last century, these husbands of her rich New York friends "all lived like kings and worked like slaves." In the horse-and-buggy days of 1882 Herbert Spencer, on a lecture-tour from England, noted of Americans that "Work has become your passion. The hair of Americans turns gray ten years earlier than in England. . . . The American almost ignores what good the passing day offers him." A new era of expatriation began. Only money seemed to count, and the artists—whether musicians, authors, painters, sculptors—fled the market place of millions and took refuge on the Arno, the Tiber, Seine or Thames. The women liked the money their husbands made but they also fled from boredom, and thought they could find a more satisfying life in foreign society and the title-market. The title-market was even more sordid than the market for leather or oil or toilets for the new bathrooms at home, but that is what happened.

The ideas of an "upper class" seep down to the "lower." In America, for a considerable time, the "upper class" had been represented by a vacuum. There was no hereditary aristocracy, and the upper class of colonial days—the "governor's set," the clergy, and large landed proprietors—had lost influence or disappeared. The new rich, heralded by the new journalism after the war, caught the attention of the crowd, so what the women of the millionaire set did and thought had an influence out of all proportion to its intrinsic value. Of the latter, there was almost nothing, but the influence was considerable and wholly bad.

Of course, American men had always wanted to "get ahead." It was in our blood, and there had been in colonial days some quite rich men, even some in the millionaire class, such as Hancock of Boston, Carroll of Maryland, and George Washington; but for them life and fortune moved at a leisurely pace and their lives and temptations were quite different from those of the big business leaders after the Civil War. Let us take just a few as samples of an age and a stage in the making of the American, for if hard-scrabble Vermont farmers were typical Americans so, in another way, were these men of a new era and a wholly different world of opportunity and moral pressures.

In 1848 a Scotch weaver and his family arrived in America as excessively poor immigrants. One of the children was Andrew Carnegie, who at the age of eleven got a job in a cotton factory at Alleghany, Pa., at $1.20 a week. We need not trace his amazing career, but by 1901 he had become the greatest steel manufacturer in America, sold his plant to J. P. Morgan who capitalized the United States Steel Company for over a billion dollars, and Carnegie spent the next twenty years in giving away his money, and hugely enjoying the job. His annual income was over $12,500,000 but at the time of his death he had donated in benefactions in Great

Britain and America over $350,000,000, and had become the close friend of such scholars and statesmen as Lord Acton, John Morley, Gladstone and others.

John D. Rockefeller was born on a farm in central New York and at thirteen was digging potatoes for a neighbor and working ten hours a day, when the sudden idea came to him that at the legal rate of interest, seven per cent, he could get as much money from the interest on $50 as he could by digging potatoes for many long days. Young John moved to Pennsylvania, walked the streets looking for a job, got a poor-paying one, and started to save money. Then came OIL, and the young bookkeeper, having risen to $25 a month, got in on it. The rest of the story need not be detailed, but his wealth was estimated at one time—such wealth and so invested is impossible to estimate accurately—at a billion and a half dollars. During his later life he gave away $530,000,000, to which his son added $170,000,000, making $700,000,000 given to every sort of project and all over the world. Rockefeller's partners all became wealthy, and one of them, Edward S. Harkness, for example, gave away $100,000,000 during *his* lifetime.

Henry Ford was born on a farm in Michigan and became a machinist at a low wage, though his father offered to give him forty acres of land if he would give up the fool idea. Ford did not invent the automobile but his genius produced the cheap one, which was such a curiosity when it was the only car in Detroit, that he had to chain it to a lamp post, when he left it, so that it would not be stolen. In 1929 he refused a cash offer of one billion dollars for his plant.

We could continue the list indefinitely with such men as Huntington, Hill, and others, who built fortunes and empires from railroads; the little publicized Weyerhaeuser whose timber lands were estimated to be worth $350,000,000; the "copper kings," coal and beef "barons," and others, of this amazing era.

We are not interested in these lives merely as success stories but as affording us a new approach to the American. Never before, in the entire history of the world, had such opportunities been opened to large numbers of men. There had been individuals, of course, Oriental or Roman Emperors, Cortez and Pizzarro in Mexico and Peru, a Clive and his satellites in India, but their situations were different. The race for this fantastic American wealth was much more of a free-for-all, and the winners, even those who did not restore huge sums to the public, felt, and to some extent truly, that they were builders and not just looters.

They were making enormous changes in the whole world, and if spreading ruin in some directions, in others were opening opportunities for literally millions of people. If in their ruthless accumulating periods they thought about the matter at all, like Clive they were probably astonished "at their own moderation." The railroads, bringing vast fortunes to a few, were also opening up empires for tens of thousands of farmers. Who can figure what infinitely varied effects were wrought on the lives of millions by the introduction of the kerosene lamp and later petroleum products, of gasoline, of the cheap motor car, farm tractor, and all the rest? Who can balance the public evil and the public good effected by the making and the distribution of such fortunes as those of Carnegie, Harkness, Rockefeller and others?

An instance of how far-reaching and unexpected the effects of this fortune-making could be is exemplified in the career of the picturesque John W. ("Bet-you-a-million!") Gates. Like nearly all the great fortune-builders this plunging gambler from the mid-West had his eye on his own financial advancement and not on the social results of his acts, yet he changed the face of a large section of the United States and the ways of living of countless individuals.

It so happened that all this frenzied activity and piling up of huge aggregations of wealth was going on just as the last and perhaps most picturesque phase of the frontier was coming into being for its short life. The great plains of the West had been considered useless for anything but cattle and sheep grazing, and a large part of them, because of blizzards, not much good even for that. Then, however, came the idea that the cows could be wintered in Texas and driven northward along the "range" for the summers. The Chisholm Trail was first blazed in 1867, and the great cattle drives began, with the rise of the gaudy "cow towns" and all the romance of the cowboy, possibly the best known of all our frontier figures, among young and old, here and in Europe. In a group of typical Americans the cowboy is entitled to one of the front seats.

The cattle business lasted for only about twenty years. Rapidly increasing population, rising land values farther east and other factors (including the almost complete extinction of the buffalo and the settling of the remnants of the Indian tribes on reservations), caused prospective settlers to cast eyes on the possibilities of the despised "cow country." That vaguely defined section was immense, perhaps larger than all the countries of western Europe combined. Obviously, however, settled farmers and ranging herds of cows could not co-exist on the same land. There were border frays in plenty between the new farmers and the old cattlemen. Then came the invention of "bob" or barbed wire, which was capable of keeping cattle out of planted land where all else in the way of fences or hedges had failed. Young Gates saw the possibilities and set up a barbed wire enclosure in San Antonio to demonstrate that it was "bull proof and horse high." It "caught on" like a prairie fire and Gates made a fortune, later capitalizing his Steel and Wire Company at $90,000,000, and continuing to make and lose fortunes. Incidentally, and more important for the American, the new fencing ended the range and cattle driving. For a while, as was said, "Bob wire played hell with Texas" but by 1890 (a date we shall soon encounter again), most of the vast ranges under private ownership was fenced; the farmer had largely taken the place of the cowboy; and the quality of the cattle within enclosures was much improved.

That a man like Gates, gambling for his own hand, could bring about such changes is an indication of what the operations of much bigger and abler men, such as some of those mentioned above, could do, even unintentionally. In spite of Lincoln's true statement that the nation could not forever remain half slave and half free, the American has nevertheless shown an amazing ability to keep his mind and his life in watertight compartments. As an old saying went when I was in business in New York, a man might be two wholly different persons when north and when south of Fulton Street, and there have been many astounding changes in the character of an American between the time when he was in process of accumulating a huge fortune and the later years after he had started to use it.

Some great capitalists have shown these two phases, but speaking generally it may be said that the business Titans of the period we are considering had only the most rudimentary social sense as to what they were doing. There was, in part, of course, pure ruthless selfishness. There was also, now and then, a trace of the early American Puritan belief that somehow you were doing God's work by making money, and that if you did make it, it was a sign of God's approval. There was also, and to a great extent, the belief that if you made a lot of money and were incidentally building up a big business, employing a lot of men, or extending railways and "developing" a section, you were rendering a patriotic service.

Many of these men, often with single-track and narrow minds, were nevertheless extremely able in their line, and probably did get things accomplished faster than others could have done. Because of this belief in themselves, they did not want to brook any interference with their plans or doings. They had no experience of public life and of public problems. Why should men—or so they thought—who could do "big things" and make their millions, bother with the routine of being a Congressman at $7500 a year, when public life was dull and brought no power or prestige? There thus came to be two bi-sections in American life—the division between the social and intellectual life of the sexes; and that between the public and private career. It was bad all around. The politician became more corrupt; the rich woman more unoccupied and restless; and the men who were big enough to "run things" more narrow and self-centered.

We may mention two results of the last point, which were to be of lasting effect on the American.

In the quarter century after the war, even with the occasional business crises, there was constant demand both for settlers and for cheap labor. As usual, conditions in Europe coincided with demands here. Things were bad over there, and in the decade 1870–80 about 5,000,000 immigrants arrived, the numbers gradually swelling until the peak year of 1907 when nearly 1,300,000 came in one twelvemonth. There was, however, a gradual change in the source, the stream shifting from the British Isles, Scandinavia and Germany to Russia, Poland, Italy, Austria-Hungary and the Balkans. Between 1900 and 1910 nearly 9,000,000 aliens entered through our ports.

In spite of laws, much of this immigration was fostered by the big employers, whose only thought was to get cheap labor to fight strikes and who had no feeling of responsibility for the people they induced to come to us or for the effect on our own nation. If many of the newer stream of immigrants provided an undue proportion of our criminals, and found it harder to become what we have called "real Americans," it was largely due not to any intrinsic bad qualities in them but to the much greater demands made upon them for deep inner readjustments.

It was not unnatural that for long they should have segregated themselves in alien language and racial "colonies," and largely in the mining and industrial centers. They were employed to a great extent in the hardest and lowest paid jobs, and we have already commented on the trait in the old American which leads him to look down upon every new and different racial group that comes here.

As a result, partly of all this, and partly of the arrogance and anti-social attitude in general of big business, the period up to 1896 was one of constant industrial turmoil, such as the extremely bitter conflicts at Carnegie's Homestead works and the Pullman strike. These newcomers were to become American, most of them in the legal and many, in time, in the real sense, but the troubles of the period were far from being confined to them, which brings us to another possible milestone in the making of the American.

There has always been the American Dream. But the very opportunities, which seemed to make that Dream more realizable in America than in any other land, have been so great that each generation has tried too avidly to seize them and make the most of them for the favored few or many. Every now and then the Dream has seemed to fade. Then a reaction has come, and the people have risen again to make the Dream true. This has occurred, like a veritable pulse-beat, about once in every generation. We had the Jeffersonian Revolution in 1800; the Jacksonian in 1828; the Lincoln election in 1860.

With very broad brush-strokes we have tried to tell something of the influences on the American, of various sections, following the Civil War, and now we have to come back to the West, that Valley of Democracy, in which, if anywhere, the regular pulse-beat might have been expected to be felt. That section had its distinct and justified grievances. The arduous task of breaking the prairies for farms, of fighting droughts and grasshoppers, the high cost of manufactured goods and the low prices for farm produce, railways which would not extend lines until they got good and ready and charged high rates, interest and mortgages to be met, with rising costs due to the vagaries of gold—these and many other factors were provoking a genuine revolt. In 1893 in Kansas alone more than 11,000 farms were taken from their owners under foreclosure. The cry went up of "Ten cent corn and ten per cent interest," and the redoubtable Mary Lease roused the farmers by her slogan of "Raise less corn and more Hell,"—good advice, given in the American way.

The pulse-beat was felt. It was felt so strongly as to frighten the moneyed East out of its wits, with Bryan demanding free and unlimited coinage of silver. Panic swept the country, and railroads, banks and great business houses failed, but when the election came, in 1896, with the "Peerless Leader" as candidate, he lost in spite of a magnificent fight, perhaps the greatest any candidate for the Presidency has ever put up with so many odds against him. The weak McKinley, who Theodore Roosevelt once said had "No more backbone than a chocolate éclair," but who was backed by all the "interests," won. Roosevelt also wrote, privately, to his friend Senator Lodge, that "The ugly feature in the Republican canvass is that it *does* represent exactly what the Populists say, that is, corrupt wealth."

Bryan may have been wrong in many of his financial and other theories, though nowadays some of them look innocuous enough in the light of the popular ones of the present, but even so, something had happened to the American. Holding the wrist of democracy one suddenly found that the pulse had stopped. Perhaps it was because of the conditions which led the Census Bureau in 1890 to announce that the frontier, that ever-present influence on America, had been declared officially *closed*. Perhaps it was many things. Perhaps it was not death but a fainting spell. Perhaps—but we are now within range of events which are part of the memory and emotional life of the older generation.

We may, however, point to a few happenings or movements which, in the next generation, appear fairly clear in their significance for our main theme.

The failure of the rhythm in the pulse-beat was more or less obscured for the time by one of those unexpected occurrences in the world at large which, in spite of our theoretical isolation, have so often affected the American without his having anything, or much, to do with them. A sudden and enormous increase began in world production of gold, with the natural effect of a rise in prices. It was not politics but mining, notably in South Africa, that relieved the farmer and other classes which had taken part in the revolt of 1896. The real difficulties were not cured but the temporary ones were, and the American could turn to other things.

Isolationism got another jolt to loosen it a bit. Ever since the Civil War, the firm settlement of the Union, and the great business prosperity following, America had been becoming more cocky. Relations with the Old World had not improved but a sudden, and even yet not wholly explained, bombshell touched off in Washington made both the Britisher and the American sit up and think. Their thoughts became deep, with more or less lasting and important effect. There had been a long-standing boundary dispute between Britain and Venezuela. The Venezuelan demands were excessive but because of the Monroe Doctrine the United States was touchy about the British pushing *their* demands too forcibly. President Cleveland had failed in his effort to have the matter settled by arbitration, and his Secretary of State, Richard Olney, sent an amazing note to Lord Salisbury, the British Prime Minister. In part, the irascible Olney remarked that "Today the United States is practically sovereign on this continent [sic], and its fiat is law upon the subjects to which it confines its interposition. Why? It is not because of the pure friendship or good will felt for it. It is not simply by reason of its high character as a civilized state, nor because wisdom and justice and equity are the invariable characteristics of the dealings of the United States. It is because, in addition to all other grounds, its infinite resources combined with its isolated position render it master of the situation and practically invulnerable as against any or all other powers."

This astoundingly worded communication was American cockiness at its worst. It was isolation raised to the nth power, combined with not merely "twisting the Lion's tail" but threatening to pull it out by the root. The public had heard almost nothing of the controversy but when Cleveland submitted it to Congress with a war-like message, there was a near panic. For various reasons the controversy was peaceably adjusted, but the chief result was that both nations, which had been making faces at each other across the ocean for nearly a century, suddenly realized what an unthinkable catastrophe war between them would be. Isolationism was still to have a long history but a third war (an actual war, not just grimaces) with the British Empire (which, for one thing, marched along our northern frontier for more than three thousand miles of undefended boundary) had loomed for a few weeks so as to exhibit all its ghastly possibilities. Americans of all sorts and origins had not instantly become Anglophile by any means but the bulk of American opinion had advanced an important step in coming to feel instinctively that, in spite of differences and clashes of interests, the fundamental relations between the United States and the British Empire were different from those existing between any other two peoples.

Then came the difficulties of the British in South Africa, and the Kaiser's famous telegram to Kruger. Germany was getting cocky and looming up as an enemy both of the British and ourselves. Next came our own war with Spain, which involved Anglo-American relations, shed important side-lights on the American, and helped to explain him to himself. Briefly, there had been misrule in the decaying Spanish empire for a long period. There had been revolts in Cuba, a most important island about 700 miles long and lying almost off the tip of Florida and flanking the Caribbean Sea, with all that that meant to us. At times, in slave days especially, the South had cast covetous eyes on it, but we might have done nothing had not certain newspapers of the yellow type undertaken to stir us up to war. The journalism, both in its intent and methods, was of the vilest, but what concerns us is not the history of war but what it meant in forming the American.

From this point of view certain facts are of great importance. Although the journals had their eye on increased circulation, and, behind the scenes, a few groups and politicians such as Henry Cabot Lodge, had theirs on imperialism and adding to American territory and business opportunities, the people could be stirred only by appeals to their chivalry and their constant sympathy for what might seem to be the under-dog. The Americans as a whole could be made to go to war on this occasion only as a holy crusade to free an oppressed people. There never was a greater contrast between the planning of the show by a few, backstage, and what the audience thought they were seeing and participating in.

During the struggle, if it can so be called, occurred the celebrated incident in Manila Bay, when Admiral Dewey and his fleet were treated by the German Admiral with a cockiness almost equal to Olney's. The British, also there, took our side and hinted to the Germans that they had better mind their own business. The details, sometimes exaggerated, are not important. What is important was that the public realized that, with practically all the European nations on the side of Spain, the British had made a gesture signifying that if we were not allowed to finish our job in our own way, the Empire might also have to be reckoned with. There was a general slinking back by the other powers, and the stock of Anglo-American good relations took a sudden rise.

The peace was also illuminating. America did not annex Cuba after victory over Spain but gave the island its freedom; and the public debate over the purchase of the Philippines and Porto Rico indicated clearly that the American was not in the least imperially minded. He had been very lukewarm over the purchase of Alaska, which had had to be made to appear as a kind deed to Russia, and the intense opposition which arose over the annexation of Hawaii, and later of the Spanish island possessions, showed markedly that the same American who had been so imbued with the idea of Manifest Destiny, as regards controlling the continental belt across America from the Atlantic to the Pacific, did not include anything farther—east, north, west or south. Practically no American has ever wanted to annex anything in Central or South America. The Monroe Doctrine has never been considered as a storage refrigerator in which to keep the food until we wanted to use it ourselves. The American, as his history has shown, is thoroughly anti-imperialistic.

From another angle we may just mention the two later wars. In both of these, in spite of anxieties over the enormous foreign population which we had added to our own stock, all racial groups proved themselves, on the whole, loyal to America, and as contrasted with earlier wars there was no difficulty in raising armies for the duration instead of for a few months, and in using conscription. The new stocks were becoming American, and the American was becoming socially more self-disciplined. As a result of conditions in Europe after World War I, we almost wholly closed our gates to further immigration, and have now had a breathing spell of more than twenty years during which comparatively few new immigrants have arrived, while those already here have had nearly a generation in which to be absorbed and Americanized. On the whole this has evidently been the case. These people have had much to contribute to the tackling of our common tasks and especially also to the zest and color of a life which tended too much towards sameness and drabness. Italian *festas* here and there, the picturesque January blessing of the boats of the Greek sponge fishermen by their Archbishop at Tarpon Springs, Florida, and innumerable other like things elsewhere, have added to the picturesqueness of our general cultural life.

There have been certain great gifts to the nation and world by such men as Carnegie, Mellon, Rockefeller, and others, who built colossal fortunes in the neighborhood of Pittsburgh. There were also those of a humbler sort but equally American. When Chancellor Bowman of the University of Pittsburgh, a genuine people's university, was raising money, five foreign-language workmen from the steel mills came to him and offered him $5000, their whole life-savings. When he said it was too much for them to do, they said America had done so much for them that they wanted to share in the responsibility of giving still better opportunities to their children. He accepted the money on condition that if they ever needed it, they could have it back with four per cent interest. Not one ever asked for a penny, and now in the magnificent central building of the University there are some thirty or more study rooms, fitted out by as many different groups of Americans of different languages and racial origins, at a cost of from $15,000 to $60,000 each, so built and furnished as to show what are the noblest attainments of their peoples and what they have to offer, not in self-laudation or as hyphenates, but to the common stock of American life.

One or two points more, before we finish with the influences which have made the American that "New Man" of Crèvecoeur.

Although our continental population is now about 135,000,000, it was in 1900 only 76,000,000. Even so, it was the largest in the world for a modern industrial state, in any single contiguous free-trade area. Despite all sectional and local differences, the needs and desires of Americans all through it were for the most part so similar that America was the ideal place for mass production and the distribution of national products. Given this fact, and the inventive and managerial skill of the American businessman, we get what happened after 1900. Mass production in innumerable lines, bicycles, automobiles, radios, any number of things, including standardized foods in cans, flooded the forty-eight states unseparated by customs barriers, languages or any great difference in traditional habits. Advertising on a scale unknown elsewhere, and warranted only by the size of the potential markets, not only brought known goods to the attention of buyers but created an infinitude of new wants. Further, mass production meant low cost. A motor car, in any of the countries of the Old World remained a luxury of the rich. In America, the Ford, and other cheap cars, became the necessities of almost every one.

All these things had profound effects on the American and his outlook. His standard of material living became the highest in the world. He not only came to look down on peoples of older lands, whom he grew to think of as hopelessly old-fashioned and unprogressive, but also to regard the new standard to which he had attained as being the only good one and one to which he was somehow entitled. The earliest Americans had been deeply affected by the American environment. The Americans of this last period were beginning to be affected by a new environment which was of their own making. They had travelled a long way from the self-sufficing household of the Virginia plantation or the New England farm.

And yet, in spite of their fondness for the new toys and gadgets and conveniences and ways, there was a profound nostalgia. We are, as yet, too near to the 1920's to be sure of just what those years meant but it seems to me that they indicated a desperate desire to recapture an earlier America. The turning away from Europe was a resurgence of the old isolationism, a desire to be in an America unspotted by the world. The popularity of Calvin Coolidge, the wish to see him in the old Vermont farmhouse with his old farmer father and the kerosene lamp, was a homesickness for a simpler America, to which Americans would never have willingly returned but which nevertheless was in their blood and doing something to them. Even the wild speculation was a defiant demonstration of the old free-for-all struggle for gain, individualism, the take-a-chance urge, on the frontier of a new world not yet understood, a world of science, of brain and not of brawn, a world which offered undreamed of possibilities and controls if its problems could be solved. Americans did not know what they wanted but in a vague way were reaching back to the various phases of the America of the past, trying somehow to find release from a world which had got a bit too complicated, and to "regain the first fine careless rapture" of what they felt they *had* been. It was all very confused, and so even yet is the American, but we must try, in a short epilogue, to sum up what we have found him to be by taking our soundings here and there in his history.

EPILOGUE

AND now at the end what have we found about the American? What is he? What are his traits and character? How, if at all, does he differ from other peoples? There is no Procrustes bed on which to fit all the members of any race or nation. If peoples and races differ, so do individuals in all of them. The first fact about the American is that there are, in our continental area alone, almost 135,000,000 of him, of all ages and more racial and language groups than live anywhere else under one government, unless it be in India. Obviously there must be immense surface variety among "Americans." Is there any common denominator?

This brief Epilogue is an effort to set down what traits we have found in him. We shall make no further effort to trace their causes or origins. We shall not try to follow their chronological order of appearance, or to arrange them in a symmetrical "character" in the old classical sense. We shall put most of them down as they occur to us in thinking over what we have already written. The result may be a hodge-podge, but that in itself is characteristic of the American. He is himself as yet a hodge-podge. He has not had long centuries of development. It is impossible even to say how long his development *has* been. Ancestors of the oldest American families may have been here over three centuries ago, but even those families have been continually subjected to new American-forming influences and to intermarriages with later Americans. Further, an American, even in the real sense, may have been here only a dozen years. So that we are all rather mixed yet, and any description of the traits we have found may be all the truer for being mixed also. These traits are going to appear not merely mixed. They are often going to prove contradictory.

For example, the American has raised woman to an almost

impossible eminence. She has been an American Golden Calf. In no other country does she get her own way as she does in America. The man has played second-fiddle in the home and in social life, and given the woman the leadership, to a great extent, in cultural life. He yields to her in an infinite variety of ways. Even when he likes to feel he is boss in the home (although he knows he is not), he lets his wife furnish it as she wishes, regardless of his own tastes, and run the entertaining as she wishes, while he hands out the checks as called for. He loves her after his fashion, is proud of her, wants her to be contented and also a symbol of his own standing and success. The two real cults in America are those of the flag and of the woman.

Yet not only is passion notably slight or absent in American literature and life; American men and women, at least mature ones, lead much less of a joint life than is found in most other countries. The men may follow their wives at a respectful distance, but they also escape to the stove of the general store or the lounge of the Millionaires Club as soon as it is decently possible. Woman is on a pedestal and has been given every opportunity but there has been no dominating woman figure in our history. We have had no Catherines the Great or de Medici, no Queen Elizabeths or Victorias to mold our destinies. We have had no Joan of Arc as national heroine and emblem.

We have spoken of the cockiness of Americans, and yet, in contrast to this they have, to a great extent, not been sure of themselves. Especially in the last century they were intensely sensitive to the criticism of such foreigners as a Dickens or a Mrs. Trollope, and even yet the vogue of the Emily Posts, who tell you which fork to use, indicates fear of not doing what is expected. The American can be the most independent cuss on earth, and give no thought to conventions or social gradations. That P. T. Barnum, with Tom Thumb at his side, could chat with Queen Victoria in Buckingham Palace as easily as with Mrs. Jones in Oshkosh, was a characteristic note, yet on the other hand, two of our traits—our "keeping up with the Joneses," and our tendency to be "joiners"—may both stem from fear of the opinion of others and of being thought "different," and so of slipping on the climb up the business or social ladder.

For the American, joining organizations not only feeds his desire for gregariousness but satisfies his desire for being thought to know "what's what" in his particular circle. It is a sort of protective coloration. The American is one of the greatest individualists in the world, yet, contrary-wise, the American man, largely for business or professional reasons, and his wife, for social ones, wants to be in the right benevolent society, golf club, garden club, charity or other organization so as not to lose the right client or the right invitation. It is natural in a completely fluid and mobile society, in which individuals rise and fall in the economic and social scales with remarkable speed, and frequently move from where they have been known to where no one knows them. Nevertheless, we have to try to combine the individualism of the American with his fear of being individually different from others, or at least those others on whom he thinks depend his own well-being and advancement.

There is another dichotomy growing out of the fundamental individualism of the American. His whole history has been such as to breed in him the desire to do as he pleases, to "get thar fustest," to make the most of himself and his opportunities. On the other hand, his history has also bred in him an intense desire for equality. The two are incompatible. Thus far, he has tried to reconcile them by rugged individualism in his economic life, and a partly supposititious and partly genuine equality, or democracy, in his social life. It has not worked out yet but both urges are strong and somehow will have to be met.

The American thinks his own country the finest in the world. He has wanted to expand it. He has done so, by war but mostly by purchase. Nothing could stop him in his military or financial conquest from coast to coast. But outside of that strip he halted, from an instinct apparently as deep and strong as that of Manifest Destiny. He was a continental expansionist but a bitter opponent of over-seas expansion. You may call him an Imperialist in conquering the continent. In stopping short at high tide on both coasts he has been anti-Imperialist.

He loves humor and a good joke, and is apt to think his own the best. He made in the last century a complete rebound from his inherited sort, and American humor is exaggeration instead of under-statement. He likes a good time and to be a good fellow and to have all around him enjoy themselves. He likes noise, as witness Times Square on a New Year's Eve. His humor is broad, and subtlety bothers him.

He is perhaps the most hospitable person in the world. He likes to talk to strangers, and has no fear that a chance conversation on a steamer or in the train may later be a social liability. He is likely to be expansive in his talk, not least about himself, his own affairs, and his country. His background is apt to be limited, in spite of constant travel throughout his own and, often, other countries. He is capable of expressing such a viewpoint as that of General Grant on his world tour, when he said, "Venice would be a fine city if it was drained."

The past means little to him. His attitude is much that of Mark Twain, in his *Innocents Abroad* or *A Connecticut Yankee at King Arthur's Court*. He is used to trying to make the best of the present but with his eye always on the future. No American, man or woman, would ever have suffered the fate of Lot's wife. Yet he founds innumerable historical societies; plasters his villages with memorial tablets; joins the Sons or Daughters of the American Revolution and innumerable similar ones; keeps hordes of workers figuring out his genealogy; pays top prices for early American furniture and silver; and prides himself on belonging to one of the "old families" of a city founded perhaps fifty years ago. He is beginning to like to think that his bank or school or what-not is a hundred, two hundred, years old, and now talks of "tradition" but is willing to scrap furniture, buildings, and all else, any year, if he thinks he has found something newer or more efficient.

The American seeks comfort, which he is likely to confuse with luxury of the latest style, and labor-saving devices which, saving him or his wife a bit of work in one direction, make him work harder to earn the money to pay for them. He wants everything around his house or office of the "best" and latest, and entangles himself in an endless round of making more to get more, even though, in comfort, he gets less. In his office, which is *his* "home" and where he has "the say," he feels he has to have what his most successful competitor—for the time being—has. In the real home, his wife has to compete with her social friends in furnishings and *hors d'oeuvres.* A worn-out carpet is a disgrace and a sign of failure. A tea with only bread and butter and conversation means a "flop" as a hostess.

He is supposed not to care about art, but not only is a large part of the art of the Old World, particularly of course in painting, now safe for the future because it is housed in America, but the unartistic American is leading the world in domestic architecture and in other directions. The huge main waiting-rooms of such terminals as the Pennsylvania and the Grand Central are temples almost, and are really beautiful, though they get cluttered up with advertisements, characteristically not even stationary but on the move, electric signs which pass rapidly before the eye like fast ticker-tape. Yet the American no longer has to go abroad to learn. He has come to a maturity of a sort and in all the arts, literature, painting, sculpture, and architecture in particular, there is no better work being done elsewhere.

He is supposed to be merely practical in his science, yet his research laboratories, built largely by his "soulless corporations," are in the van of all, and by an odd trick of contradiction the American leads in that seemingly least practical of the sciences—astronomy, and a considerable part of the business of a corporation which has orders for perhaps $2,000,000,000 worth of goods may be based on applications of the formula for the square root of minus 1.

The American has never liked war. He has been a leader in movements for peace, yet he has been ready to fight at the drop of a hat. For nearly five years Americans fought between themselves the greatest Civil War in history. War is a job Americans may feel they have to do, and they do it as well as those of any of the so-called military nations who have been taught to believe in and love war. Yet the American thinks it a stupid way of ironing out differences. He finds it hard to believe it necessary, and when his mind is taken off it, he finds it hard to hate his enemy. He relapses easily into a spirit of friendliness and becomes the "big boy" which the French called him in World War I. But he can fight; *wow*, how he can fight!

The American of each generation looks down on the alien immigrant of later generations and strata. He calls them "Wops," "Dagoes," "Micks," and so on; but when he is in contact with them he gets along with them all right, and cannot understand why they cannot get along with one another in their own lands. "Minority Groups," bah! "Haven't we the largest minority groups of any country in the world," he says, "with newspapers printed in some sixty foreign languages, and yet we don't fly at each other's throats all the time." It makes him feel that foreigners in other countries must be fools or have an exceptionally large dose of original sin in them. He knows as little of foreign history as of foreign exchange, and both wars and war debts are incomprehensible to him. He tends to feel that the starting of the one or the failure to pay the others are just stupid or dishonest.

He enjoys making money, for the sake of the game and for what he can do with it, not only for himself in prestige and power, but for his wife and children, his community and the rest of the world. With very rare exceptions he is never a miser. Life and opportunity have been free and open for him. He can be hard as nails in making money, but when he has it he throws it away lavishly. He knows he is no "Uncle Shylock," and he resents the imputation but does not think too much about it. He knows what is going on in every American community, the Community Chest, Hospital and other "drives," and what they turn up. He knows of the $100,000,000 or so that Carnegie gave to the British Isles, that Americans rebuilt the Belgian Library at Louvain which the Germans had destroyed, that the Rockefellers have given tens of millions to many countries, that we helped to build the University of London, put a new roof on the palace at Versailles, and innumerable other things—tens of millions poured out to other countries, not for cancelling war debts but for all sorts of help in times of peace. So he shrugs his shoulders, says "Oh, to hell with them," and goes on giving.

The attitude of the American toward money is quite different from that of almost any other people, if not of all. In the past the chances have been so great, the natural wealth of the country so enormous, its resources so apparently illimitable, its growth so rapid in population and industry, that the American has come to think of money in almost wholly new terms. Making it has been more exciting and more of a game than anywhere else, and when made, because made so easily, it has not been something to be hoarded and conserved but to be spent and given away. With regard to wealth, the American mind thinks in an economic world of a fourth dimension.

Because of all this, the American has developed other cognate qualities. One of the most outstanding of these is his willingness to take a chance. In old countries where opportunities are limited but where a man may have got a little ahead, either in money or position, he hesitates to risk them, because once down from where he has got, he fears he may never get up again. Under such conditions failure carries a certain stigma. In America, it may be said to carry almost none at all. A man tumbles, tries something else, and very likely comes back, though it may be in a wholly new line. As a bit of Americana I like a story which I happen to know is true. A woman, who was a social leader in one of the larger cities of the Rocky

Mountain states, asked a plumber to come and do a job. He sent the usual assistant, who happened to be drunk. The lady complained and the assistant was fired. He went to the mountains, struck it rich and ten years later returned, sobered and worth millions, and the lady who had ordered him out of her house, opened the fashionable cotillion with him, unknowing. That could happen only in America.

This brings out another characteristic. The American is amazingly versatile. If a man has been thirty or forty years with one company, that is usually enough to get him a silver service, a banquet and a notice in the papers. Few successful Americans have not turned their hands to many different sorts of things in the course of their lives. They will try anything or go anywhere if it seems to offer a chance. During the depression in England in the 'twenties social workers there told me that one of the most difficult problems was to get the unemployed to change either their location or the nature of their work. Most Americans simply would not understand that attitude.

Americans have been such jacks-of-all-trades, and often have had so many ups and downs, that any kind of a job, except the most menial ones as permanent, is all right. For many, it starts in college and the list of things boys and girls do to work their way through runs almost the entire gamut of occupations, and none has the slightest effect on social standing, except to raise the student, who is working his own way, higher in general estimation.

Perhaps partly because the game of business and of life has been made so strenuous, the American has little of the amateur spirit. He prefers his music, good or bad, "canned" on the radio to making any himself, good or bad. He has a sort of fear of not doing a thing well, and therefore often prefers not doing it at all. He is afraid he may be laughed at or thought conceited. At college, students do not play ball or row, and so on, unless they think there is some chance of getting on the team or crew, but they go by tens of thousands to stadiums or riversides to watch others, and then when older are too busy for sport, or still shyer of being a duffer, except at golf.

As we have seen, the Americans have always been rather isolationist, yet when they have the chance they travel in hordes to other countries and want to do business all over the globe. They are apt, however, to do both in a hurry and with the feeling that everything is better in America. Their isolationism is military and political. They fear tying themselves up definitely for a long period in international relations and want to be free of entanglements, much as they want to keep themselves free to change their personal careers at home. You could get very few Americans to sign on for a job for many years ahead at even the handsomest of salaries. Yet, isolationist as the American is in one sense, there is perhaps no more internationally minded person in the world. His interests and benefactions go all over the world as do those of no other people. He is as ready to finance antiquarian exploration in Mesopotamia as in Arizona; to hunt fossils in Mongolia as in Montana; to help a hospital in Paris or Pekin as in any American city; to send aid to the sufferers from a flood of the Yellow River as from that of the Mississippi.

The sense of hurry seems inborn in the American. He loves speed, even to get nowhere. He wants to "get rich quick," do everything "quick." I used to watch an incoming commuters' train at Hoboken. Men were hanging on the steps like bees, ready to jump even before the cars stopped, and run for the Tube Train. Yet when they got to their offices they might sit around half an hour before doing anything. The advertisements tell the same story. How to be cultured in fifteen minutes a day. Books are printed in condensed editions so as to be just an easy evening's reading. This love of speed, combined with the love of mechanical things and gadgets, made the automobile the "perfect gift" to the American. No other nation has ever dreamed of having so many cars per capita, or of sacrificing so many other wants or desires to get them, or of spending so much of one's waking life in them.

Another trait of the American is his love of bigness. He likes to watch his cities grow, though he is still enamored of the farm tradition and the small town is still perhaps the most characteristic thing in America, with its front porch life, its easy neighborliness, and its "folksiness." He is proud of the size of his fruits, of the dams he has built, of having the biggest railway stations in the world, of his skyscrapers. The old concept of "bigger and better," which held much truth at one time, still has strong hold on him. One of his buildings, that of the War Department in Washington, is a mile square and has seventeen miles of corridors, requiring tricycles and roller-skates to get about in, so that a general is said to have got lost there on several occasions.

The American is easy-going, not only in making money and spending or giving it away, but even when it is stolen from him. He knows there is enormous waste in government, municipal, state and Federal, and also much graft; he is busy, and thinks everything will come out all right somehow. After all, he himself has always been wasteful. When land was worked out he would abandon it and move to other land. He burned his forests or cut them down, with no thought of any future scarcity. It has often been said that many a European family could live on what an American one threw out, except perhaps in New England. In the fierceness of the struggle to get ahead, all sorts of sharp corners were turned and queer things done. The main thing was to get something done or won, and to do it first. If the politician did queer things too, well, the country was rich and if the smell did not get too bad or the taxes too high, why worry?

There we come on another trait, the "why worry" one. It is linked to all our past. We were always moving on to something new. No one knew what was ahead, what situations he might meet, what lay over the mountains. If you took a wrong turn, settled on the wrong spot, came a cropper in a business venture, well, start again, but why worry? Everybody was doing it, and somehow, after all, most people were getting somewhere.

The frontier gave us that, as well as our typical American philosophy of Pragmatism, whose only test of the truth is "will it work?"

Another American trait is the desire to be helpful and kindly, to work together—the husking bees and quilting bees and barn and house raisings of the early days translated into terms of modern life. With this goes perhaps another one of our traits, our instinctive sympathy for the under dog, regardless of which dog is right. The under one *is* under, and that is enough for us for the moment. Throughout our long story, so many have needed, got, and *given* help, that it has become an instinct.

The ordinary American subordinates his mind to his will. He is happiest when he has a job to do, and if it has to be done in a hurry, so much the better. Most Americans do not want to tax their "think-tank," as the slang phrase has it, too much. They want to use their will and driving power to get something done, but do not want to analyze too far its possible future effects. The seventeenth-century preoccupation with thought, which then took largely the form of theological hair-splitting, has been followed to a great extent by such religion as avoids critical thinking (like Fundamentalism), or which is motivated by emotion, often altruistic and generous, or which has become merely a form of social service. I doubt if one American man or woman in a thousand who goes by preference, inheritance or habit, to this church or that, could give any clear statement of how its creed differs from that of others.

It has been the easy-going habits of the American which have accounted for much of our crime, so appalling to other countries, who get it in concentrated doses in the movies or sensational news items. Like our politics, we let it slide until it gets too bad, and our attitude toward it is much the same.

The American has an exalted belief in the possibilities of education for any and every one. Partly allied to what I have said about "joining" and the uncertainty of position in our mobile life, is the feeling of the American that, like a national brand of food, he is safer with a label. There is no Education

Act, like the Pure Food Act, which helps to guarantee quality of product, but a High School Diploma, a College Degree, and especially that of Doctor of Philosophy, are passports to consideration for a job and other things. Particularly in the teaching profession the letters after your name have much to do with the number of figures after the dollar sign in your salary check. It is all part of the right Golf Club, Garden Club complex and saves the bother of thinking or the possible risks of testing. It doesn't, but is supposed to, and it at least provides an alibi.

The American wants as little government as possible, except when he can get something out of it. For the most part, however, the things he has asked of it have been such as created general conditions. He hates red tape, hates having the government stick its nose into his business, or tell him what to do in detail, though he may ask for a tariff, bonuses for veterans, help for the farmer, or sops to silver. It is all very mixed, unthinking, illogical, and American.

The American loves freedom. He came from Europe to get it, has moved to frontier after frontier to get it again when he thought he was losing it. He has always wanted to be his own boss. Possibly one of his strongest traits has been that he has wanted to "go to Hell in his own way," or indeed anywhere else he chose. It shows in the Southerner; in the Yankee farmer; in the hunters, trappers, and other frontiersmen; in the Forty-niners and the cowboy; in the whaling and clipper-ship captains; in the squatters and pre-emptors of lands; in the business men, big and little; in a word, in all Americans, from the beginning.

A final word as to what heroes the American chooses. First, we may note that our heroes have all been chosen by the people. None has become one permanently who was just built up either by himself or the press, though he may be one as transiently as a shooting star. The heroes whose names have lasted and grown in the national consciousness have all been, as Wector says in his book on *The Hero in America,* "men of good will." They have been honest and forthright, not using what Theodore Roosevelt called "weasel words." They have been greater than the average run of the people but have been such as the people could understand, and have never boasted of their power nor have they forgot that they have owed that power *to* the people. They have been men of brave deeds, of inventive genius, of social idealism, from all grades of society, rich or poor, of humble or distinguished family, but they have been men who have *done* things and led forward and upward. On the whole, the list of heroes indicates an American sound at heart, distinguishing the real from the spurious, the lasting from the passing, service from selfishness, the leader from the demagogue, the man from the stuffed shirt.

Well, we are at the end of our journey. Perhaps we have not been able to paint a clear portrait of the American. We have been able to put in a touch here, a touch there. There is no *one* American. There are tens of millions of them. Yet possibly from all we have found, we do get some idea of what *the* American, the real one, is. At least, we would know him anywhere we met him, wherever it was; and if we had never seen him before, could say, like Stanley in the African jungle, "Mr. Livingstone, I presume?" or, in American slang, "I know *you*, Al."

This sketch of the American is imperfect. It is not a finished portrait. He himself is still young. What he may become, what he *can* do and *will* do in the future cannot be forecast. But whatever he may prove, it will be of profound import to all mankind. His numbers, his skills, his combination of fertility in research and of practical ingenuity, the vast resources of his country, all these and other like things will be of enormous weight in the scales of the world to come. But above all, perhaps, what will count most for the generations that shall succeed those now struggling in this crisis of the human spirit will be his *dreams*. He has always had them. With all his Yankee "notions," his pioneer spirit, his mass production, and the rest, he has ever been essentially the *dreamer.* He largely dropped the Past, as a weary traveller at the end of the day's hike undoes and slips his pack from off his back. He has scarce lived in the *present* even. "There is gold in them thar hills," he murmurs, and starts again on his endless quest. He has looked to the heights and to the future. But if he has lifted himself, he has lifted others as well. He has not echoed Kipling's "He travels the fastest who travels alone."

Today there is no greater concentration of wealth and power than that in America, an almost empty continent three centuries ago. It has been made by dreams—dreams of opportunity, dreams of reward, dreams of equality, dreams of freedom. Perhaps, after all, dreams have unknown power, and the greatest dream humanity has dreamed as yet for its daily life has been the *American Dream*, which has brought millions of disillusioned and ambitious to our shores from all the nations of the earth. It has been a dream for all men to follow in freedom and in their own way. As far as I have been able to depict them, here are the American and his Dream. God bless and guard them both!

INDEX

INDEX

C

D

E

N

O

T

U

X

Y

Z